Joanne,

Wishing you all the best!

Richard

Question and Insight in Everyday Life

Question and Insight in Everyday Life

A Blueprint for Transformative Problem Solving

Richard Grallo

LEXINGTON BOOKS
Lanham • Boulder • New York • London

Published by Lexington Books
An imprint of The Rowman & Littlefield Publishing Group, Inc.
4501 Forbes Boulevard, Suite 200, Lanham, Maryland 20706
www.rowman.com

86-90 Paul Street, London EC2A 4NE

Copyright © 2022 by The Rowman & Littlefield Publishing Group, Inc.

All rights reserved. No part of this book may be reproduced in any form or by any electronic or mechanical means, including information storage and retrieval systems, without written permission from the publisher, except by a reviewer who may quote passages in a review.

British Library Cataloguing in Publication Information Available

Library of Congress Cataloging-in-Publication Data

Names: Grallo, Richard, 1947- author.
Title: Question and insight in everyday life : a blueprint for transformative problem solving / Richard Grallo.
Description: Lanham : Lexington Books, [2021] | Includes bibliographical references and index. | Summary: "In Question and Insight in Everyday Life: A Blueprint for Transformative Problem Solving, Richard Grallo examines the nature and patterns of human problem solving. The book's conclusions apply equally to the problems of everyday life as well as to challenges that arise in educational, counseling, political, engineering, and science fields"— Provided by publisher.
Identifiers: LCCN 2021042237 (print) | LCCN 2021042238 (ebook) | ISBN 9781793643902 (cloth) | ISBN 9781793643919 (epub)
Subjects: LCSH: Problem solving,
Classification: LCC BF449 .G73 2021 (print) | LCC BF449 (ebook) | DDC 153.4/3—dc23/eng/20211102
LC record available at https://lccn.loc.gov/2021042237
LC ebook record available at https://lccn.loc.gov/2021042238

*I dedicate this book to my parents,
Jennie and Frederick Grallo,
of happy memory,
with love and gratitude.
They loved learning
and encouraged it in others.
May this book also encourage others.*

Contents

List of Figures and Tables	ix
Acknowledgments	xi
Introduction	1
1 Problem Solving in Overview	5
2 Pattern 1: Seeking Understanding by Considering Possibilities	31
3 Three Patterns of Critical Thinking: Filtering Possibilities for Something More	45
4 Experiencing and Its Functions in Learning and Problem Solving	73
5 Problem Solving in Larger Contexts	89
6 Examples of Facts of Consciousness in Other Perspectives	119
Epilogue: Problem Solving as Mindful Practice	139
Bibliography	157
Glossary of Terms	165
Index	175
About the Author	181

List of Figures and Tables

FIGURES

Figure 1.1	Patterns of Problem Solving and a Mode of Pause	8
Figure 2.1	A Markov Model of Problem Solving Pattern 1—Seeking Understanding	36
Figure 3.1	A Markov Model of Problem Solving Patterns 2, 3, and 4—Critical Thinking	50
Figure E.1	Comparison of Three Types of Critical Thinking	146

TABLES

Table 3.1	Examples of Reflective Questions	50
Table 3.2	Judgment Outcomes for Mary's Reflective Question	55
Table 5.1	Passive and Active Mental Events in Distinct Patterns of Problem Solving and Basic Experiencing	94

Acknowledgments

Ideas for this book have developed over many years. In various symposia and articles I have attempted to identify, describe, and explain the importance of specific mental events for the entire problem solving process.

I am triply grateful for the contributions that others have made to making this book a reality and I wish to acknowledge my indebtedness to them. While they may be too numerous to mention, I take note of the lasting influence of these few. In particular, I draw heavily on some of the work of Canadian philosopher Bernard Lonergan, especially his cognitional theory, intentionality analysis, and generalized empirical method. From Albert Ellis I draw the idea that the products of our thinking can be distorted or undistorted, and that the quality of our thinking will affect our emotions, behaviors, and future habits. From Martin and Cynthia Deutsch I take the insight that all learning occurs within developmental contexts. From Theresa Jordan I draw the idea that life itself can be regarded as one giant open-classroom in which learning may (or may not) be occurring in different places and at different rates.

The published work of many Lonergan scholars has been very helpful. Included among them are Joseph Flanagan, Richard Liddy, Ken Melchin, Pat Byrne, Terry Tekippe, Brian Cronin, Hugo Meynell, William Mathews, and Mark Morelli. I am also grateful for many conversations that have occurred in the past with Bernard Bommarito, William McArdle, and with faculty members at Metropolitan College of New York such as Steven Cresap, Charles Gray, Clyde Griffin, Heide Hlawaty, Grace Roosevelt, Louis Tietje, and Rachel Yager. More recent conversations with David Rosner and with Michael Stebbins, Ken Melchin, and Paul LaChance have also been very helpful in specific details and conceptualization.

Fred and Sue Lawrence and Pat Byrne of Boston College, Richard Liddy of Seton Hall University, and Theodor Damian of Metropolitan College of

New York have been very gracious over the years by inviting me to present and publish my ideas in various conferences and journals. Thanks also to the administration at Metropolitan College of New York for research leaves to work on the book: presidents Alida Mesrop, Stephen Greenwald, Vinton Thompson, and Joanne Passaro; vice presidents Tilokie Depoo and Humphrey Crookendale; and deans Ruth Lugo, Adele Weiner, and Joanne Ardovini.

The extraordinary debt I have to Bert F. Breiner and to my cousin Diane Grallo cannot be overstated. From them I always received encouragement and many constructive suggestions.

Finally, I am grateful to editor Kasey Beduhn and the staff at Lexington Press and to the outside reviewers for professional and encouraging work on behalf of this book.

Introduction

This book is about complex human problem solving: its nature, conditions, and place in human living and development. Problem solving is a type of learning that addresses novel or chronic situations that confront us with gaps in our experience, understanding, knowledge, or practice. The most common types of gaps encountered are cognitive, emotive, and performative. Problem solving differs in important ways from simpler forms of learning such as memorization, paired associate learning, concept attainment, or stimulus-response learning. The simpler forms of learning are quite useful for effectively dealing with routine situations. In contrast, problem solving is more suitable to dealing with new situations and relatively intractable difficulties. It is more complex, takes more time and effort, and is often open to interference. Yet both types of learning, simple learning and the more complex problem solving, play central roles in our individual and collective development.

Without learning, simple or complex, there simply is no human development. There is no development of knowledge or skills, no discoveries or inventions, no personal growth and no human progress. For these and other reasons, the topics of learning and problem solving have been of interest to philosophers, psychologists, educators, and inventors throughout history. Human history itself can be regarded as a succession of successful and unsuccessful attempts to solve problems. Human problems can range anywhere from the practical and mundane to the momentous existential questions of philosophy and religion. Yet problems they all are. Hence any light that can be shed on the nature of problem solving should be of interest to anyone who engages in it, not just psychologists or philosophers. This includes educators and problem solving groups of all sorts.

Interest in problem solving has been renewed since the 1970s, when there commenced an explosion of related research and theory. Accounts of simple learning were insufficient to explain all that humans do when we actually attempt to solve problems. Yet while problem solving has been explored from a variety of perspectives, often crucial facts have been overlooked. The focus in this book will be on a limited set of "facts of consciousness" or "mental events." Included among these mental events are questions and insights, the desire to know, sensation and perception, images and evidence, formulations, judgments and decisions, and expressive actions and habits, and finally the social trust that is necessary for all effective collaborative problem solving.

Problem solving is not an easy topic to study for a number of reasons. First, there is no generally accepted standard language with which to describe mental events. Secondly, mental events are fleeting and often not easy to identify, let alone describe. They may not be familiar to some readers. Finally, mental events have a mixed reputation in well-established fields such as philosophy and psychology.

Nevertheless, this book approaches the mental events of problem solving by addressing five aims: (1) to identify and distinguish some basic facts of consciousness, (2) to describe the experience of each fact of consciousness, (3) to place these facts of consciousness in an explanatory and functional relation with one another as these exist in distinct patterns of problem solving, (4) to identify possible interferences with cognitive functioning and describe how they work, and (5) to describe some larger contexts in which the patterns of problem solving function. To further these aims, the facts of consciousness described in this book are presented and re-presented from a variety of different perspectives.

This book was written because recent approaches to learning and problem solving have only focused on some facts of consciousness to the neglect of others, and few have attempted to place all in an explanatory account that relates them to each other. More specifically, the emphasis here will be on three basic points: (1) The mental events of question, insight, and the desire to know are most important of the facts of consciousness mentioned above. Questions move learning forward by identifying gaps that need to be addressed. Insights provide a unifying synthesis that illuminates the viable answers. (2) Questions, insights, and the desire to know naturally organize themselves into four "patterns of problem solving" and their absence defines a mode of pause from the work of problem solving. (3) Problem solving efforts are made by individuals as well as by small problem solving groups. Therefore, "social trust" becomes an important fact to examine. (4) Knowledge of the facts of consciousness and their related patterns can provide a blueprint for all past, present, and future problem solving and learning.

While some of the published works referenced in this book may mention some of the facts of consciousness, they rarely describe all of them in any detail. Of the facts of consciousness mentioned, most significant in the list of missing items are question, insight, the desire to know, and the processes of social trust. Yet many of the approaches to be cited do address some specific aspects of problem solving and are therefore important, if partial, contributions to a more complete analysis of complex human learning. Moreover, all of these approaches are themselves the product of inquisitive and insightful persons, and therefore they provide some evidence of a desire to know and of problem solving itself. Finally, each approach also inherently relies on the work of predecessors, thus exemplifying some measure of social trust.

To reiterate, this book assumes that the following are basic facts of consciousness that the reader can verify in personal experience: questions and insights, the desire to know, sensations and perceptions, images and evidence, judgments and decisions, actions and habits, the various ways in which all of these can be formulated and expressed, and finally social trust. Any approach to problem solving that does not acknowledge all of these cannot possibly place all of them in an explanatory context with one another.

In light of these considerations, it is the overall thesis of this book that transformative problem solving and human learning involve distinct patterns or modes of mental events. Each pattern is a different group of cognitive acts and operations coordinated by a guiding intention; hence, each pattern is a distinctive process and type of cognitive functioning. Central to each pattern is the presence or absence of question, insight, and the desire to know. When the patterns are working together, they provide learning that is attentive to experience, deeply insightful, supported by evidence, guided by time-tested values, and transformative of situations and self. In addition, human problem solving proceeds in an intersubjective context that requires the presence and operation of social trust. In addition to this overall thesis, each chapter has its own goals or objectives and may be approached as an independent essay.

More specifically, the book may assist readers in two ways. First, it should facilitate attaining a special type of self-knowledge. This would be knowledge of the acts, operations, and processes involved in one's own problem solving efforts. Second, it should offer some guidance in self-management, allowing the reader to put this knowledge to use by better coordinating the mental events which enable human problem solving. Without this kind of self-knowledge, future problem solving is likely to remain a hit or miss affair. Without a related self-management, the self-knowledge will be ineffective. In contrast, with this self-knowledge and self-management one is positioned to develop a "learning personality" wherein the primary motivation is the desire to know and the related desire to grow in accordance with it. This kind of personality includes a habitual approach to situations that is focused on transformative problem solving and the constructive change it invites.

Chapter 1

Problem Solving in Overview

Problems are a fact of life and problem solving is a way to deal with them. The medical researcher engages in the problem of attempting to understand disease and to find a cure for it. The detective seeks to uncover the mysteries involved in a crime. The inventor works to discover a better way of doing things. The small business owner strives to attract customers and to make a reasonable profit. Individuals and families struggle to manage household finances in the hope of a better future. Individual persons work to manage their own education, worklife, and health. All of these are involved, at least to some extent, in the attempt to solve problems.

Yet individuals vary greatly in their attempts to solve problems, yielding a wide spectrum of "results" ranging from spectacular successes to demonstrable failures. In addition, despite invitations to the contrary, few can say what specifically they are doing when they attempt to solve problems and move toward increased and effective learning.

This book asserts that effective problem solving has a few central components: questions, insights, the desire to know, and social trust. Questions and insights play different roles in thinking, and they operate in different patterns or modes of thinking. While there are other components to problem solving, it is the questions that give shape to the process, if we cooperate. It is insights that bring things together in at least apparent solutions. Hence, acquiring knowledge and solving practical problems is essentially a matter of asking and answering questions—of question and insight. The desire to know, in ourselves and others, propels the entire enterprise forward. Finally, since much of our problem solving involves collaboration with others and assistance from them, social trust is a vital component of the process that makes collaboration possible.

The problem solving process that will be described here is not some deterministic mechanism with automatic results, but a probabilistic phenomenon that may or may not succeed. The process is not completely predictable and is often full of surprises. Problem solving is not entirely in our control, but it can be managed to some extent by our conscientious efforts. Problem solving results are not guaranteed to be satisfactory, but are subject to further testing. Embedded in the problem solving process is the possibility for transformation not only of the problem situation but of the problem solver. Without any attempts at problem solving we are left to the shaping forces of the environment, whether those forces are physical or social.

The ease with which a person can recognize the main components of problem solving described here depends on the habits of thinking and personality that are currently in place. Extroverts, by habit, tend to focus on data that are external to themselves. With this habit, they will tend to overlook aspects of the consciousness that are beyond the five senses. Introverts may be more at home with their internal world of feeling and thought, but that alone does not guarantee that they will easily recognize the events of consciousness discussed here. Each reader will need to judge for themselves how easy it is to recognize these components of problem solving.

Because problem solving is a process, it can be supported or sidetracked. Disruptions from within the individual and interruptions from the environment will be considered. Because problem solving is a human effort, it can be conducted by individuals or small groups, and it relies on past human experiences. When problem solving relies on the work of others, social trust enters the picture. Most problem solving does not get very far without relying on the reported contributions of others. The quality and reliability of those contributions will impact future problem solving efforts.

INITIAL CONSIDERATIONS

The aim of this chapter is to provide an overview of problem solving in its component parts and patterns. Knowledge of one's own problem solving activities and efforts is a form of self-knowledge. It is not the sort of self-knowledge that one might obtain by undergoing psychoanalysis, but it is knowledge of those aspects of self that are involved in thinking things through. As such it can function as a kind of blueprint for all problem solving efforts. This self-knowledge can then open up options for the problem solver and lead, with practice, to more efficient self-management of one's own learning, and to more efficient self-management in general. Some philosophers have labeled this second aim as "self-appropriation"[1] or "elements of effective thinking"[2] or "self-possession of conscious performance"[3] or "self-regulation of learning."[4]

In this chapter and throughout most of the book distinct patterns (or processes) of problem solving activities will be introduced, described, and placed into an explanatory context. In addition, a mode of pause from the work of problem solving will be described. Subsequent chapters will elaborate on each of these four patterns and the mode of pause by describing them, placing them in relation to one another, exploring how one can insure high-quality thinking in each pattern and then locating the patterns in larger contexts of personality, society, culture, and history.

As important as problem solving is, it is not the only type of learning. It operates side by side with simpler forms of learning such as paired-associate learning, stimulus reinforcement, concept attainment, and sheer memorization. Yet, as a more complex form of learning, problem solving is designed to deal with situations that are new and perplexing to us and that in some sense press for a solution. It also deals with chronic problems that seem to defy solution. Such problematic situations, whether large or small, new or chronic, confront us with the challenge to engage in the work of problem solving or to withdraw. Whatever we choose to do will accumulate over a lifetime into either habits of problem solving or habits of avoidance and drift. These habits of problem solving will contribute to the shaping of a learning personality; while the habits of drift will result in a personality that is less engaged with learning.

It should be emphasized that, if left free to operate, the patterns of problem solving will more likely than not produce solutions that are attentive to experience, deeply insightful, supported by evidence, guided by time-tested values and transformative not only of problematic situations in the world but also of the problem solver. Hence the implications of problem solving reach not only to the environments in which we live but to the very development (or stagnation) of ourselves.

Each of the four patterns is a sequenced series of conscious acts and operations, guided by an intention and resulting in an endpoint. These patterns are named as follows: "seeking understanding," "factual judging," "values judging," and "deciding." In addition, there is a mode of pause labeled "basic experiencing" (see figure 1.1). Each pattern consists of elements that are in fact mental events, and each pattern is a functional grouping of such events. Since mental events are involved throughout, their existence can be verified in one's own conscious activities.

The four patterns of problem solving and the mode of pause will later be placed in the larger contexts of personality, social trust, culture, and history. These larger contexts are important because they can support or interfere with

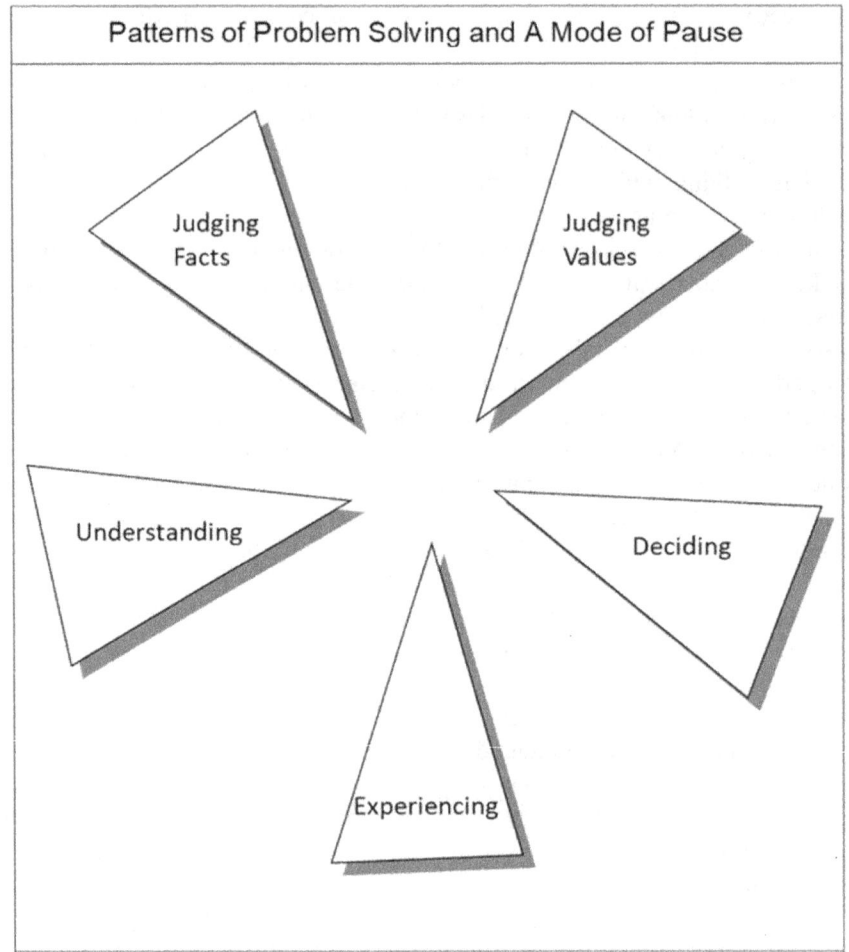

Figure 1.1 Patterns of Problem Solving and a Mode of Pause. *Source*: Author.

problem solving. In addition, the larger contexts are also the beneficiaries of problem solving efforts. Chapter 5 will explore these topics in greater detail, and chapter 6 will compare and contrast them with a few other accounts of problem solving drawn from philosophy and psychology. Chapter 7 will consider how the four distinct patterns of problem solving and the mode of pause may be viewed as a form of mindful practice and used as a blueprint for learning in any area.

Throughout the book reference will be made to relevant works of some philosophers and psychologists. From philosophy, inspiration is drawn from the work of Canadian philosopher Bernard Lonergan, especially his work in cognitional theory and generalized empirical method. Inspiration is also drawn from the history of psychology. Psychology has a relatively brief history since the founding of the psychological laboratory of Wilhelm Wundt in 1879. In particular, some reference will be made to the schools of psychodynamic psychology, radical behaviorism, cognitive behaviorism, and more recent trends and themes of the twenty-first century. Psychodynamic psychology is associated with Sigmund Freud, Carl Jung, Erik Erikson, Karen Horney, and others. It emphasizes unconscious processes in personality development and functioning. Radical behaviorism is associated with Ivan Pavlov, John B. Watson, and B.F. Skinner. It focuses on environment, observable behavior, and habits in its study of personality development, and functioning. Cognitive behaviorism is associated with thinkers such as Aaron Beck, Albert Ellis, and others. It admits the causal role of thoughts and feelings in the development and functioning of personality.

PROBLEM SOLVING IS A LEARNING PROCESS

Problem solving is a cognitive process. It is a "process" because it is a sequence of events that take place over time and that result in a product. Brewing coffee is a process resulting in a beverage. Playing a baseball game is a process resulting in a final score. Sometimes the events that make up a process are instantaneous and sometimes they are extended over time. Problem solving is a cognitive process because it involves the analysis and transformation of information. Since we learn through the analysis and transformation of information, problem solving is therefore essential to the learning process.

Many of the events in problem solving are mental events. Question and insight are clearly mental events. They cannot be discovered with the five senses, yet they can be experienced. Questions have no sound, but they do occur to us. Insights have no shape, yet we all have had them. These are conscious events that function at the heart of the problem solving process. We also formulate and express our questions and insights in language. Events of "formulation" and "expression" are also part of the problem solving process. Expressions can be seen and heard by others. Of course, that is not enough; they also need to be understood, not only by ourselves but also by others. It will also become clear that problem solving also relies on experiences such as sensations, perceptions, memories, and images. Moreover, problem solving relies on communication with others and on the reports of the problem solving efforts by others.

Finally, problem solving results in learning. Yet learning can be regarded as either a relatively stable change in consciousness or a change in behavior. These changes in consciousness and behavior provide the opportunity for the problem solver to become a bit more experienced, insightful, knowledgeable, guided by value, and responsible. Hence, problem solving is not merely an accumulation of information; it is a transformation of ourselves. To the extent that problem solvers actually make use of these changes they are in a position to bring change to real-world situations. The learning experience becomes transformational not only of the problem situation but of the problem solver.

MENTAL EVENTS IN PROBLEM SOLVING

Problem solving is not simple learning, but it presupposes it.[5] As mentioned, simple learning consists of paired associate learning, stimulus response learning, concept attainment, and memorization. This type of learning typically results in memories or habits that can be used easily in routine, previously encountered situations. This is a form of "System I thinking." This is "a mode of thought comprising, rapid, implicit, and automatic cognitive operations."[6] In addition, these memories and habits may be applied in dealing with problems presented by novel situations. It is clear from work on memory and its loss that new learning relies heavily on memory. It is also clear that the development of specialized cognitive habits contributes to success in many fields.[7]

In contrast to simple learning, problem solving is a discursive process, extended over time, consisting of many events. It is a form of "System II thinking" which is defined as "a mode of thought comprising slow, explicit and controlled processes."[8] Some of the events of problem solving, like question and insight, are purely mental events; others have physical aspects, such as the expression of questions and insights in writing and speech. Some of these events are instantaneous, like the sudden emergence of insight. Others have a longer duration, such as the adequate "formulation of a researchable question." Also, because this process is a chain of events it can easily be upset, either through interruptions from the environment or from disruptions in the individual thinker.

Complex problem solving may emerge in the face of challenging situations that demand a response. Those situations may be entirely new or they may be a chronic annoyance. Yet complex human learning rarely occurs without a presenting problem, and it proceeds slowly if the problem is poorly defined.

As indicated, question, insight, and the desire to know are mental events that are central to any careful problem solving effort. Without questions, there is no recognized problem to be solved. Without insight, there is no apparent solution. Without the desire to know, problem solving efforts are not sustained and are easily derailed.

But what is "question" as a mental event? Questions emerge from an often unclear recognition of a gap in our experience, understanding, knowledge, or practice. If that recognition is pursued, once it is clothed in appropriate language, the question becomes formulated. Hence a formulated question is a representation of a problem, understood as a gap, and expressed as an interrogative.[9] If the question is pursued, it becomes an intention to fill the gap and the question itself is a concrete instance of the desire to know. This desire and intention distinguish "authentic questions" from "inauthentic questions." The emergence and pursuit of authentic questions constitute a dynamic attitude of questioning. With an attitude of authentic questioning, questions become "operators" and move the process of learning forward. Questioning as described here is not simply a general attitude of wonder, but a desire specifically focused on perceived gaps. Inauthentic questions, in contrast, are not really questions at all, but are often complaints or delaying tactics disguised as a question. They are moved by an entirely different intention, and it is not the desire to know.

Not all inquiry is problem solving. Some questions are routine and have been encountered before. Insights to answer them have become encoded in memory and are summoned subject to the conditions of memory. Problem solving, in contrast, is an extended process that usually kicks in when problems are novel, chronic, or difficult in some other way. A more extended process is required to move toward a solution.

What is insight as a mental event? Insights emerge as a potential solution to a problem or potential answer to a question. They bring together a variety of disparate but relevant elements into a coherent synthesis. As such, insights serve as "integrators" and consolidators in a protracted process of learning. As a partial fulfillment of the desire to know, insights are often associated with an emotional release of the tension generated by the effort to solve a particular problem or answer a particular question.[10] In addition, insights frequently give rise to further questions.[11]

As mental events, questions and insights often make their first appearance in an unformulated manner. They are to be distinguished both from their later formulation and expression. Regarding questions, it is one thing to recognize a gap (the unformulated question), according to which we know that something is missing. But because the nature of that gap is not formulated, we cannot quite articulate it. It is another thing to formulate that recognition in the words of a question (formulated question). With the formulation we are beginning to get a better handle on what is missing. It is a third event to express that question to another person (expressed question). Questions that we have may or may not be expressed to others for a variety of reasons. Regarding insights, it is one thing to come up with the beginning of a bright idea (the unformulated insight). One might refer to these as "partially baked ideas." We know that we seem to be on the right track, but because it is not formulated, we cannot work with it easily. It is another thing to formulate the insight in words or in a formula. This becomes a formulated insight. This formulation gives us a clearer idea of what is happening. It is a third event to express that insight to another person (expressed insight). Insights that we have may or may not be expressed to others for a variety of reasons.

It is useful to compare philosopher Bernard Lonergan's five conclusions about aspects of insight with the conclusions reached by psychologists using methods that are more indirect. In particular, Lonergan concluded that insight (1) comes as a release to the tension of inquiry, (2) comes suddenly and unexpectedly, (3) is a function not of outer circumstances but of inner conditions, (4) pivots between the concrete and the abstract, and (5) passes into the habitual texture of the mind.[12]

Robert Sternberg and Janet Davidson have compiled a specialized collection of empirical studies devoted to the description of insight and of some conditions that seem to favor its emergence.[13] (1) While Lonergan refers to a release of the tension of inquiry, Mary Gick and Robert Lockhart address the affective aspects of insight[14] that they regard as a natural correlate. In some cases the "aha" experience is accompanied by delight, and in others by chagrin, depending on the content of the insight. Howard Gruber[15] considers insights and associated emotions using specific examples of learning throughout history. (2) Lonergan adverts to the suddenness of insight as do Gick and Lockhart and Gruber. Janet Davidson[16] focuses primarily on this aspect of insight in her review of the literature and her related empirical study. (3) For Lonergan, insight is a function not of outer circumstances but of inner conditions, such as the emergence and formulation of a question and the desire to know. Psychological researchers may attend to both inner and outer conditions. Instead of questions, they may refer to the formulation of a problem.[17] In addition, they often attend to the behavioral and social contexts in which problem solving occurs.[18] (4) While Lonergan adverts to how insight pivots between the concrete and abstract, psychological researchers routinely examine the extent to which insights can be generalized (which would not be possible were it not for abstraction). (5) Finally, Lonergan writes about insight passing into the habitual texture of the mind. That refers to the diminished attention it receives as it moves into the background of our consciousness. Such settling "into the habitual texture of the mind" may signal the emergence of expert knowledge, which has been the focus of some research attention: with some emphasizing the automatic aspects of it,[19] and others emphasizing the consciously controlled reflective aspects of it.[20]

In contrast with insight, question as a conscious event has received even less attention.[21] Occasionally, questions are addressed from a linguistic point of view, as a formulation of an interrogative proposition.[22] Yet questions seem neglected as a pre-verbal recognition of a gap in our understanding, knowledge, or practice, and they are also neglected as an intention to fill the gap (through learning). The literature in cognitive psychology approaches the function of the question when it examines the way in which we "find problems" and "represent problems."[23] The probability of successful problem solving is heightened if the nature of the gap is clear and if the intention to learn is preserved in spite of disruptions and interruptions.

The nature of the question anticipates the nature of the insight sought and the kind of conscious mode or pattern of which it is a part: whether it is "understanding," "judging," or "deciding." Questions as mental events have characteristics which are functionally complementary to the characteristics of insight. In particular, questions (1) initiate the tension of inquiry, (2) they may come suddenly and unexpectedly, (3) they are likely a function of both outer circumstances and of inner conditions, (4) they pivot between the concrete and the abstract, and (5) they have the potential of passing into the habitual texture of the mind.[24]

Questions and insights play alternating roles in the expansion of consciousness. As the intentions of further questions change, the inquirer's viewpoint expands and it becomes deeper and more comprehensive with every accumulating insight. As questions continue, the urgency of different patterns of problem solving becomes more apparent.[25] The pattern of seeking understanding can achieve a grasp of possibilities, but at some point possibilities are not enough. The activities that constitute the pattern of factual judging are needed to distinguish true from false, and probable from improbable. This is factual critical thinking. The activities in the pattern of values judging are needed to align what we have come to know with tested values. This is values-oriented critical thinking. The activities of the pattern of deciding include activities needed to determine what valuable knowledge should be acted upon and what worthless activities are to be abandoned. This is deliberative critical thinking.

While questions and insights are not the only mental events, they are very important in their respective and recurrent roles in the patterns of problem solving. Distinct questions move the process forward and insights consolidate gains. As mental events they are not hypothetical constructs, namely something that is simply inferred from indirect evidence. Rather, mental events can be directly experienced by the person having them. No inference or logical proof is required. No one can have the experience of a mental event for someone else. For example, one cannot have an insight for another, or one cannot hear a symphony for another. Also mental events are not abilities, understood either as a summary of what a person can do or as a prediction of what they might do in the future. Rather, they are time-limited changes in conscious experience.

In problem solving, question and insight function in conjunction with other conscious activities such as the desire to know, sensing and imagining, remembering and perceiving, formulating and expressing, collecting evidence and reasons, weighing evidence and reasons, judging (fact and value), deciding and engaging in action, and social trust. Throughout this book these mental events will also be referred to as "facts of consciousness." Some of these events are in our control, while others are not. Problem solving that is unfettered and that is dominated by the desire to know is to be distinguished from "problem solving" efforts in which the desire to know is blocked or upset.

Historically mental events have acquired a poor reputation in both philosophy and psychology. For example, in philosophy, the logician Gottlob Frege developed a project to reduce all linguistic statements to rules of logic.[26] Following this, Ludwig Wittgenstein, in his later writings, developed a project of attempting to fully describe human language as a social game.[27] In both projects, mental events were seen as irrelevant to the projects' goals and were banished. Other examples are found in psychology; early structuralism ran into a different kind of trouble trying to describe a seemingly endless variety of mental contents.[28] As a result, the study of mental events came to be seen as unfruitful. Later radical behaviorism, popular in the 1950s and 1960s, sought to limit psychology's subject matter to publicly observable behavior and to exclude mental events. This was part of a project to make psychology more scientific.[29]

By the twenty-first century, all of these projects involving the "elimination" of mental events have run their course. In retrospect, they have come to be seen as addressing smaller goals and answering more limited questions than once predicted. Yet mental events exist anyway in spite of these systematic efforts to ignore or banish them. Ironically, each of these projects can be understood as positive examples of an attempt at problem solving and as a product of insight arriving to address specified questions. Yet, despite these projects' rules for banishing mental events, complex problem solving went on before these projects were conceived, and it will continue after their passing. Problem solving itself will be at the heart of future advances in every field. Any attempt to eliminate problem solving and its constituent activities will also eliminate any possibility of solutions and thereby eliminate the future projects themselves.

The very complexity of human problem solving consists in its makeup of multiple cognitive acts and operations tending toward a goal or toward multiple goals. To answer the question "How does complex human problem solving work?" requires the isolation and identification of distinct activities and operations, and relating each to the others in a dynamic system of functional interrelationships. The remainder of this chapter will identify and describe patterns or modes of consciousness associated with complex problem solving or with a pause from problem solving. It will explain how each pattern relates to the others. It will also describe in general terms the mental events that repeatedly occur in each pattern.

Looking ahead, chapters 2 and 3 will examine four distinct patterns of problem solving in greater detail, along with their associated mental events and interferences with these events. In addition, since problem solving is work, chapter 4 will consider a mode of pause from problem solving labeled "basic experience." This is a problem-free and question-free zone of conscious experience. In it no problems present themselves and no questions are pursued. In some instances, the mode of pause becomes a zone of relaxation and of the regeneration of energy and focus. These chapters will also address the topic of quality assurance in problem solving patterns and in rest.

PATTERNS OF PROBLEM SOLVING AND A MODE OF PAUSE

A "mental event" can be defined as a change in consciousness. It can be an instantaneous act, such as the sudden occurrence of a bright idea, or it can also be an operation that is extended over time and is not instantaneous, such as solving a puzzle.

A "pattern of problem solving" is a functionally interrelated collection of mental events, motivated by the desire to know and designed to address questions. What makes a group of mental events (acts and operations) into a pattern of problem solving is that among them is a guiding intention, some intervening consolidating events and an endpoint (or product). Each pattern of problem solving is a structured group of mental events that differs from the others mainly in its guiding intention and its endpoint. In the patterns of problem solving, the intervening consolidating events are drawn from the facts of consciousness mentioned above: sensing and imagining, remembering and perceiving, question and insight, formulating and expressing, collecting evidence and reasons, weighing evidence and reasons, judging (fact and value), deciding, and engaging in action. In the language of contemporary psychology, each pattern of problem solving is also a "cognitive process." As such, they are extended over time and they are thereby subject to interferences from the outside environment (e.g., interruptions, confirmation bias, or group bias) or from within the problem solver (e.g., disruptions such as fatigue, confirmation bias, or process bias).

The first pattern of problem solving to be considered in the book is Seeking Understanding. (Hereafter, it will also be called "Problem Solving Pattern 1," "PS Pattern 1," or just "Pattern 1.") When operating in this pattern the thinker is open to considering a variety of meaningful possibilities and attempting to gain an initial grasp of a situation. The attempt may take the form of asking questions. The more questions asked and answered the better the grasp or comprehension of the situation will be. Consider the example of an accident investigator who is faced with the task of making a preliminary report on a train derailment that occurred a few hours ago. While the report is not the final word, it should be a balanced consideration of available relevant information. It will be a preliminary grasp of what happened, what were the circumstances and some early hypotheses about why it happened. The primary question that guides the process could be something like this: "What might have happened here?" Early answers to this and related questions will later be subjected to tests for accuracy. (See also chapter 2.)

While understanding grasps possible solutions, critical thinking aims to put these possibilities to the test by assessing the solutions against some criterion of truth, value, or action. Hence three types of critical thinking can be distinguished wherein we primarily seek to resolve matters of fact (Factual Critical Thinking), apply and coordinate values (Values-oriented Critical Thinking), or take responsible action (Deliberative Critical Thinking).

Three patterns of problem solving are instances of specific types of critical thinking. (Hereafter these will be called "Problem Solving Patterns 2, 3, and 4," or "PS Patterns 2, 3, 4," or just "Patterns 2, 3, 4.") The patterns of critical thinking are more convergent than Seeking Understanding (PS Pattern 1), because they are filters designed to weed out all previously considered possibilities with the exception of those that pass some additional test. In Factual Critical Thinking (PS Pattern 2) the test is a test of truth or probability. In Values-oriented Critical Thinking (PS Pattern 3) the test is some standard of value or worth. In Deliberative Critical Thinking (PS Pattern 4) the test is a worthwhile course of action. These tests do not infringe on one another but coordinate with one another. Patterns 2, 3, and 4 are similar forms of critical thinking since they involve consideration of evidence or reasons, and the application of a criterion in an attempt to answer a reflective question. "Reflective questions" always take only "yes" or "no" as an answer. Yet Patterns 2, 3, and 4 are distinct from one another because each pattern addresses different reflective questions and has different end-points.

In Factual Critical Thinking (PS Pattern 2) the task is primarily to establish the facts: that is, to determine which of the possibilities considered in Pattern 1 happens to be true. Consider the example of a jury which has been assembled to determine whether or not John Doe committed a robbery at ABC Market last June 11. The primary question that guides this process is: "Did John Doe do it?" Evidence and reasons will be assembled by the opposing attorneys. The judge will instruct the jury in the law and a criterion of truth and probability. In criminal cases the criterion is that the evidence should show beyond a reasonable doubt that John Doe committed the crime, otherwise he is considered not guilty. The jury itself will then weigh the reasons and evidence according to this criterion. As a group they will need to have a "reflective factual insight" into whether or not the evidence is sufficient to indicate that John Doe committed the robbery. A "judgment of fact" is simply an answer to the reflective question of fact: "Did John Doe do it?" This is the primary question guiding this process. The achieved judgment is the endpoint of the process and it is simply the affirmation or denial of the truth of some previously considered possibility. The entire pattern of factual judging has been labeled here as "Factual Critical Thinking" (PS Pattern 2). The jury is the judge of facts and will either affirm that John Doe committed the crime or they will acquit. (See also chapter 3.)

In Values-oriented Critical Thinking (PS Pattern 3) the task is primarily to resolve issues of value: that is, to judge which of the possibilities considered and facts established happen to be worthwhile. Just because something is true does not mean that it is automatically worthwhile. We may wish to apply other criteria of value to what we understand and know to be true. This process may also involve the application or adjustment of a scale of values. A question such as "Is this worthwhile?" will be the primary guiding question in this process. Consider the voter who is faced with the choice of voting for one person from a field of four candidates. As a preliminary step the voter may wish to determine whether the various proposed policies of the candidates are generally valuable. Does she approve of them? Evidence and reasons will be assembled and then weighed according to some criterion of value. The common question, "Is it worth it?" illustrates the breadth of values being considered in PS Pattern 3. The question can evoke a response in terms of moral/ethical values or of pragmatic considerations of possible outcomes. A "reflective values insight" will indicate whether or not the evidence is sufficient to answer the reflective question of value. A "judgment of value" is the endpoint of this process and is simply an answer to the reflective question of value: "Is this position worthwhile?" This kind of judgment is the approval or disapproval of the worth of some previously considered possibility. The entire pattern of judging values will be labeled here as "Values-oriented Critical Thinking" (PS Pattern 3). (See also chapter 3.)

In Deliberative Critical Thinking (PS Pattern 4) the task is primarily to decide on a course of action: that is, to select which of the possible courses of action it is most appropriate to implement in a given context. Just because something is true and worthwhile generally does not mean that it is something we would choose to act on in our own lives. This process definitely involves the application of a scale of values to ourselves and to situations in which we operate. A question such as "Should I do it?" will be the primary guiding question in this process. Consider the case of a patient considering medical options for treating a medical condition. The patient may opt for surgery, medication, or to wait. The surgery may be successful, but it may also result in difficult complications. The medication, while less effective, may fully treat the condition. If the patient chooses to wait the condition may or may not get worse.[30] In careful deliberative critical thinking, evidence and reasons will be assembled and then weighed according to some scale of values. In this case it will include the scale of values of the patient. A "reflective deliberative insight" will indicate whether or not the evidence and reasons are sufficient to answer the reflective deliberative question "Should I have the surgery?" A "decision" is the endpoint of this process and is simply an answer to the reflective deliberative question. Because the question it answers is reflective, it only takes "yes" or "no" as an answer. Because the question is deliberative, it is always formed in the first person "I" or "we." Should I do that? Should we refrain from doing that? "Decision" is the personal endorsement of a course of action. It is a limited personal resolution, commitment, or imperative to realize some value in one's life, or to eliminate some disvalue. The full expression of a decision is the actual action it endorses. That course of action may have multiple consequences such as complications, side effects, and worsening disease. Decisions to be fully implemented must be backed up by action, in this case actually following the course of treatment. The mode of deciding will be labeled as "Deliberative Critical Thinking" (PS Process 4). (See also chapter 3.)

A special mode of consciousness associated with effective problem solving is an experienced state of pause from the work of problem solving. It is labeled here as "basic experience." In this mode, no problems present themselves and no questions are pursued. This is difficult to describe because the word "experience" itself has multiple meanings. In its widest meaning, experience is anything that we live through. In this sense, all the patterns of problem solving are part of experience: in the patterns experience can be used as a source for discovering problems and as a resource and as a testing ground for solving problems.

But is there another meaning for "experience" and is there another function that is being overlooked? Here an affirmative answer is given by noting that there is a form of conscious awareness that is devoid of all problem solving efforts. Let us name this "basic experience." In this form of consciousness, problem solving efforts are placed on pause. Its main function is to be a haven from problem solving. Excluded from it is all the work involved in problem solving and the emotions associated with it. Ruled out are not only questions, seeking insights, formulations, and expressions of various sorts, but also as many images and sensations as possible as well as distractions and interruptions. This is not an easy state of consciousness to achieve without practice.[31] For each individual, we can also inquire about the extent they make use of experience as a haven from the work of problem solving. (See also chapter 4.)

THE FOUR PATTERNS OF PROBLEM SOLVING IN FUNCTIONAL RELATION TO ONE ANOTHER

Each of the patterns of problem solving constitutes a different way of thinking; basic experiencing provides the material for thinking as well as a possible haven from the work of thinking. All these groupings of mental events have some guiding intention to move forward. They all have some endpoint. They all have intermediate mental events. Yet each differs from the others in motivating force and endpoint. Experiencing is moved by attention and ends in memories. Seeking Understanding (PS Pattern 1) is moved by questions for understanding and ends in insights as possible answers. Factual Critical Thinking (PS Pattern 2) is moved by the reflective question of fact ("Is it true?") and terminates in the judgment of fact. Values-oriented Critical Thinking (PS Pattern 3) is moved by the reflective question of value ("Is it worthwhile?") and ends in the judgment of value. Deliberative Critical Thinking (PS Pattern 4) is moved by the question for deliberation ("Should I/we do it?") and ends in a decision to act.

While every pattern of problem solving has its own functions, those functions naturally lead to other patterns. Experiencing provides the material to which we can attend and note discrepancies. Experience of discrepancies naturally gives rise to questions for understanding and the attempt to comprehend or understand what is presented. But understanding yields only possibilities. This naturally calls forth the quest for knowledge (verified understanding). Is our understanding correct? Is it true or likely to be true? Further, the verification of facts invites further questions of value: Is what we understand and know worthwhile? Is it valuable? Finally, in a world of lived experiences, meaningful possibilities, verified facts, approved values the question arises as to whether or not we will do something about it.[32]

Experiencing, Seeking Understanding, Factual Critical Thinking, Values-oriented Critical Thinking, and Deliberative Critical Thinking naturally call forth each other. They do this not mechanistically but according to probabilities. If one has a desire to know then it will be deeply dissatisfying to live without pursuing questions or addressing problems. If one has a desire to know then it will be deeply dissatisfying to remain in a world of mere possibilities without attempting to nail down what in the world is true and what is worthwhile. And what is the point of all this prior work of gaining factual or moral knowledge without actually using it?

PATTERNS OF PROBLEM SOLVING IN LARGER CONTEXTS

Problem solving does not occur in a vacuum. It occurs in successively larger contexts of personality, society (and social trust), culture, and history. Each of these contexts may affect and be affected by individual problem solving efforts. Each of these larger contexts may be regarded as a "field of forces" as understood in the work of psychologist Kurt Lewin.[33] Force field analysis is a method of social-psychological analysis designed to describe, predict, and explain change or no change in individuals and groups. In each force field (or larger context) there will be "driving forces" that move change in the direction of the growth of learning, as well as "restraining forces" that interfere with learning. The acts and operations that make up each pattern of problem solving are personal driving forces that facilitate learning. They are supplemented by other forces in the environment that also propel learning. In contrast, both within the person and in the larger environment there are restraining forces that hold learning back, distort it, or prevent it altogether.

Personality is a force field or larger context in which problem solving occurs. By "personality" we mean a relatively stable constellation of cognitive, emotive, and behavioral aspects of individual persons. While some authors regard the term as notoriously difficult to define,[34] others have indicated that "there is a core agreement in considering personality as an integration of traits that can be investigated and described in order to render an account of the unique quality of the individual."[35] For psychologists, "traits" are aspects of the person that are relatively stable over time. Personality traits include those that are cognitive, emotive, and behavioral. Cognitive traits pertain not only to habitual thoughts but to the cognitive processes that produce them. This includes all of the patterns of problem solving. Emotive traits refer to characteristic or predictable affective responses. Behavioral traits refer to recurrent trajectories of observable behavior. To the extent that traits are automatic, they are often rooted in habits not only of behavior, but habits of thought and emotion as well.

Within the context of personality, the patterns of problem solving are also related in terms of increasing levels of personal commitment and associated levels of anxiety. Each pattern of problem solving is an exploration of the unknown and each requires an increasing commitment of both resources and reputation. Anxiety is particularly relevant here since it is an emotion that directly concerns an unknown future. Specifically, "anxiety" is defined as "an emotion characterized by apprehension and somatic symptoms of tension in which an individual anticipates impending danger, catastrophe or misfortune. . . . Anxiety is considered a future-oriented, long-acting response broadly focused on a diffuse threat."[36]

Experience is something that one cannot help but do; to be alive and conscious is to experience. There is no choice about it or special aptitude that is required. Seeking Understanding (PS Pattern 1) involves a bit more commitment to follow questions and insights where they lead. Yet, since we are dealing with mere possibilities, anxiety levels tend to be low. The activity of brainstorming (or generating possibilities) is often viewed as a pleasant activity by students. Factual Critical Thinking (PS Pattern 2) requires a greater personal commitment by affirming or denying the truth of some idea. This often requires making a knowledge claim in front of others. There is the possibility of error, which could make one appear ignorant. With that possibility anxiety may increase. Values-oriented Critical Thinking (PS Pattern 3) requires an even greater commitment of approving or disapproving the value of something. While the facts may be something that we cannot help, approval and disapproval require taking a more deeply committed stand in front of others. There is the possibility not only of error but of being misguided in later allocation of resources and decisions. With that possibility anxiety may increase even further. Deliberative Critical Thinking (PS Pattern 4) requires the greatest commitment of all through engaging or refusing a course of action. At stake are one's time, reputation, and other resources. There is the possibility of revealing something about ourselves in what do and do not choose. Here the anxiety level may be the highest.

This connection between the patterns of problem solving and anxiety in particular may be formulated as the "pattern-anxiety hypothesis": As one moves from basic experiencing to understanding to factual critical thinking to values-oriented critical thinking to deciding, the hypothesis predicts that the level of personal anxiety will increase. The subjective experience of anxiety can range from a mild awareness of discomfort through heightened concern to the extreme of panic. The predicted increase in anxiety is due in part to increasing levels of personal commitment. As one moves through each pattern, more is required of the thinker, and the individual is confronted with greater personal risks. Hence there is a magnification of attention, concern, and anxiety.

The learning history of each person and their experience in dealing with anxiety will likely result in habits of thinking in which some patterns of problem solving come to be preferred and over-practiced while others are avoided and neglected. There would result a "problem solving profile" of relative strengths and weaknesses based on the patterns of problem solving. Let us identify these profiles as descriptions of "problem response styles."[37]

Problem response styles provide a descriptive account of the extent to which an individual does or does not routinely engage effectively in each of the patterns of problem solving. Some individuals function well in generating possibilities (Seeking Understanding) but do less well in activities involved in putting possibilities to the test (Factual Critical Thinking). Some have a heightened sense of values and of what is ethical (Values-oriented Critical Thinking) but are less effective at getting things done (Deliberative Critical Thinking). Some are very effective in getting things done, but at a loss when it comes to deep appreciation of experiences (as in basic experiencing). The permutations are many.[38]

Society and our social relations constitute another larger force field in which problem solving occurs. By "society" we mean "an enduring social group living in a particular place whose members are mutually interdependent and share political and other institutions, laws and mores, and a common culture"[39] Society exists within physical environments but also provide a group context for human interactions. The nature of these interactions will be crucial to any person's development. Social trust will play a crucial role in facilitating growth-producing or growth-limiting interactions with others.[40] By "social trust" we mean the reliance on the word and the assumed competence of others in thinking and in getting things done. When we ask someone for the time and then act on it, we are engaging in social trust. When we place a stamp on a letter and mail it, we engage in social trust. Other names for social trust are "belief" and "believing." By whatever name, social trust is an indispensable aid for persons living and working in groups. With it we can regard others as our eyes and ears in the environment and as partners in effective problem solving efforts. Without it we become isolated and are reduced to the impossible task of finding everything out for ourselves.

Culture provides an even larger force field in which problem solving occurs. By "culture" here is meant "the distinctive customs, values, beliefs, knowledge, art, and language of a society or a community. These values and concepts are passed on from generation to generation, and they are the basis for everyday behaviors and practices."[41] Bernard Lonergan offers a more succinct definition: "Culture is a set of meanings and values informing a common way of life."[42] As such, culture has cognitive, behavioral, and emotive components as well as a habitual aspect. This set of meanings provides for individuals and groups a blueprint for living, and it supplies standard answers to basic questions such as "Who are we?" "Where did we come from?" and "What is our future?"

Culture is important to problem solving because it provides a basic roadmap in which individual and group problem solving efforts may occur. It also provides resources for some of these efforts. When problem solving occurs in individuals and in small groups the results become available as contributions to the general culture. On the other hand, culture also provides boundaries beyond which individual and group problem solving efforts are discouraged or may not occur at all. Therefore, problem solving both influences culture and is influenced by culture.

History is the largest force field of all for problem solving. By "history" here is meant both the succession of events lived by a people and the scholarly discipline of recorded history. Lived history is the sum total of all events experienced by a people during a certain time period. The number of such events is vast and probably countless. Included somewhere among them are likely to have been attempts at problem solving. Recorded history, in contrast, consists in narrative accounts of some of those events, based on available historical evidence.

Recorded history is important to problem solving because it provides a chronicle and descriptive account of previous individual and group problem solving projects. It becomes a resource for the present by offering models that may be imitated and improved by later problem solvers. When problem solving occurs in individuals and in small groups the results are then available to future historians as contributions to the general history of a people or of a field of study. On the other hand, recorded history also provides boundaries beyond which individual and group problem solving efforts may find it difficult to go. Traditions from the past may interfere with innovations that are effective yet quite unprecedented. Therefore, problem solving both influences history and is influenced by history.

ENSURING PROBLEM SOLVING QUALITY

From the beginning, philosophers and psychologists have been concerned with the quality of problem solving and with the possibility of its corruption. If accurate problem solving and knowledge acquisition is conceived of as a simple process such as perception or sensation, then ensuring quality becomes a matter of simply "seeing what is there to be seen." In contrast, if accurate problem solving and knowledge acquisition is conceived of as a complex process involving experiencing, understanding, judging, and deciding, then ensuring quality becomes a matter of ensuring the quality and integrity of each pattern of problem solving and basic experiencing according to the inherent norms of each. Here, "problem solving quality" is the extent to which the activities of the problem solving patterns are guided by the desire to know.

In addition, if problem solving is to be really thorough, there must be a balance involving all the patterns of problem solving and basic experiencing. Elimination or curtailment of any one will result in a product that is less attentive, insightful, factual, valuable, and practical than it might otherwise be. More specifically, limiting experience results in a limitation of the scope of what is to be learned. Limiting the flow of relevant questions and insights interferes with the processes of Seeking Understanding and of the three types of Critical Thinking. The result is diminished understanding, knowledge, and effective practice. In contrast, if all the patterns work together over time, they result in a kind of knowledge and transformative problem solving that is attentive to experience, deeply insightful, grounded in evidence, guided by time-tested values, and transformative of situations and of self. Such knowledge is both thorough and expert.

How can we ensure quality in our problem solving? It can be ensured by isolating, identifying, and reversing those factors that interfere with the natural unfolding of the processes of experience, understanding, and critical thinking.

What are some of these limiting factors? There are personal limiting factors that may arise within the individual and there are environmental limiting factors that come from the outside. Personal limiting factors may be regarded as disruptions of the processes and patterns of learning, while environmental limiting factors may be regarded as interruptions of learning. Included among the personal disruptions would be any bodily, emotive, cognitive, or behavioral state that interferes with the attention required for thorough learning. Included would be states such as hunger, fatigue, pain, stray emotions, or thoughts. Many emotions, including anxiety, can interfere with the patterns of problem solving and the unfolding of the desire to know. Interfering emotions could be positive or negative; they become interferences when they crowd out the desire to know. In addition, forms of personal bias are also included here. In contrast, there are the environmental interruptions which include any outside influence that interferes with the attention required for thorough learning. These are almost too numerous to catalog. In addition, forms of group bias are also included here.

Among all the interferences with learning, "bias" is particularly difficult to address because it is poorly defined and because we may not know that it is operating. At present, bias is not clearly and unambiguously defined. Some accounts have identified dozens of uses for the word "bias."[43] This situation is a prescription for chaos. To address that, let us define "process bias" as any systematic disruption, distortion, or interference of problem solving efforts. In contrast, unbiased problem solving efforts are described in patterns of problem solving 1, 2, 3, or 4. The systematic disruption of any relevant information or mental event from a problem solving effort is pertinent here. The existence of bias in this sense requires that: (1) there be an identified problem that is being investigated, (2) information and problem solving activities that would significantly change the outcome are being excluded, and (3) the relevant information or activities are disrupted over an extended period of time. Relevant information includes primarily questions and insights about the problem. Bias can also exclude relevant images, language, collection and weighing of evidence. When the bias is operating, the exclusion of relevant information is ongoing.

Biases may arise through accident or deliberate choice in response to stimuli that are painful, uncomfortable, or threatening. Bias is a mental moving away from such stimuli, and in the extreme, from the people who produce them.[44] The process of moving away gets reinforced by an immediate feeling of relief.[45] When bias is practiced over a stretch of time, it becomes a cognitive habit and it takes on all of the traits of a habit: it is done without thinking, done easily, done efficiently, and has some pleasant aspect to it (i.e., reducing anxiety and "keeping one safe").

Reversing biases is no easy matter. It requires identifying them when and where they exist. It also requires installing a new habit of reversing and removing them by finally examining the uncomfortable questions, insights, images, language, and evidence that have been excluded from consideration for so long.

Looking ahead, as each pattern of problem solving is explored in subsequent chapters, the issue of ensuring a quality result will again be addressed for each specific context. Of course, the matter of quality assurance in problem solving will be intimately connected with the facts of consciousness, especially question, insight, the desire to know, social trust, and various forms of bias in the sense defined here.

ADDITIONAL CONSIDERATIONS: PREDICTIONS

If this book is to be any real use to readers, it should assist in bringing about clear effects that can be verified in personal experience. These effects may be immediate, intermediate, or long-term. Each effect is a step of partial self-appropriation and each effect advances the overall goal of "self-appropriation" which is the self-managed developmental process of achieving ever more differentiated experiencing, understanding, judging, and deciding about one's own experiencing, understanding, judging, and deciding. In addition, as one moves through experiencing, understanding, factual judging, values judging, and deciding, the level of personal commitment increases.

The immediate predicted effects can be listed as follows. By the end of chapters 1–5, readers will (1) recognize and identify cognitive acts, operations, events, and processes in terms of their own experience, (2) distinguish cognitive acts, operations, events, and processes from one another, (3) engage in each cognitive activity as appropriate to a given problem stimulus, and (4) manage cognitive activities of a given pattern by generating appropriate responses. Furthermore, by the end of the book, readers will have (5) demonstrated to self and others: specific instances of Seeking Understanding, Factual Critical Thinking, Values-oriented Critical Thinking, and Deliberative Critical Thinking by means of question, answer, and action. In addition (6) readers will acknowledge themselves as a thinker and problem solver who engages in the patterns of problem solving and the mode of pause. Taken together, these six immediate effects constitute forms of "partial self-appropriation." As one is learning to be a better learner, moving from experiencing, understanding, judging, and deciding will likely be associated with increasing levels of anxiety, because each pattern requires more work and exposes oneself to criticisms by others. This connection is the "pattern-anxiety hypothesis." Readers can test it for themselves.

Intermediate predicted effects would be that by the end of one year, readers will have demonstrated to self and others: markedly increased frequency and effectiveness in attentiveness to experience, Seeking Understanding, Factual Critical Thinking, Values-oriented Critical Thinking, and Deliberative Critical Thinking by means of question, insight, desire to know, social trust, and related action. In short, after repeated practice the appropriate unfolding of the patterns and modes of consciousness will be on the way to becoming a habitual practice. As expertise increases, levels of anxiety may level off or diminish. Also, as one becomes more adept at moving from one pattern of problem solving to another, the level of anxiety decreases and becomes simply a manageable state of focused attentiveness. In addition, one can expect greater progress toward "self-appropriation" and to the emergence of a "learning personality" whose primary motivation is the desire to know and the related desire to grow in accordance with it.

Among the long-term predicted effects, the following may be included: (1) Readers will have achieved a change in cognitive, emotional, behavioral, reflective, and self-regulatory habits. They will routinely and effectively engage in Seeking Understanding, Factual Critical Thinking, Values-oriented Critical Thinking, Deliberative Critical Thinking, and strive for comprehensive learning by means of question, answer, and action. In addition, they will routinely make effective use of their own experience. As with any change in habit, the predicted changes in habits of thinking will now be easier to perform than the earlier habits they replaced. (2) This change in problem solving habits will reveal to the reader implications for a specific area of interest (with its expert knowledge) and for a more general wisdom (with its practical knowledge of prudence). In sum, they will have produced a "learning personality" which involves a habitual orientation toward facing problems and engaging in transformative problem solving. They will have achieved a change in disposition, that social psychologist M. Csiksentmihalyi describes as a "control of inner experience."[46]

Whether these predictions will actually come true in any individual case is largely a matter of implementing a personal decision to experience, understand, judge, and decide more carefully and more mindfully, and with a view to an improved knowledge and management of oneself as a thinker, problem solver, and learner. It is a choice for a practical form of "wisdom," which can be defined as an ongoing and developing knowledge of how to live life well.

NOTES

1. Bernard Lonergan, *Insight: A Study of Human Understanding* (Toronto: University of Toronto Press, 1992).
2. Edward Burger and Michael Starbird, *The Five Elements of Effective Thinking* (Princeton, NJ: Princeton University Press, 2012).
3. Mark Morelli, *Self-Possession: Being at Home in Conscious Performance* (Boston: Lonergan Institute, 2015).
4. Dale Schunk and Barry Zimmerman, *Self-Regulation of Learning and Performance: Issues and Educational Applications* (Mahwah, NJ: Erlbaum, 1994).
5. Daniel Kahneman, *Thinking, Fast and Slow* (New York: Farrar, Straus and Giroux, 2011).
6. American Psychological Association, *APA Dictionary of Psychology* (Washington, DC: American Psychological Association, 2015), 1061
7. Charles Duhigg, *The Power of Habit: Why We Do What We Do in Life and Business* (New York: Random House, 2014); Ann Graybiel and Kyle Smith. "Good habits, bad habits." *Scientific American, June 2014*, 38–43.
8. *APA Dictionary of Psychology*, 1061.
9. C. Hamblin, "Questions." *The Encyclopedia of Philosophy* (New York: Collier Macmillan, 1972).
10. Lonergan, *Insight*, 28; Jonathan W. Schooler, Marte Fallshore and Stephen M. Fiore, "Putting Insight into Perspective." *The Nature of Insight*, 559–587.
11. Lonergan, *Insight*, 28–31; Colleen M. Seifert, David Myer, Natalie Davidson, Andrea L. Palatano and Ilan Yaniv. "Demystification of Cognitive Insight: Opportunistic Assimilation and the Prepared-Mind Perspective." *The Nature of Insight*, 65–124.
12. Lonergan, *Insight*, ch. 1.
13. Robert Sternberg and Janet Davidson (Eds.) *The Nature of Insight*.
14. Mary Gick and Robert Lockhart, "Cognitive and Affective Components of Insight." *The Nature of Insight*, 197–228.
15. Howard Gruber, "Insight and Affect in the history of Science." *The Nature of Insight*, 397–432.
16. Janet Davidson, "The Suddenness of Insight." *The Nature of Insight*, 125–156.
17. Maria Ippolito and Ryan Tweney, "The Inception of Insight." *The Nature of Insight*, 433–462.

18. Mihalyi Csikszentmihalyi and Keith Sawyer, "Creative Insight: The Social Dimension of a Solitary Moment." *The Nature of Insight*, 329–364.

19. Malcolm Gladwell, *Blink: The Power of Thinking without Thinking* (New York: Little-Brown, 2005).

20. Robyn Dawes, David Faust and Paul Meehl, "Clinical vs. Actuarial Judgment" *Science, 243,* 1668–1674 1989; Joachim Kreuger (Ed.) *Rationality and Social Responsibility* (Mahwah, NJ: Erlbaum, 2008).

21. Richard Grallo, "The Absence of Question and Insight in Accounts of Knowledge." *Symposium*, XIV, No. 1 (2007), 33–43.

22. Sylvan Bromberger, *On What We Know We Don't Know: Explanation, Theory, Linguistics and How Questions Shape Them* (Chicago: University of Chicago Press, 1992)

23. Alan Newell & Herbert Simon, *Human Problem Solving* (New York: Pearson, 1972).

24. Lonergan. *Insight*, ch. 1.

25. Patrick Byrne. "Consciousness: Levels, Sublations and the Subject as Subject." *Method*, 13, No. 2 (1995), 131–150; Richard Grallo."Learning, Functional Interferences and Personality Dynamics."*Symposium*, XIII, No. 1 (2006), 15–22; G. Wallas. *The Art of Thought* (New York: Harcourt Brace Javanovich, 1926).

26. Gottlob Frege, *The Foundations of Arithmetic: A Logico-Mathematical Enquiry into the Concept of Number* (New York: John Wiley & Sons, 1980.)

27. Ludwig Wittgenstein, *Philosophical Investigations* (Hoboken, NJ: Wiley-Blackwell, 2009)

28. "Structuralism" has been described as an early movement of scientific psychology that regarded psychology as "the study of mental experience and that sought to investigate the structure of such experience through a systematic program of experiments based on trained introspection." *APA Dictionary of Psychology* (Washington, DC: American Psychological Association, 2015), 1039; see also Edwin G. Boring, *A History of Experimental Psychology (2nd Ed.)* (Englewood Cliffs, NJ: Prentice-Hall, 1957).

29. B. F. Skinner, *Science and Human Behavior* (New York: Free Press, 1953.)

30. For a case example, see Theresa Jordan, Richard Grallo, and Richard Montgomery. "Combining Decision Analysis and Experimental Data to Study Bias in Educational Settings: Impacts of Patient Age on Medical Students' Treatment Decisions." *Journal of Research in Education*, 4, No. 1 (1994), 58–67.

31. Morelli, *Self-Possession*, 178–180; Peter Harvey, *An Introduction to Buddhism: Teachings, History and Practices* (New York: Cambridge University Press, 1990), 246–252; Charles Prebish, *The A to Z of Buddhism* (London: Scarecrow Press, 2001), 221 entry on *samatha*.

32. Morelli, *Self-Possession*, ch. 7.

33. Kurt Lewin. "Defining the 'Field at a Given Time.'" In *Resolving Social Conflicts and Field Theory in Social Science* (Washington, DC: American Psychological Association, 1997).

34. Arthur Reber and Emily Reber. *Dictionary of Psychology* (New York: Penguin Books, 2001).

35. J. P. Chaplin. *Dictionary of Psychology. (2nd Ed.)* (New York: Laurel Books, 1985, p. 334); American Psychological Association, *Dictionary of Psychology. (2nd Ed.)* (Washington, DC: American Psychological Association, 2015, p. 782).

36. American Psychological Association, *Dictionary of Psychology. (2nd Ed.)*, 66.

37. Richard Grallo. "Learning, Functional Interferences and Personality Dynamics." *Symposium,* XIII, No. 1 (2006), 15–22.

38. The formula being: n!/(n-k)!

39. American Psychological Association, *Dictionary of Psychology. (2nd Ed.)*, 1002.

40. Erik Erikson. *Childhood and Society,* (New York: W.W. Norton, 1993); Lev Vygotsky. *Mind in Society: The Development of Higher psychological Processes* (Cambridge, MA: Harvard University Press, 1978); Mary Ainsworth, M., Blehar, E. Waters & S. Wall, S. *Patterns of Attachment* (Hillsdale, NJ: Erlbaum, 1978).

41. American Psychological Association, *Dictionary of Psychology*, 274.

42. Bernard Lonergan. *Method in Theology* (New York: Herder, 1971).

43. Craig Carter, Lutz Kaufmann & Alex Michel, "Behavioral Supply management: A Taxonomy of Judgment and Decision Making Biases," *International Journal of Physical Distribution and Logistics Management*, 37, No. 8 (2007), 631–669.

44. Karen Horney, *Our Inner Conflicts: A Constructive Theory of Neurosis* (New York: W.W. Norton, 1993).

45. Technically this is *negative reinforcement* [feeling good after escaping unscathed]. See American Psychological Association, *Dictionary of Psychology*, 694.

46. Mihalyi Csikzentmihalyi, *Flow: The Psychology of Optimal Experience* (New York: Harper & Row, 1990), ch. 1.

Chapter 2

Pattern 1

Seeking Understanding by Considering Possibilities

INTRODUCTION

Imagine that you are waiting for friends at a train station. They are supposed to arrive on a train scheduled to come in at 3 PM. It is now 3:30 PM and you wonder where the train is. You do not know what is happening. An announcement is made that the train is delayed. A person next to you reports that she has received a text message that the train has been derailed.

The questions start to arrive. What might be happening? Was any one injured? What has happened to my friends? The process of seeking to understand has begun. Any answers we get now may likely be only provisional, and they may be revised later. However, we have embarked on a process of considering initial possibilities based on available information. This chapter focuses primarily on the first pattern of problem solving, named "Seeking Understanding." This pattern of problem solving is a search to grasp possible meaning in various situations.

GOALS AND OBJECTIVES

There are three goals of this chapter. (1) To explore the process of Seeking Understanding in concrete detail. The specific acts and operations associated with this pattern of problem solving will be identified, described, and then related functionally to one another in a sequenced pattern. (2) In consequence, to promote a deeper grasp of our own capability to understand anything by introducing quality assurance checks to our understanding. (3) To identify some practical steps that can be taken to solidify this knowledge and make it part of a habitual approach to learning and problem solving.

To address these aims, we will regard Seeking Understanding as a specific pattern of conscious problem solving activity. It is a mode of problem solving performance that consists of definite acts, operations, and processes that can be verified in one's personal experience. In fact, if the reader is unwilling, not ready or unable to verify them, then much of what follows will have no clear meaning.

The facts of consciousness referred to here have already been identified by Canadian philosopher Bernard Lonergan in his work on cognitional structure, intentionality analysis, and generalized empirical method.[1] In this work, Lonergan identified four "levels of consciousness" specified as experience, understanding, judging, and deciding. For example, "experience" is the sum total of all that we have lived through. It provides the data or raw materials for our use in understanding, knowing, and acting in the world. "Understanding" is the search to grasp possible meaning in various situations. "Judging" aims for factual or moral knowledge by subjecting our insights to criteria of truth and worth. "Deciding" orients us toward reasoned action based on what we experience, understand, and know. Each of these areas of consciousness has different specific functions, different products, and different guiding intentions. In addition, each area has different specific acts, operations, and processes associated with it.

In chapter 1, these four "levels of consciousness" have been reframed as four structured groups of mental events or "patterns of problem solving" and one "mode of pause" from the work of problem solving. In addition, the area of judging has been further refined to include two distinct types, with two different guiding intentions and two distinct end-products: there is "factual judging" and "values judging." These are explored in greater detail in chapter 3.

In all of this work, whether one speaks of "levels of consciousness" or "patterns of problem solving," all are related through a process of "sublation," whereby the activity of one pattern of problem solving takes up where previous ones leave off and adds a new dimension to that work.[2] In addition, this progression from one pattern to another is not automatic and in some cases progress may be made by moving back and forth from one to another. As indicated in chapter 1, embedded in each pattern of problem solving is the possibility for transformative growth that not only changes the problem situation but the problem solver as well.

By the end of this chapter, the reader will have demonstrated knowledge of Seeking Understanding (PS Pattern 1) by meeting the following objectives: (1) identify and distinguish the component acts and operations of Pattern 1, and (2) provide examples of them from personal experience as well as the reported experience of others.

In a railroad crash a large number of questions will need to be addressed about the train itself, the tracks, the key persons involved, and so on. The insights that address those questions are only possibilities. Considering the initial questions and the possibilities they suggest, as practiced in Pattern 1 (*S*eeking Understanding), paves the way for establishing facts and getting at a true or probable account of what happened. Considering initial questions and the possibilities they suggest also allows for the later identification and prioritizing of what is valuable in problem situations. What is most important to address in order to insure railroad safety and timeliness? Considering possibilities also helps to identify options for choice and later action, for example in adopting better railroad policies or technologies.

To the extent that individuals undergo and practice the acts and operations of Pattern 1 (Seeking Understanding) they constitute themselves as questioner, investigator, formulator, and intelligent witness to whatever is being investigated. Taking the information of this chapter seriously increases the probability of a deep-seated understanding developing in the learner regarding any topic of choice. From that basis, the learner is in a better position to generalize when appropriate and to refrain from generalizing when appropriate. In other words, the learner will be developing those habits of thinking associated with expertise.

LIMITATIONS

A number of conditions limit the discussion of this chapter. First, in exploring the details of Pattern 1 (Seeking Understanding) no mention will be made of understanding in terms of abstractions, as is done in many of the taxonomies of learning objectives and goals. For example, there is Bloom's taxonomy which discusses human capabilities largely in terms of abstractions such as "comprehension," "knowledge," or "evaluation."[3] Since its introduction in the 1950s, this scheme has enjoyed wide application, especially in American education. Largely in response to the "cognitive revolution" of the 1970s and 1980s, Anderson and associates offered a revision of Bloom's taxonomy which moves from abstract nouns to abstract verbal nouns in an attempt to capture the dynamic reality of cognitive process, something that has come to be highly emphasized in cognitive psychology and education.[4] In contrast, the focus here is on concrete acts and operations of thinking found in one's own thought experience.

Second, there will be no discussion of understanding in terms of hypothetical constructs such as "learning styles" or "locus of control." Hypothetical constructs have been defined as "processes that are inferred to have real existence and to give rise to measurable phenomena."[5] Such processes are not directly observed or experienced. As such they not only have all of the limitations of abstractions, but they can be verified only indirectly through their effects. In contrast, no mention is made here of hypothetical constructs at all.

Finally, we will not be discussing understanding in terms of neuroscience. Typically neuroscience descriptions and explanations of psychological events take the following form:

> Conscious event X, which we know from our own experience or from the self-reports of others, seems to be related to brain activity Y as determined by special means (e.g. PET scan, CT scan, MRI or fMRI). Therefore, conscious event X is identical with brain event Y, or at least, conscious event X must be caused by brain event Y.

Once statements of this kind are asserted, alternative descriptions and explanations are frequently excluded. In addition, these types of statements are rarely put to the test. Hence the offered descriptions and explanations and accompanying narrative are simply put forward along with some vague extra-scientific hope about what will be demonstrated someday. In contrast, here no reference is made to the projects and evidence associated with neuroscience research.

SETTING A CONTEXT FOR UNDERSTANDING

Whatever Seeking Understanding is, it does not operate in a vacuum. It operates in the psychological context of the individual person's cognitive-emotional-behavioral life, as well as in wider social contexts. There are the even larger contexts of culture and history which set the background. All of these contexts affect and can be affected by what we come to understand. Chapter 5 explores this in greater detail.

Since understanding can be situated within the context of a shared language and its history, several points can be made regarding the history of words such as "understanding" and the related terms "apprehension" and "comprehension." In English, both are related to the act of "prehension" (or grasping) done automatically by infants, without any training. Educational psychologist Jean Piaget traced the connections of this physical grasping to a "grasping with the mind" (i.e., apprehension or comprehension). This mental grasping was recognized in ancient times by Aristotle in his description of insight as "mind grasping form in images."[6]

More specifically, Seeking Understanding (Pattern 1) can also be situated within a psychological context of other modes of consciousness. As noted above and in chapter 1, Seeking Understanding and the mental events associated with it comprise only one pattern of problem solving activity. There are three others that can be differentiated from it: these are forms of critical thinking (PS Pattern 2—Factual Critical Thinking, PS Pattern 3—Values-oriented

Critical Thinking, and PS Pattern 4—Deliberative Critical Thinking). In addition, there is a mode of pause from problem solving labeled "basic experiencing."[7] The mode of pause (basic experiencing) and the mode of Seeking Understanding may be regarded as "pre-critical thinking." The last three areas can be regarded as explicit attempts to get things right according to some criterion (as in Factual and Value-oriented Critical Thinking) or to set things right through intended action or inaction (as in Deliberative Critical Thinking).

There are some commonalties among all four patterns of problem solving and the mode of pause. First, some people will become more adept in one pattern or mode than in others. This is what might be named "problem solving response style" and it is a form of individual differences in psychology.[8] Second, attempts to manage one's thinking amount to the same thing as regulating the four patterns and the mode of pause, insofar as they can be regulated. Third, each area is distinguished from the others in terms of its end-products. For example, end-products of experience are often images and memories. End-products of understanding are possibly true ideas. End-products of judging facts are affirmations or denials about putative facts about the world, self, or others. End-products of judging values are approvals or disapprovals about what is or might be. End-products of deliberating are engagement in or refusal of proffered courses of action. Fourth, each pattern of problem solving is distinguished as well as in terms of its guiding questions. A guiding question is the central purpose toward which the conscious activity works.

PATTERN 1: SEEKING UNDERSTANDING BY CONSIDERING POSSIBILITIES

With[9] these wide contexts in mind (shared language and history, and the psychological context), we can now focus our attention on the specific area of consciousness labeled "Seeking Understanding." Here it is well to keep in mind the following three questions: (1) What are the acts and operations that make up this pattern of problem solving? (2) What is the function of each act, operation, and process? and (3) Can the reader verify their presence in conscious life?

Seeking Understanding is a pattern of problem solving that is initiated by the primary question: "What might be happening in situation X?" The process is moved forward and expanded the more questions are asked. Poet Kipling has enumerated a list of questions that take non-numerical answers, such as "Who? What? When? Where? Why? and How?."[10] In addition, there are questions that take numerical answers, such as "How much? How many? How often? How far? and How long?" All of these are "questions for understanding" and they lead to a preliminary grasp of a situation. Insight provides a synthesis that functions as a potential answer to such questions. Both questions and insights must be formulated or captured in language in order to be available for continuation of the process. Once formulated, questions and insights can be expressed to others. Figure 2.1 presents a visual representation of the acts and operations involved in the pattern of Seeking Understanding.

The most obvious thing about PS Pattern 1 is its end-products: these are answers to our preliminary questions. To work properly, it assumes that there is some situation to be investigated. The process itself leads to understandable answers to our questions, but it is unclear whether the answers are true or even likely. Even less obvious are the mental events that led up to the preliminary answers and where those answers might lead in the future.

Pattern 1 (Seeking Understanding) is nothing more than the series of mental events that constitute it. (See figure 2.1.) Since it is a process extended over time, it can be disrupted. Since possible disruptions can be identified in advance, measures can be taken to exercise some quality control over the process.

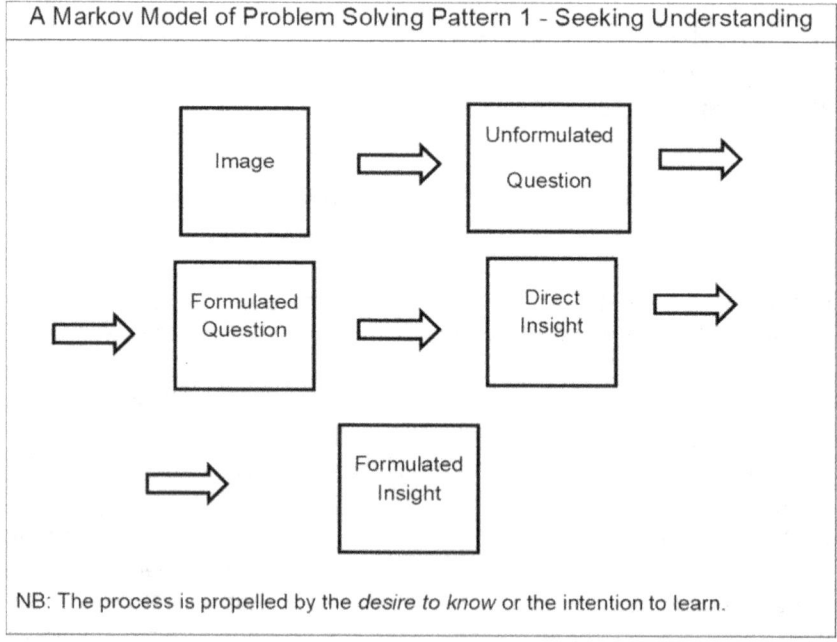

Figure 2.1 A Markov Model of Problem Solving Pattern 1—Seeking Understanding.
Source: Author.

As the first event in this process, consider what we will call the "unformulated question." Did you ever have the experience of recognizing that there was a gap in your understanding, but at the same time being unable to even put into words a question that expresses that gap? The experience mentioned above of waiting at the train station for a train that might be derailed could be an example. Let us call this event the "unformulated question." We know that there is something missing in our understanding of the progress of the 3 PM train, but it is hard to put our finger on it.

Another example of this is offered in the 2011 film *Moneyball*.[11] The protagonist in the film is a baseball team manager who is addressing his senior staff and trying to determine what the main problem is with their losing team. The senior staff demonstrates a persistent inability in identifying gaps in their knowledge. The manager works to make clear to them that there is a gap in their understanding and that they cannot even express that gap in words.

A second mental event occurs at the point where the question is formulated, usually in words. Sometimes we can create our own formulations. Sometimes prefabricated formulations already exist, such as the memories and habits mentioned in chapter 1. These provide a limited list of recurring questions that can be posed regarding any topic whatever.

Consider an example to see how the events described so far might operate in sequence. Suppose that at the station we finally hear an announcement about a railroad crash. It is the 3 PM train. Images may come to mind or may flash on a screen. Consider brainstorming questions regarding this example in order to gain a preliminary but comprehensive understanding of the event. What happened? Where did it happen? Who was involved? How did it happen? When did it occur? Why did it happen? In addition, there are all the quantitative questions that could be asked. Through such a brainstorming of questions and pursuing them we begin to expand our search for understanding in terms of its breadth.[12]

In addition, there is what might be termed an "echo exercise" of repeating the same question in order to determine greater depth in our search. For example, if we begin with the train leaving the station, we could repeatedly ask: "and what happened then? . . . and then? . . . and then?" By pursuing repeated questions of this kind, we expand our search for understanding in terms of its deeper, perhaps less obvious connections.

So, when we first hear the news of the crash we have the original unformulated question wherein we know that there is some gap in our understanding but we do not have it yet formulated into words. This can be followed by what might be called a series of "formulated questions." Such questions may come from our list of questions or it may be specially formulated for this occasion. Some authors offer pre-formulated lists of questions that may be useful in specific instances.[13] In any case it may take a while to move from the unformulated question to the formulated questions.

Third in this series would be the appearance of an "insight," which has been defined as "the sudden appearance of a potential solution to a problem or answer to a question."[14] Since a comprehensive understanding would require the answers to a number of questions, there would need to be a corresponding series of insights. The occurrence of such insights is not guaranteed and it is not under our control. The correctness of these insights is also not guaranteed and would have to be subjected to another pattern of problem solving that deals specifically with fact checking. (This is Factual Critical Thinking—PS Pattern 2, discussed in chapter 3.)

Fourth in the series would be the "formulation of the insight." Insights themselves are fleeting events and it is well known that if they are not written down, they may very well be lost. Therefore, following up an insight by formulating it in some encoding system has the function of "freeze drying" the thought for future use. The encoding system could be any natural language, or mathematics, or visual or acoustic symbols, and so on.

This entire patterned sequence of events from an unformulated question to formulated questions to insight to formulated insight may be regarded as a cognitive process. It is what we have labeled "PS Pattern 1—Seeking Understanding." This process is motivated by what Lonergan describes as "the desire to know" and what others have called "preserving the intention to learn." As a process it is extended over time, and as such it is subject to disruptions from within the thinking person and interferences from the environment. (See figure 2.1.)

Sometimes, in Pattern 1, an inverse insight occurs. An "inverse insight" is a recognition that there is something wrong with our question or its formulation. Perhaps the question includes vague or undefined terms, or perhaps it assumes a falsehood. The occurrence of an inverse insight is an opportunity to revisit the answerability of our question.

To summarize, PS Pattern 1 (Seeking Understanding) is a problem solving process that generates insights by examining experience. The insights generated here are possibilities that may stand in need of further examination by other processes of problem solving. Pattern 1 begins with an unformulated question for understanding: this is a recognition that there is a gap in our understanding of a situation of interest (see figure 2.1). Sooner or later we may place this recognition into words, for example, "What happened?" or "What is going on here?" These are formulated questions. The process is propelled forward and sustained by a desire to know and all the related questions it generates. It terminates in a set of insights, which fill the gap of the unformulated questions, and which answer them. Along the way, many questions may be considered and pursued. At the right point in time, all the elements of this process are held together and grasped by direct insight. This direct insight grasps that a real possibility exists for answering the initial questions.

The acts and operations of Pattern 1 are functionally related to one another and they emerge probabilistically not mechanistically. The occurrence of a mental event earlier in the sequence increases the probability of later events, but it does not guarantee them. In addition, it is also possible to shuttle back and forth. Sometimes we formulate and pursue questions only to find that the questions are inadequate. We have arrived at what some have called an "inverse insight": the point is that there is no point to the questions as formulated.[15] We need to reformulate our questions and pursue improved reformulations.

ADDITIONAL CONSIDERATIONS: KEY POINTS AND IMPLICATIONS

To the extent that the "facts of consciousness" described in this chapter can be verified in experience, a number of points follow:

1) Because the acts and operations of Seeking Understanding (PS Pattern 1) are functionally interrelated, it is a cognitive process. A cognitive process is a sequence of interrelated mental events and operations (see figure 2.1).
2) Seeking comprehensive understanding requires a serious consideration of the finite set of recurrent questions. The fact that the list is finite suggests that learning may be manageable. The fact that the questions on the list are recurrent suggests that the acquisition of understanding will likely not proceed in some linear fashion but in a spiral surrounding the topic.[16] To address the recurrent set of questions we can take steps to ensure that all questions in the recurring list are being considered. To ensure comprehensiveness, a team of investigators may brainstorm possible answers and the follow-up clues.
3) Because Pattern 1 (Seeking Understanding) is a process, this type of thinking takes time. Some elements of this process, such as insights and questions, may be instantaneous; but others, such as formulating, are often time-consuming. The process could extend from hours to months or years.
4) Because Pattern 1 is extended over time, it can be disrupted by personal or environmental interferences. Anyone who seriously attempts to practice Seeking Understanding as described here will be guided by the desire to know. The influence of other desires or emotions, whether positive or negative, may very well distort the process. Of special

interest is the human tendency to exclude further relevant questions. Excluding questions reduces the quality of understanding by blocking the insights they seek. If the exclusion is systematic, the investigation becomes biased. "Process bias" is this systematic exclusion of further relevant questions and the insights associated with them. This systematic exclusion routinely occurs in many print and electronic media due to unstated agendas and limitations of space and time. To address the operation of this kind of bias, we can insist that all recurrent further relevant questions be addressed. The team of railroad investigators, if they are motivated by a desire to know what happened, can act as a check to make sure that further relevant questions and insights are not excluded.

5) To the extent that one practices the acts and operations of Pattern 1 (Seeking Understanding) that person constitutes themselves as a questioner, investigator, and formulator of insights.

6) To the extent that one continues in this practice, habits of problem solving develop. Since Seeking Understanding takes time, it therefore requires perseverance in the desire to know and keeping track of one's efforts. No one is exempted from the extended interactions of questions and insights over time. How can one come to live effectively with them? To address the requirement of perseverance in the desire to know requires no less than the development of an intellectual habit in the inquiring person. Promoting the practice and occurrence of questions and insights and taking them seriously will require habits that reinforce these realities: a set time and place for study, elimination of distractions, a method for recording questions and insights, and so on.

7) Elsewhere, rules have been presented for addressing any problem whatever under the title Interrogative Problem Representation.[17] This is a method that formulates problems in terms of questions that an adequate solution would answer.

8) In problem solving groups, team members can check on each other to make sure that each is proceeding under the guidance of the desire to know. If the railroad investigators have lost the desire to know, then they have really "lost it" and they are not much used to any investigation.

9) Because Pattern 1 (Seeking Understanding) is a time-consuming process, it is not possible to practice it in reference to everything. The scarcity of time requires that topics for exploration and understanding must be selected.

10) Because of this limitation, the everyday practice of Seeking Understanding invites the development of intellectual habits, a specialization of topics of interest and collaboration with others.

11) Only part of PS Pattern 1 is in our control. The explosion of questions that occurs in Pattern 1 may increase the probability of recognizing both the vastness of our chosen topic and our own ignorance about it.
12) To address our ignorance, we can chart its nature by mapping the remaining unanswered questions. Field notes are likely to make clear the remaining unanswered questions, which then become leads in further investigative steps. In general, insights are not in our control. We cannot determine when or where they will occur. Questions sometimes arise unbidden, and so are not in our control, but we can also sometimes pose questions on our own initiative. Pursuing questions that have emerged is mostly in our control. Formulating questions and insights is generally in our control. (See figure 2.1).
13) To some extent, PS Pattern 1 (Seeking Understanding) functionally precedes other patterns of problem solving (Patterns 2, 3, and 4). Pattern 2 (Factual Critical Thinking) examines the possibilities generated in Pattern 1 in terms of their truth, accuracy, or likelihood. Pattern 3 (Values-oriented Critical Thinking) examines the possibilities of Pattern 1 and the facts of Pattern 2 in terms of their value or worth. Pattern 4 (Deliberative Critical Thinking) examines possible options of Pattern 1 in terms of whether or not they should be engaged or rejected. The facts established in Pattern 2 and the values identified in Pattern 3 also serve to inform the decisions of Pattern 4.

SUMMARY

Seeking Understanding (PS Pattern 1) is clearly a process. In other words, it is a temporal sequence of functionally related mental events. Since this process unfolds over time, it can be delayed or disturbed. Successful management of the process requires minimizing or eliminating various interferences. In our example of the railroad crash, investigators could experience any number of interferences that could disrupt or interrupt efforts to come to some preliminary grasp about what happened.

Interferences with understanding can be environmental or personal. "Environmental interferences" involve interruptions caused by the physical environment or by the activities of others. Curious onlookers could be upsetting the crash site and delay investigators in their work. "Personal interferences" are disruptions caused by the state of one's body, emotions, or habitual thoughts. In our example, the crash investigator could be fatigued or emotionally distracted by some news from home. Whatever interferences are operating they are not likely to be of assistance in the investigation.

As indicated previously, unique among all the interferences is the role played by bias. Over seventy uses for the word "bias" have been cataloged.[18] In this context, we refer to a "process bias" which may be defined as is any systematic disruption, distortion, or interference of problem solving efforts. This bias frequently manifests as a systematic exclusion from an investigation of further relevant questions or insights. Because the questions excluded are relevant, the information they convey may change the findings of the investigation. Because the exclusion is systematic, this information is ruled out repeatedly, not just on one occasion. In our example, imagine if our investigators would in advance decide to consider no possibility that involved mechanical failure. They ask no questions related to that possibility. They make no inspection of the mechanical equipment. What kind of an accident investigation would that be? How trustworthy would be the resulting report?

Successful management of Pattern 1 (Seeking Understanding) requires being very clear about the questions being addressed. In effect, it consists of the injunction to NOT proceed in investigating any problem whatever without first reframing the problem in terms of clear, researchable questions. The initial entry into a field of investigation is accompanied by and guided by an explosion of questions. Only as these questions are satisfactorily answered does understanding grow and knowledge (or tested understanding) make its appearance. More specifically, to handle the explosion of questions, it is well to chart the course of progress with each question. Investigators of the train crash are likely to take comprehensive notes to describe what was present at the scene and to document the progress of the train prior to the event.

Sometimes, the questions as formulated are unclear or based on false assumptions. In this instance, an inverse insight is needed to grasp that, with regard to this question, the point is that there is no point. We are on the wrong track and need to reframe the question.

Successful management of the process also requires minimizing or eliminating various interferences. More specifically, "process bias" is a particularly difficult form of interference with problem solving. With it, questions and the associated insights are choked off from ever emerging. They are systematically excluded from consideration. To counter process bias and to have any hope of achieving a comprehensive understanding, all further relevant questions must be seriously examined.

In light of these considerations, it can be stated that managing the process of Seeking Understanding for maximum benefit involves the use of two correlated strategies: (1) ask and pursue all further relevant questions and insights, and (2) avoid any systematic exclusions of relevant questions and insights. Promoting one strategy automatically promotes the other. Neglecting one automatically neglects the other.

One means of promoting both of these strategies is to record and keep track of the relevant questions and insights associated with a problem under investigation. A record of questions and insights would provide a map of one's current understanding (as indicated by formulated insights) and one's current lack of understanding (as indicated by one's unanswered questions). This type of record not only provides evidence of the state of one's understanding and confusion, but it can serve to curtail extravagant claims to an "understanding" that is greater than what actually exists.

NOTES

1. Bernard Lonergan, *Insight: A Study of Human Understanding* (Toronto: University of Toronto Press, 1992).

2. Patrick Byrne, Consciousness: Levels, sublations and the subject as subject. *Method,* 13 No. 2 (1995): 131–150; Morelli, Mark. "Beyond the Metaphor of Levels of Consciousness: Appropriation of Sublative Transformations." *Method,* 9 No. 2 (2018): 47–74.

3. Benjamin Bloom, M, Engelhart, E. Frost, W. Hill, and David Krathwohl, *Taxonomy of Educational Objectives. Handbook I: Cognitive Domain* (New York: David McKay, 1956).

4. Lorin Anderson, and David Krathwohl, eds. *A Taxonomy for Learning, Teaching and Assessing: A Revision of Bloom's Taxonomy of Educational Objectives* (New York: Longman, 2001).

5. American Psychological Association, *Dictionary of Psychology* (American Psychological Association, Washington, DC, 2015, 239, 515). For an example, see Harold Pashler, Mark McDaniel, Doug Rohrer, and R. Bjork. "Learning Styles: Concepts and Evidence." *Psychological Science in the Public Interest*, 9 (2008): 105–119.

6. Aristotle, *De Anima* (Cambridge, MA: Loeb Classical Library, 1964).

7. Richard Grallo, "Thinking Carefully about Critical Thinking." *Lonergan Review*, IV, No. 1 (2013): 154–180.

8. James Adams, *The Care and Feeding of Ideas: A Guide to Encouraging Creativity.* (Addison-Wesley, Boston, 1986); Richard Grallo. "Personal Differences in the Application of G.E.M." *Lonergan Review*, VII, No. 1, (2016): 49–61.

9. This section is based on a previously published article that appeared in *Symposium*: Richard Grallo, "On Seeking Understanding." *Symposium*, XXI, No. 1 (2014): 19–28.

10. "Six Serving Men." Rudyard Kipling, accessed March 16, 2021, http://www.kiplingsociety.co.uk/poems_servingmen.htm ("I have six faithful serving men. They taught me all I knew. What? and Why? and When? and Where? and How? and Who?).

11. Bennett Miller. (director) *Moneyball.* Film (Hollywood, CA: Columbia Pictures, 2011). This film presents the successful baseball strategies of Oakland A's manager Billy Beane.

12. Alex Osborne, *Applied Imagination* (New York, Charles Scribner & Sons, 1953). Osborn is credited with popularizing the strategy of brainstorming of ideas. In this procedure potential "solutions" to problems are offered without any initial editing or censoring. The focus is mainly on potential solutions. More recently, Marilee Adams (2009) has explored the strategy of brainstorming questions.

13. Marilee Adams, *Change Your Questions – Change Your Life* (San Francisco: Berrett-Koehler Publishers, 2009); Dorothy Leeds, *Smart Questions: A New Strategy for Successful Managers* (New York: Berkley Books, 1987); Andrew Sobol and Jerold Panas, *Power Questions: Build Relationships, Win New Business and Influence Others* (Hoboken, NJ: Wiley, 2012).

14. Lonergan, *Insight*, 3.

15. Lonergan, *Insight*, 43–50.

16. Jerome Bruner, *THE process of Education* (Cambridge, MA: Harvard University Press, 1976).

17. Richard Grallo, "Principles of Interrogative Problem Representation (IPR) – A Preliminary Sketch." *Symposium*, XIX, No. 1 (2012): 21–31.

18. Craig R. Carter, Lutz Kaufmann, and Alex Michel, "Behavioral Supply Management: A Taxonomy of Judgment and Decision Making Biases." *International Journal of Physical Distribution and Logistics Management*, 37, No. 8 (2007): 631–669.

Chapter 3

Three Patterns of Critical Thinking
Filtering Possibilities for Something More

INTRODUCTION

In[1] situations where problems are unsolved and the available results of thinking are inadequate, the need for critical thinking is heightened. In environments where the quality of thinking is poor and the nature of its defects remain unidentified, some sort of special thinking is required to sort fact from fiction and distinguish the valuable from the worthless. In circumstances where action is required, some filter is needed to exclude thoughtless impulsivity and timid inaction. Critical thinking is a vaccine against "cognitively transmitted diseases" of epidemic vagueness, falsehood, runaway wishes, untestable propositions, and incoherent projects. Yet what exactly is critical thinking and how can it be implemented?

In light of these questions, this chapter has three related aims: (1) to invite readers to reflect on the thought processes they routinely use when they seriously attempt to solve problems, (2) to clarify what is meant by "critical thinking," and (3) to identify three distinct types of critical thinking and the patterns of problem solving associated with them.

First, inviting readers to reflect on their own thought processes represents both a turn toward the concrete as well as a turn toward the self as problem solver. Neither of these is an easy task because by "turning to the concrete" it is easy to get lost in a forest of seemingly unrelated details. "Turning toward the self as problem solver" is also no easy task since we live in a culture in which the "external world" seems to demand attention, and there seems little support for such introspective reflection.

Second, by clarifying at least one account of critical thinking, the goal here is to relate specific cognitive acts and operations to one another and to such related topics as "judgment," "reasons," "evidence," and "criteria." Whatever critical thinking is, it somehow involves all of these. In addition, the goal involves relating everything mentioned to a specific type of question—a "reflective question" that permits only "yes" or "no" in its range of possible answers. On this later point, it is worth repeating how adequate analysis of the role and function of questions and questioning in critical thinking has been remarkably absent from both philosophic accounts of knowledge and psychological accounts of problem solving and intelligence.[2]

Third, if there are different types of reflective questions, then it follows that there will be different types of critical thinking designed to address those questions. Each type of critical thinking would be guided by its own reflective question, and, therefore, each type would serve a unique purpose. There are three processes of critical thinking to be described here. They work to filter the possibilities generated in Problem Solving Pattern 1 (Seeking Understanding). The possibilities emerging from Pattern 1 are not enough and through critical thinking they are subjected to further tests.

Fourth, for any pattern of problem solving to work, the desire to know must not only be present but controlling. Intrusion of personal or environmental interferences will likely deflect problem solving from its aims.

Fifth, each type of critical thinking (Factual, Values-Oriented, and Deliberative) could then be situated as part of a larger whole involving all thinking, indeed all consciousness. Any theory of this larger whole would need to include a unified theory of problem solving.

Finally, whatever critical thinking is, it is a human achievement, and it does not operate in a vacuum. Since it is a human achievement, it is possible to miss the mark, to err, to fail in one's effort. Since it does not occur in isolation, some consideration must be given to forces operating in the larger context of the thinker's personality and social milieu, as well as culture and history. Do those forces propel or restrain the effort to think critically? If so, how?

The aims for this chapter can be succinctly summarized in this way: "The aim is not to set forth a list of abstract properties of human knowledge but to assist in . . . effecting a personal appropriation of the concrete, dynamic structure immanent in and recurrently operative in . . . cognitional activities."[3]

SOME BACKGROUND FOR CRITICAL THINKING

Etymology: Consider some preliminaries arising from etymology. Whatever critical thinking is it is somehow related to judgment, evidence, and reasons. If critical thinking is in any way related to knowledge, then it must serve to answer questions of some sort. The very word "critical" derives from the Greek κρινειν (to judge). Therefore, whatever critical thinking is, it may very well involve an account of judgment. If the judgment involved is to be well-founded according to almost any tradition of logic, then it will require reasons, and in the case of experience-based judgments, evidence. If the judgment involved constitutes some contribution to knowledge, then it should answer a particular question. Moreover, it may turn out that questions answered by judgments and judgment-like activities have a characteristic form.

Thinking about Learning in the 20th Century: The last century saw the rise of educational psychology as a distinct subspecialty of psychology. With it came systematic explorations of the nature, conditions, and consequences of human learning. It has resulted in sustained thinking about thinking and the guided action that can flow from it.[4] Prior to the recent interest in critical thinking, the topics of thinking and learning were often related to abilities, aptitudes, and learning objectives, and then later to competencies or proficiencies and just plain careful thinking. At the present time, it is appropriate to look back and inquire whether critical thinking is any one of these.[5]

Is critical thinking an "ability" or something any person can do in their current circumstances? Much of the pioneering work of L. L. Thurstone and his associates in the 1930s and 1940s in the area of "primary mental abilities" took issue with the concept of general intelligence. They identified distinct abilities in the areas of verbal use and fluency, numeracy, spatial and perceptual ability, memory, and reasoning.[6] While critical thinking was not identified as such in this work, the allied ability of reasoning was included in it. Throughout the brief history of educational psychology, work on abilities has continued in one form or another with the work of Howard Gardner on "multiple intelligences" providing a well-known more recent example.[7]

Is critical thinking an "aptitude" or something a person would be able to do after focused training? While many readers will be familiar with the well-publicized work of Howard Gardner on "multiple intelligences," a parallel empirically based research program was conducted by J. P. Guilford over the span of at least five decades. Guilford's ongoing project was to identify and to measure the most elementary types of thought, or "micro-thinking." The goal was to do for educational psychology what the periodic table of elements did for chemistry. He argued that each of the most elementary forms of thinking or "aptitude" consisted of a cognitive process operating on a content to yield a product. Just as a three-dimensional object in the material world would not exist without the dimensions of length, width, and height, so also an element of the mental world (an aptitude) would not exist without the three dimensions of content, operation, and product. In the most classic statement of his theory, he identified 120 aptitudes.[8] While his theory of "structure of intellect" is not much used today, the project of a periodic table of elements for thinking remains a potentially useful one. In this theory also the phrase "critical thinking" was not explicitly used. However, the operation of *evaluating* various kinds of content was always contained within this literature and survives in contemporary discussions of critical thinking.

Is critical thinking a "learning objective"? In the 1950s Benjamin Bloom and his associates developed a taxonomy of what they termed "learning objectives" in the cognitive, affective, and motor areas of student performance.[9] The most widely used part of this work centered on the cognitive (or thinking) domain. In it these authors discussed educational aims of greater cognitive complexity proceeding through the following range: knowledge of facts, comprehension, application, analysis, synthesis, and evaluation. Over the years this work was amended by Anderson and associates to include a consideration of the dynamic nature of cognitive processes as a replacement for lists of abstract concepts, as well as incorporating the possibility of metacognitive or reflective thought.[10] While the phrase "critical thinking" was not explicitly used in this work, the ability to evaluate and reflect on various kinds of material was always discussed in this literature and has found its way into contemporary discussions of critical thinking.

Thinking about Critical Thinking in the 21st Century: Is critical thinking a "competency" or "proficiency"? Contemporary accrediting agencies in American higher education have often focused on what they call "competencies" or "proficiencies," with their pragmatic emphasis on doing as guided by some form of careful thinking. Competencies and proficiencies often appear as some form of "literacy" or "numeracy": for example, computer literacy, information literacy, writing across contexts, etc. In spite of this, higher education has come under increasing critical scrutiny with rising tuition costs, mitigated employment prospects for graduates, and an unclear record of documented educational effects.[11] In this cultural context, some accrediting bodies and colleges specifically mention critical thinking as a core competency and some external tests do the same.[12]

Is critical thinking just "careful thinking"? Since the early 1970s, Alverno College has developed a curriculum with core competencies, one of which is quite explicitly critical thinking. In much of their literature, "critical thinking" is used in a wide sense to embrace many types of thinking, whether or not the thinking in question leads directly to judgment or decision making, as long as the thinking involved is done carefully and according to appropriate standards.[13]

If critical thinking is to continue to develop as some distinct areas of interest, then clear definitions will be needed to avoid the pitfalls of unfettered abstractions and all-inclusive lists. Any such definitions should fulfill the primary function of indicating what is included and what is excluded. For critical thinking, a well-formed definition would distinguish "critical" thinking from all other forms of thinking, specifically from thinking that does not lead directly to judgment or decision making.

In fact, in the developing literature on critical thinking, definitions of the phrase differ widely in their range of reference, from rather specific definitions to very wide definitions. The more narrow definitions focus on "judgment" or "decision" as a direct product of critical thinking. The wider definitions do not do this and instead seem to include all types of thinking as long as it is done carefully. The definitions by Ennis[14] and Facione[15] fall into the category of narrow definitions that focus on judgment and decision, and the work of Levy,[16] the Alverno group (Cromwell and Halonen), and Nosich[17] falls into in the wider category that seems to focus on "careful thinking" in all areas whether or not it leads directly to a judgment or decision.

ELEMENTS OF CRITICAL THINKING

This chapter adopts Peter Facione's 2006 definition of critical thinking that clearly relates it to the activity of judgment. This is not "judgment" in the popular sense that has been loosely identified with blame, condemnation, or sweeping ratings of persons. It is judgment as a cognitive act that comes in answer to reflective questions. In this role, it constitutes a resolution or completion of a reflective inquiry.

> We understand critical thinking to be purposeful, self-regulatory judgment which results in interpretation, analysis, evaluation and inference as well as explanation of the evidential, conceptual, methodological, criteriological, or contextual considerations upon which that judgment is based.[18]

This definition can be expanded to include decisions as an end-product as well as judgment. Hence, "critical thinking" is a form of thinking characterized by the use of a criterion to achieve a judgment or decision.

This definition can be applied by first considering some purposes to which critical thinking might be put, and then by examining it in light of a specific model of critical thinking. Purposes in critical thinking may often be formulated as "reflective questions." As we have seen, these are yes/no questions that require that we evaluate previously obtained information in order to resolve issues of fact or value or to reach a decision. Consider the examples in table 3.1.

While referring to diverse topics, these questions have a number of structural similarities. A first similarity is that they each anticipate "yes" or "no" answers: "yes" indicating a personal affirmation of some kind, and "no" a personal denial. Such affirmations or denials are in fact judgments and represent a personal commitment on the part of the person making them. A second similarity is that the questions in table 3.1 each presuppose that specific

Table 3.1 Examples of Reflective Questions

1) Does vitamin C reduce cold symptoms?
2) Was the 2008–2009 U.S. economic stimulus good for the country?
3) Should more money be invested in highways?
4) Should I exercise for one hour five times per week?
5) Is it a good health idea to take aspirin once per day?
6) Should we teach writing in all undergraduate courses?
7) Does the U.S. "Affordable Health Care Act" of 2010 cover catastrophic medical emergencies?
8) Should I invest in gold?

(*Source*: Author)

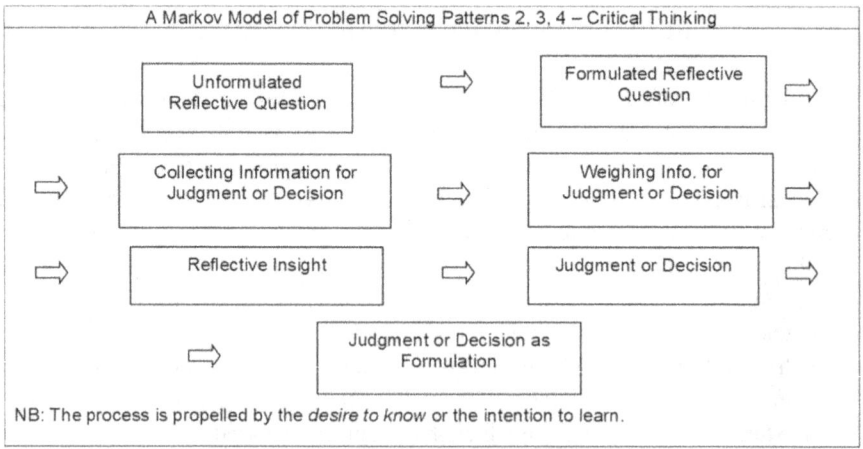

Figure 3.1 A Markov Model of Problem Solving Patterns 2, 3, and 4—Critical Thinking. *Source*: Author.

concepts are understood. For example, question 1 presupposes some understanding of what vitamin C is and of what cold symptoms are. Question 7, to be intelligible, presupposes some understanding of the 2010 U.S. Affordable Health Care Act and what a "catastrophic medical emergency" is.

Figure 3.1 presents a Markov model[19] of cognitive acts, operations, and states that lead up to and condition the act of judgment (or the structurally similar act of decision). A Markov model is a representation of a finite sequence of observed and unobserved events such that the probabilities of earlier events condition the probability of occurrence of later events in the series.

The judgments referred to in figure 3.1 may be either judgments of fact or judgments of value. A "judgment of fact" is a limited affirmation or denial offered to resolve an issue of fact or about states of affairs in the world (broadly conceived). A "judgment of value" is a limited approval or disapproval of something, whether it exists or not. The model presented in figure 3.1 may also be extended to include the critical and reflective process of deliberation and its resolution in decision. In such an extension, the role of decision replaces that of judgment. A "decision" is a limited personal resolution, commitment, or imperative to incorporate some value in one's life or to eliminate some disvalue.

As a Markov model, figure 3.1 presents a sequence of events that occur probabilistically and not mechanistically; if the first item in the sequence occurs, the probability of the second item occurring is increased.

The questions in the model give critical thinking its purposive character mentioned in the Facione definition: the purpose is to correctly answer the question considered. Since there are three distinct reflective questions, it follows that there are three distinct collections of mental activities and operations that may be distinguished as different types of critical thinking. Factual Critical Thinking (PS Pattern 2) is a collection of mental events designed to address reflective questions of fact and to establish facts. Values-Oriented Critical Thinking (PS Pattern 3) is a collection of mental events designed to approve and prioritize values and to address reflective questions of value. Finally, Deliberative Critical Thinking (PS Pattern 4) is a collection of mental events designed to address reflective questions of deliberation and to commit to a particular course of action.

In terms of "guiding questions" they may be compared as follows. Factual Critical Thinking (Pattern 2) is guided by reflective questions of the form, "Is this [proposition] true [or likely]?" (See table 3.1: questions 1 and 7.) Value-Oriented Critical Thinking (Pattern 3) is driven by reflective questions of the form, "Is this good (or worthwhile, or useful)?" (See table 3.1: questions 2, 3, and 5.) Deliberative Critical Thinking (Pattern 4) is oriented by reflective questions of the form, "Should I (or we) do (or refrain from doing) this?" (See table 3.1: questions 4, 6, and 8.)

Prior to "questions-as-formulation," there may occur an "unformulated question." The question-as-formulation is simply the familiar interrogative sentence expressed in everyday language. The unformulated question is a prior conscious event whereby we recognize a gap in our knowledge or practice. That gap might be in our knowledge of the facts ("Is this really true?") or it might be a gap in our knowledge of values ("Is this really worthwhile?"). The recognized gap might also pertain to the manner in which we operate in the world ("Should I/we do this?"). These unformulated questions are only partially under our control; we can routinely ask them according to some protocol, but sometimes they emerge in consciousness quite suddenly and unbidden. We can choose to pursue them or not. This choice gives our critical thinking its "self-regulatory" character mentioned in the definition.

Pursuit is likely to increase the probability of later events in the Markov series.

To be well founded, both judgments and decisions need to be based on information that has been collected. Such "collection of information" is a mental process and fact of consciousness that takes time, and it presupposes that we know what to look for. Clues regarding what to look for can be found in the question that is being pursued as well as in the criteria that we plan to use to weigh the collected information. Such information may be in the form of evidence or some sort of reasons. The intimate role of evidence and reasons are also characteristic of critical thinking, as mentioned in the definition.

"Weighing information" for judgment or decision is also a mental process and fact of consciousness that involves the use of a criterion or multiple criteria. "Weighing information" is the comparison of collected evidence and reasons with a criterion for judgment or decision making and the application of that criterion of judgment or decision in one direction or another. Without criteria, evidence and reasons can roll about in some unanchored fashion leading to results that are unclear and ambiguous. The use of clear criteria is what gives critical thinking its criteriological character, also mentioned in the Facione definition.

Reflective insight, like all insight, is an event that is not directly under our control. We can simply improve the statistical chances that it will occur. An insight is, by definition, a sudden act of understanding that emerges to organize disparate elements.[20] As a "reflective insight" it grasps the sufficiency (or insufficiency) of the evidence or reasons to support the proposed answer to the question. Without the reflective insight, a thinker may be awash in conclusive evidence and still "not get it." As crucial as the insight is, it is not in our control; however, the more expert we become in a field, the more likely it is that reflective insight will occur.

Judgments and decisions may or may not be formulated clearly in some language or symbol system. Judgments and decisions may or may not find public expression in speech, writing, or action. "Expressing" is a mental process and fact of consciousness that serves as part of all of the patterns of problem solving by making formulations of mental events more explicit by committing them to writing or speech, sometimes in the presence of others. Unlike the insights themselves, formulation and expression are generally under our control.

"Judgments" or "decisions" are resolutions of reflective questions of fact, value, or deliberation. They each involve increasing levels of personal commitment. The judgment of fact is a personal affirmation that something is (or is not) true. The judgment of value involves the higher stakes of personal approval that something is (or is not) worthwhile. The decision involves the highest stakes: commitment to action and character development by importing values into one's life (or exporting disvalues from it).

Each of the cognitive acts and operations discussed above has a distinct function within the sequence. To eliminate or avoid that function will be to disrupt the process of critical thinking. Moreover as previously indicated, in all of these acts and operations, questions and insights play central roles. They are, as it were, the catalysts of critical thinking. Questions function as an operator for the entire sequence if they are pursued. That pursuit will happen only if there is a sustained desire to know. Insights function as an integrator, bringing prior elements together in a comprehensive and intelligible act of understanding.

Critical thinking (in any of its three forms) assembles in one time and place the reasons or evidence that might be sufficient to support a prospective judgment or decision, guided by and in answer to a reflective question. Any display of all these elements will likely illuminate, through reflective insight, the strengths and weaknesses of the assembled argument.

PATTERN 2: FACTUAL CRITICAL THINKING: WHEN POSSIBILITIES ARE NOT ENOUGH

In some problem situations, it is quite unsatisfying to be left adrift on an ocean of possibilities. Consider the example of Mary who has just completed a physical examination. Mary does not like to visit doctors or hospitals, but for a while she has been feeling lethargic and had a vague sense that something might be physically wrong. Many possibilities jump into her head and she worries what might be going on. For her, at this point, possibilities are not enough. She begins to transition to a new mode of problem solving: Factual Critical Thinking (PS Pattern 2). (See figure 3.1.)

Mary's uncomfortable recognition that there is a gap in her knowledge about her health is an unformulated factual reflective question. It may first appear as a recurring, if amorphous, sense of unease. This recognition may later take shape in the formulation of a reflective question such as "Is there something seriously wrong with me?" From a medical point of view, it will not be possible to answer this question immediately. Further tests will be needed. Mary has a desire to know and does not desire to swim in a sea of imagined possibilities. She takes steps to establish what the facts are in her case. She consults her physician and submits to a physical examination. Together they agree to collect information that will address Mary's question. Lab work is ordered and an x-ray is taken. A routine x-ray has indicated a spot on her lung. A fully reformulated question jumps to the forefront of her consciousness, "Is it cancer?" More tests will be ordered to address this question. Results of those tests will need to be considered before a judgment can be made. The judgment of fact is simply an answer to the reflective factual question. Together, all of the results will be weighed by the physician to answer the reflective question about cancer. A biopsy indicates cancerous tissue in the area of the spot. The answer to the reformulated reflective question is yes. The judgment is made and expressed to Mary.

This "judgment of fact" is a personal (and professional) affirmation by the physician that cancer is present in Mary's lung. The judgment is limited in scope, and it does not require knowledge of everything to successfully make it. The judgment is triply anchored in evidence and reasons, in the medical criteria for weighing them, and in the reflective question of fact. All three of these sources are understood by the physician in a reflective factual insight. This reflective insight grasps all three as sufficient to support the judgment of fact. It is the element of "social trust," to be discussed later, that enables Mary to affirm the doctor's judgment in this matter.

In general, "judgments of fact" are answers to reflective questions, and as such they take "yes" or "no" as an answer. Well-founded judgments of fact come as answers to reflective questions of fact and are supported by sufficient evidence and reasons as determined by relevant criteria. The reflective insight grasps the sufficiency of these elements to support the proposed judgment. This entire process is propelled by a desire to know, not by any other desire or emotion. Once the judgment is made it can be formulated and communicated in a variety of ways.

The most obvious thing about Factual Critical Thinking (PS Pattern 2) is its end-products: judgments of fact. To work properly Pattern 2 assumes a less obvious series of mental events leading up to the judgment: a reflective question of fact that guides the process, an assembly of reasons and evidence relevant to the judgment, and a weighing of the assembled reasons and evidence. The process leads to a reflective factual insight that either grasps or does not grasp the sufficiency of assembled evidence. Also, it may not be immediately clear what the unintended consequences are that may lead down from judgments.

Factual Critical Thinking (Pattern 2) is nothing more than the series of mental events that constitute it. (See figure 3.1.) Since it is a process extended over time, it can be disrupted. Since possible disruptions can be identified in advance, measures can be taken to exercise some quality control over the process.

There are different kinds of judgments of fact: concrete judgments of fact, generalizations, mathematical and logical judgments. Each comes with its own criteria. Mary's situation pertains to a concrete judgment of fact. That judgment indicates that cancer exists in Mary. However, the facts of consciousness described in Pattern 2 will apply to any judgment of fact, whether it is concrete, general, mathematical, or logical.[21]

The mental events discussed here are facts of consciousness that are essential to Factual Critical Thinking (Pattern 2). Without Mary's recognition (unformulated reflective question) that something was missing in her knowledge about her health, nothing would have started her on the process to find out what really was happening. Without her formulated reflective question, she would have experienced a difficult time in expressing her concerns to her physician. Also, she really desires to know whether or not she has cancer. Without her physician and the collection of evidence, there would have been nothing on which to base any answer. Without her physician weighing the evidence according to medical criteria, Mary would not have had the benefit of medical expertise nor would she be able to hear a definitive answer to her question. Without the judgment of fact communicated to her, Mary would remain without concrete knowledge about the state of her health. Mary and her physician constituted a team in this investigation.

In what ways can a judgment of fact go wrong? Table 3.2 presents judgment outcomes for the reflective question "Does Mary have cancer?". In this case there are two ways to be correct: Mary has cancer and that is judged to be the case. Or, Mary does not have cancer and that is judged to be the case. However, there are two ways to be incorrect and depart from the factual situation. A first error is the false positive, wherein we make a positive judgment ("She has cancer"), but that judgment is false. In statistics, this is referred to as a "Type I error." We can also refer to it as an "error of hallucination" because we are seeing something that is not there. This error is serious since it could lead to invasive and painful treatments that Mary does not need at all. The second error is the false negative, wherein we make a negative judgment ("She does not have cancer"), and that judgment is false. In statistics, this is referred to as a "Type II error." We can also refer to it as an "error of

Table 3.2 Judgment Outcomes for Mary's Reflective Question

	Reflective Question: Does Mary Have Cancer?	
	Factual Situation	
Judgments	Mary has cancer.	Mary does not have cancer.
Judgment of Fact [YES]	Correct	False Positive Type I Error "Error of Hallucination"
Judgment of Fact [NO]	False Negative Type II Error "Error of Blindness"	Correct

(*Source*: Author)

blindness" because we fail to see what is there. This error is serious because the cancer is missed and Mary does not get treatments that may restore her health.

In judging facts, our goal should be arriving at truth (or at least likelihood) and avoiding error. In Mary's case, we really want to know whether or not she has cancer. Practice of Factual Critical Thinking as described here will increase the probability of achieving that knowledge. In general, judgments of fact go wrong when any of the facts of consciousness of Factual Critical Thinking is missing or impaired.

More particularly, judgments of fact go wrong when the available evidence does not match the size of the judgment. It is difficult to find sufficient evidence to support judgments containing quantifying words such as "none," "never," "most," "all," or "always." More modest judgments would include quantifiers such as "a few," "some," "sometimes," "many," or "this one." These latter judgments are more likely to be well-matched with available evidence.

Judgments of fact also go wrong when a preferred judgment drives the whole process and not the desire to know and the available evidence. If anyone is bound and determined to prove a particular judgment, then they are vulnerable to at least the "confirmation bias."[22] In this case, they only seek evidence that proves their point and omit any evidence that disproves it. Politicians and advertisers are especially weak in this area. In contrast, if the desire to know and the available evidence drive the process, then the "cherry picking" of the confirmation bias is less likely to happen, and the judgment obtained is more likely to rest on sufficient evidence.

Defects in judgments of fact may emerge over time, when it is discovered that some reasons were false or unclear, that some evidence was defective or missing, or the constituent parts of Factual Critical Thinking (PS Pattern 2) were disrupted at key points. In contrast, judgments of fact will stand the test of time when the supporting reasons remain clear and true, when the assembled evidence still supports the judgment, and when participants would make the judgment again.

To summarize, Factual Critical Thinking (PS Pattern 2) is a problem solving process that builds on Pattern 1 (Seeking Understanding) by filtering ideas in terms of criteria for truth or likelihood. The possibilities generated in Pattern 1 are not enough, and they are subjected to further tests to affirm what is true and to rule out error. Pattern 2 begins with an "unformulated reflective question" - a recognition that there is a gap in our knowledge. (See figure 3.1) Sooner or later we may put this recognition into words, for example, "Is this true?" or "Is this likely?" These are formulated reflective questions. The process is propelled forward and sustained by a desire to know. It terminates in a judgment of fact, which fills the gap of the unformulated reflective question, and which answers the formulated reflective question. Along the way, evidence and reasons are collected and weighed according to relevant criteria of truth and likelihood. At the right point in time, all the elements of this process are held together and grasped by the reflective factual insight. This special insight grasps that either the evidence is or is not sufficient to support the proposed judgment of fact.

Over the course of a lifetime, judgments of fact will coalesce into a unique lifetime or developmental perspective for each individual. Relevant parts of this developmental perspective may become available, as a problem solving perspective, for problems that present themselves in the future. Future experience will indicate whether a particular problem solving perspective is helpful for growth or not.

PATTERN 3: VALUES-ORIENTED CRITICAL THINKING: WHEN TRUTH IS NOT ENOUGH

In some problem situations, knowing most of the facts is not enough; we need to weigh the worth of something. Consider the example of John who is a research and development executive with a major manufacturing company. His job includes examining new technology to determine if it should be adapted to company operations and distribution. By attending periodic technology conferences a number of new products are presented to him. These products are possibilities, and in the spirit of PS Pattern 1 (Seeking Understanding), he attempts to understand them. In the spirit of PS Pattern 2 (Factual Critical Thinking) he collects evidence about how these technologies do or do not work. At these conferences, John makes no decision, but merely considers the extent to which a new development might be worthwhile for his company. In the case of each technology, he makes a "judgment of value." As he proceeds, he also prioritizes these technologies according to some scale of values, indicating what is better than what and for what purpose. For this part of his job, neither mere possibilities nor facts are enough. John is functioning in Problem Solving Pattern 3, Values-Oriented Critical Thinking. (See figure 3.1.)

From a managerial point of view, it will not be possible to answer John's values questions merely on factual grounds. John will need to determine what the company can reasonably live with in accordance with its values. He is not just interested in facts associated with each new technology, but in the extent to which a specific technology would be useful for his company. He seeks a definitive answer to the question, "Is technology X better than the one we currently use?" or "Is technology X better than technology Y?" given the purpose and goals as reflected in the company's mission statement. At this point, he really does not know; that is, he does not have answers to these questions.

As he enters the conference, John recognizes that there is a gap in his knowledge about the potential usefulness of some new technologies. Initially, this recognition is an unformulated reflective question. This recognition may later take shape in the formulated reflective question "Is there something worthwhile for us in technology X?" From a business point of view it will not be possible to answer this question right away. Further information will need to be collected. John has a desire to know about new technology and does not desire to languish in a forest of useless possibilities. He takes steps to establish what the facts are regarding those technologies that seem promising. He may consult with others at the conference and with colleagues at work. He spends time collecting information that will address his values questions. He tries interesting technologies in mini experiments. He interviews vendors and consumers alike. A fully reformulated question jumps to the forefront of his consciousness, "Is technology X useful for our work in distribution?" More information will be collected to address this question. Results of this information gathering will be needed before a judgment of value can be made. The judgment of value is simply an answer to the reflective value question. Together, all of the results will be weighed by John to answer the reflective value question about Technology X. It turns out that certain specifications in Technology X will not make it a good fit for John's company. The answer to the reformulated reflective value question is no. The value judgment is made and expressed by John to his superiors at the company.

"Judgments of value" emerge as approvals or disapprovals of the worth of something. In this case, John's judgment of value is a personal (and professional) disapproval of technology X for use in his company. The judgment is limited in scope, and it does not require knowledge of everything to successfully make it. The judgment is triply anchored in evidence and reasons, in the business criteria for weighing them, and in the reflective question of value. All three of these sources are understood by John in his reflective values insight. This reflective insight grasps all three as sufficient to support his judgment of value.

In general, well-founded "judgments of value" come as answers to reflective questions of value, are supported by sufficient evidence and reasons, as determined by relevant criteria. The "reflective values insight" grasps the sufficiency or insufficiency of these elements to support the proposed judgment of value. This entire process is propelled by a desire to know, not by any other desire or emotion. Once the judgment of value is made it can be formulated and communicated in a variety of ways.

The most obvious thing about Values-Oriented Critical Thinking (PS Pattern 3) is its end-products: judgments of value. To work properly Pattern 3 assumes a less obvious series of mental events leading up to the judgment of value: a reflective question of value that guides the process, an assembly of reasons and evidence relevant to the judgment, and a weighing of the assembled reasons and evidence. The process leads to a reflective values insight that either grasps or does not grasp the sufficiency of assembled evidence. What is less obvious about Pattern 3 is this series of mental events that leads up to the judgments of value, as well as the unintended consequences that may lead down from the judgments themselves.

Values-Oriented Critical Thinking (Pattern 3) is nothing more than the series of mental events that constitute it. (See figure 3.1.) Just as it was the case with Patterns 1 and 2, this process is extended over time and can be disrupted. Since possible disruptions can be identified in advance, measures can be taken to exercise some quality control over the process.

Each of the mental events discussed here are facts of consciousness that are essential to Values-Oriented Critical Thinking (Pattern 3). Without John's recognition (unformulated reflective values question) that something was missing in his knowledge about new technologies, he would not have started to find out what was really valuable with some new technology. Without his formulated reflective values questions, he would have experienced a difficult time in expressing his interests to vendors and colleagues at the conference. Without his collecting evidence and other relevant information, there would have been nothing to support any answer. Without his weighing the evidence according to business criteria, John would not have had the benefit of a thorough review nor would he have been able to arrive at a definitive answer to his question.[23] Without the judgment of value emerging from this process, John would remain without knowledge about the value of technology X for his company's goals.

In what ways can a judgment of value go wrong? In general, the judgment of value can go wrong if any element of Values-Oriented Critical Thinking (PS Pattern 3) is missing or impaired, including the desire to know. John's dilemma was to determine whether or not Technology X would be a good fit for his company. He was not at the technology conference in order to make a decision, but simply to make a judgment about the value of this or that technological innovation. His judgments of value could go wrong in a manner that is analogous to the errors of judgments of fact. In his investigations he could come to the conclusion that X is worthwhile for his group and he approves it, when it is not (error of hallucination). In contrast, he could come to the point where he sees little value in X and disapproves it, when there is such value (error of blindness). These errors may be detected by John or others immediately or only after a certain amount of time. In addition, John may not have really identified clearly the values he is using and he may fail to prioritize those values he adopts.

In addition, judgments of value also go wrong when a preferred judgment drives the whole process and not the desire to know and the available evidence. Sometimes this is another instance of the confirmation bias. In other instances, values become rigidly held as demands and commands on self, others, and the world.[24] In these circumstances, judgments of value are not mere approvals or disapprovals, but instruments of mental distress and punishment.

Defects in judgments of value may emerge over time, when it is discovered that some reasons were false or unclear, that some evidence was defective or missing, or the constituent parts of Values-Oriented Critical Thinking (PS Pattern 3) were disrupted at key points. In contrast, judgments of value stand the test of time when the supporting reasons were clear and true, when the assembled evidence still supports the judgment, and when participants would make the judgment again.

To summarize, Values-Oriented Critical Thinking (PS Pattern 3) is a problem solving process that builds on Pattern 1 (Seeking Understanding) and Pattern 2 (Factual Critical Thinking) by filtering ideas in terms of their worth according to some criterion of values. The possibilities generated in Pattern 1 and the facts affirmed in Pattern 2 are subjected to further tests to approve what is worthwhile and to rule out what is worthless. Pattern 3 also begins with an "unformulated reflective question" that is a recognition that there is a gap in our knowledge of value. (See figure 3.1.) Sooner or later we may put this recognition into words, for example, "Is this good?" or "Is this worthwhile?" These are formulated reflective questions. This process is also propelled forward and sustained by a desire to know. It terminates in a judgment of value, which fills the gap of the unformulated reflective questions and which answers the formulated reflective question. Along the way, evidence and reasons are collected and weighed according to relevant criteria of value. At the right point in time, all the elements of this process are held together and grasped by the reflective values insight. This special insight grasps that either the reasons and evidence are sufficient to support the proposed judgment of value or they are not. The entire process is extended over time and may take weeks, months, or years.

Over the course of a lifetime, judgments of value will also coalesce into the problem solver's unique developmental perspective. Year after year a wide variety of judgments of value will be made: some things approved and others disapproved.[25] Over time the need may emerge to introduce some order into this list by establishing a ranking of values.[26] Parts of this lifetime perspective may become available in a problem solving perspective for problems that present themselves in the future. Future experience will indicate whether the values identified and prioritized in everyday life are helpful for growth or not.

PATTERN 4: DELIBERATIVE CRITICAL THINKING: WHEN GOOD INTENTION IS NOT ENOUGH

In some problem situations mere good intentions are not enough. Responsible action is needed. "Responsibility" here is understood as the active, ongoing alignment of one's decisions and actions with one's ever expanding factual and moral knowledge.[27] In contrast, "irresponsibility" is understood as the active, ongoing defense of one's current decisions and actions against newly emerging factual and moral knowledge.

Consider the example of Stacey who has just graduated from college. She has received a few job offers. One is in a small town close to where she grew up and the other is in a large city. Stacey will need to make a decision by next month. On this issue, she cannot consider possibilities, verify facts, and clarify values beyond that time. She will need to choose. The options presented are possibilities, and in the spirit of Problem Solving Pattern 1 (Seeking Understanding), she attempts to understand them. In the spirit of Pattern 2 (Factual Critical Thinking) she collects evidence about what these jobs entail and what these places of employment are like. In the spirit of Pattern 3 (Values-Oriented Critical Thinking) Stacey examines the extent to which each option promotes values that are important to her. She also prioritizes these options according to some value scale. At this time for Stacey, mere possibilities or facts or tested values are not enough. Stacey is now functioning in Problem Solving Pattern 4, (Deliberative Critical Thinking). (See figure 3.1.)

Stacey has visited both the small town and the large city several times. She is familiar with their neighborhoods and culture. Stacey's upcoming decision is very important since it will affect various areas of her life for at least the next five years. For this part of her life, possibilities, facts, and values are not enough. Stacey needs to function in Deliberative Critical Thinking (Pattern 4).

From a personal point of view it will not be possible to answer Stacey's deliberative questions merely on factual grounds or on the grounds of abstract values. Stacey will need to choose what to import into her life. She is not just interested in facts or abstract values, but in the specific quality of two different life paths. She seeks a definitive answer to the question, "Is the small town option better than the big city option?" At this point, she does not have an answer to this question. She is undecided. She has not chosen. When she does decide, she will be importing one option into her life and excluding the other.

As she comes to think about her next steps, Stacey recognizes that there is a gap in her knowledge about the specific job options that face her. This recognition is an unformulated deliberative reflective question. This recognition may later take shape in the formulation of a deliberative reflective question such as "Should I choose the small town option?" or "Should I choose the big city option?" If Stacey deliberates carefully, it will not be likely that she will answer this question immediately. Further information will likely need to be collected. Because Stacey is very interested in the course of her life, she has a desire to know about the quality of each option and does not desire to get lost in indecision. She may consult with friends and family and with colleagues at school. She will spend time collecting information that will address her deliberative questions. The deliberative question may be reformulated in a number of ways.[28] More information will be collected to address this question. Results of this information gathering will be needed before a decision can be made. The "decision" is simply an answer to the deliberative reflective question. Together, the pros and cons of each option will be weighed by Stacey to answer the deliberative reflective question about job choice. The decision, whatever it will be, can be expressed verbally to others and is most fully expressed by Stacey's actions to follow-up on it.

"Decisions" emerge as engagements with or refusals of available options. In the decision, we import or dismiss something from our life. Embedded within every decision is a trajectory of growth, stagnation, or decline. Stacey's decision will be an engagement with one or another career and life option. The decision is limited in scope, but it can have a profound effect on future events for Stacey. The sound decision is triply anchored in evidence and reasons, in the relevant criteria for weighing them, and in the reflective deliberative question. In a well-founded decision all three of these sources are understood by Stacey in her reflective deliberative insight. This reflective insight grasps all three as sufficient to support her decision.

In general, well-founded decisions come as answers to reflective questions of deliberation and are supported by sufficient evidence and reasons as determined by relevant criteria. The reflective deliberative insight grasps the sufficiency of these elements to support the proposed decision. This entire process is propelled by a desire to know, not by any other desire or emotion. Once the decision is made it can be formulated and communicated in a variety of ways.

The most obvious thing about Deliberative Critical Thinking (Pattern 4) is its end-product: decisions. To work properly Pattern 4 assumes a less obvious series of mental events leading up to the decision: a reflective deliberative question that guides the process, an assembly of reasons and evidence relevant to the decision and a weighing of the assembled reasons and evidence. The process leads to a reflective deliberative insight that either grasps or does not grasp the sufficiency of assembled evidence. What is less obvious about Pattern 4 is this series of mental events that leads up to the decision as well as the unintended consequences that may result from the decision itself.

"Deliberative Critical Thinking" (Pattern 4) is nothing more than the series of mental events that constitute it. (See figure 3.1.) As is the case with the other patterns of problem solving, it is a process extended over time and it is subject to disruption. Since possible disruptions can be identified in advance, measures can be taken to exercise some quality control over the process.

Each of the mental events discussed here are facts of consciousness that are essential to Deliberative Critical Thinking (Pattern 4). Without Stacey's recognition (unformulated reflective question) that something was missing in her practice about new job offers, nothing would have prompted her to settle on a particular option. Without her formulated reflective deliberative questions, she would have experienced a difficult time in expressing her concerns about future life choices to friends and family. Without her collecting evidence and other relevant information, there would have been nothing to justify any decision. Without her weighing the pros and cons according to relevant criteria, Stacey would not have had the benefit of a thorough review of her options nor would she have been able to arrive at a definitive answer to her question. Without the decision emerging from this process, Stacey would remain indecisive about her options.

In what ways can decisions go wrong? Decisions can go wrong if any element of Deliberative Critical Thinking (PS Pattern 4) is missing, including the desire to know. In the area of decision making, Stacey was faced with a simple decision involving two attractive options: accepting the offer of a good job in a small town or a good job in a large city. Since it is a decision, she will be importing something into her life and excluding something else. Her decision could go wrong in a manner that is analogous to the errors of judgments of fact. In Stacey's deliberations she could come to the conclusion that the small town job is best and she chooses it. However, there might be things she thought about this option that are not really part of it. This involves not just an error of hallucination but living with the hallucination, since by choosing, she has imported it. In contrast, she could have refused the big city job because of what she did not see about it, but since she has refused it, she cannot go back. Another way in which Stacey's decision could go wrong is that she may have not considered all the available options. Generating the possible options is the prior work of Pattern 1 (Seeking Understanding).

In addition, decisions also go wrong when a favorite option drives the whole process and not the desire to know and the available evidence. Sometimes this is another instance of the confirmation bias. In this case, a particular option eclipses all others in terms of its initial attractiveness. In these circumstances, decisions are not the result of a deliberative process carefully weighing options, but merely an echoing of what we instinctively want without much thought.

Like defects in judgment, defects in decisions can emerge over time, when it is discovered that some reasons were false or unclear, that some evidence was defective or missing, or the constituent parts of Deliberative Critical

Thinking (PS Pattern 4) were disrupted at key points. In contrast, decisions stand the test of time when the supporting reasons remain clear and true, when the assembled evidence still supports the decision, and when participants would likely make the decision again.

To summarize, PS Pattern 4 (Deliberative Critical Thinking) is a problem solving process that builds on Pattern 1 (Seeking Understanding), Pattern 2 (Factual Critical Thinking), and Pattern 3 (Values-Oriented Critical Thinking) by filtering options (possible courses of action) in terms of practical criteria of whether or not they should be imported into or excluded from our lives. The possibilities generated in Pattern 1, the facts affirmed in Pattern 2, and the values approved in Pattern 3 are not enough, but they are subjected to further tests to identify options that are optimal for Stacey. Pattern 4 also begins with an unformulated reflective question; it is a recognition that there is a gap in what we are currently doing. (See figure 3.1.) Sooner or later we may place this recognition into words, for example, "Should I do this?" or "Should we refrain from that?" These are formulated reflective questions. This process is also propelled forward and sustained by a desire to know. It terminates in a decision, which fills the gap of the unformulated reflective questions, and which answers the formulated reflective question. Along the way, pros and cons for each option are collected and weighed according to relevant criteria of practice. At the right point in time, all the elements of this process are held together and grasped by the reflective deliberative insight. This special insight grasps that pros and cons for the various options that identify the optimal decision. The entire process is extended over time, but the nature of decision is to cut off internal debate and to choose.

Over the course of a lifetime, decisions and their expressions in actions coalesce into the problem solver's unique developmental perspective and a unique list of achievements as well as the problem solver's character. "Character" is a collection of relatively stable cognitive, emotive, and behavioral traits of personality. Parts of this assembled personality are likely to become available as a problem solving perspective for problems that present themselves in the future. As mentioned, the extent to which the accumulated achievements and adopted traits of personality promote growth will be determined by future experience.

ADDITIONAL CONSIDERATIONS

Implications

To the extent that the facts of consciousness described in this chapter are verified in experience, a number of points follow:

1) Because the elements of critical thinking are functionally interrelated, each type of critical thinking is a cognitive process. A cognitive process is a sequence of interrelated mental events and operations.
2) Because each type of critical thinking is a process, these forms of thinking take time. Some elements of these processes, such as insights and questions, may be instantaneous; but others, such as collecting and weighing information and formulating, are time intensive. The process could extend from hours to months.
3) Because each pattern of critical thinking is a process, each one can be disrupted by personal or environmental interferences. Anyone who seriously attempts to practice Factual Critical Thinking or Values-Oriented Critical Thinking as described here will be guided by the desire to know. The influence of other desires or emotions is likely to distort the process. Anyone who seriously attempts to practice Deliberative Critical Thinking must be guided not only by the desire to know but also by the desire to grow in a manner consistent with their approved values.
4) To the extent that one practices the acts and operations of PS Pattern 2 (Factual Critical Thinking) and PS Pattern 3 (Values-Oriented Critical Thinking) they constitute themselves as a critical questioner, investigator, formulator, and competent judge of fact and value.
5) To the extent that one practices the acts and operations of PS Pattern 4 (Deliberative Critical Thinking) they constitute themselves as a deliberative, responsible, questioner, investigator, formulator, and competent decision maker.
6) Not all acts and operations within the three patterns of critical thinking are in our control. This was explored in the last chapter with its discussion of Problem Solving Pattern 1 (Seeking Understanding). This is also true of all the types of critical thinking discussed here. In particular, questions are only partially in our control: we can routinely ask them according to some protocol, but sometimes they emerge in consciousness quite suddenly and unbidden. Insights, on the other hand are not in our control. However, through study and constant practice in problem solving, we can set up conditions that increase the probability of their occurrence. If we are to practice critical thinking, or any other type of thinking, we should focus on what is in our control. Activities such as formulating questions and insights, and collecting and weighing evidence are generally in our control.
7) Because each type of critical thinking is a time-consuming process, it is not possible to practice any form of critical thinking about everything. The scarcity of time requires that topics for critical examination must be selected.

8) Because of this limitation, the everyday practice of critical thinking also invites both the development of intellectual habits and collaboration with others. (See chapter 5.)
9) If critical thinking is to become a long-term feature of the way a person thinks, it must become a habit. Yet the acquisition of habits is not a straightforward matter. It may involve a difficult process of eliminating old habits and acquiring new ones. Practice will play an important role in this but that is only a part.[29]
10) Growth in critical thinking will not be easy. It will not proceed in a straight line without setbacks, personal struggle, and opposition from others.[30] It will require perseverance, since establishing facts, identifying and prioritizing values and making well-founded decisions all take time. Stories from the history of psychology, as well as other disciplines, amply demonstrate this.[31]
11) Specifically, some authors have offered particular exercises designed to assist with the development of one or another aspect of critical thinking.[32] Increased facility in each of these aspects is likely to come with perseverance and continued practice. Ongoing practice in these areas will allow us to make fewer and better judgments and decisions. These will be designed for the problem at hand, evidence-based, and not overly generalized.
12) In order to develop the patterns of critical thinking into intellectual habits one would need to identify and exploit opportunities to practice them. Areas of life where truth, identifying and prioritizing one's values and making well-founded decisions are important candidates. Examples might include a critical review of one's personal finances, management of one's fitness and health, assessing the effectiveness of a program at work, evaluating social policies, various personal and professional choices. They could also include addressing the key existential questions presented by philosophy and religion.
13) In specific instances of practice one can assure the quality of the process by being guided by the desire to know, and not by other interests, motives, or emotions. One can also identify and keep track of the mental events of each mode of critical thinking as they appear. If any are missing, the process has been disrupted. For example, judgments are often put forward with little or no consideration of the question that they allegedly answer. Decisions are often presented with little to no detailed exploration of the problem that is being addressed.
14) Since all the patterns of problem solving are complex, it is useful to keep track of mental events by means of an intellectual journal. The dated entries can include the relevant mental events as they occur. (See figure 3.1.) The journal itself maps how the process has probabilistically

unfolded over time, with prominence given to the emergence of questions and insights. It will indicate false starts, breakthroughs, limitations, and growth in a given area of study. It will also indicate the social trust we have invested in others as they assist our problem solving efforts. Such detail will lead to greater self-knowledge and through that to a greater capacity to regulate and manage one's own problem solving.

15) Each pattern of critical thinking is designed for distinct problem solving situations. Factual Critical Thinking (PS Pattern 2) is designed to fill gaps in our knowledge. There are some situations where that is all that is needed. Values-Oriented Critical Thinking (PS Pattern 3) is designed to fill gaps in our value system. There are situations where our values system is being put to use, or is under construction or has been assaulted by some catastrophe or crisis.[33] In clarifying and sorting our values we may rely on facts that have previously been established, so in some sense Pattern 3 does need established facts to operate. Deliberative Critical Thinking (PS Pattern 4) addresses gaps in our practice. We are often faced with decisions requiring us to choose from a list of options. In making our choices, we will also rely on previously established facts and currently operative values. Hence, Pattern 4 presupposes the work of Patterns 2 and 3. Moving from Pattern 2 to Pattern 3 to Pattern 4 is probabilistic and not mechanistic, and it is determined by the current situation, the problems at hand, and the diligence of the problem solver.

16) The more complex a process is and the more it requires perseverance, the fewer the number of people who are likely to engage in it.[34] However, there is clear evidence many persons and small groups practice these forms of thinking in various walks of life. Readers are invited to find examples in their own experience of how they or others do this. Establishing expertise in any area through Factual Critical Thinking (PS Pattern 2) may take many years. Identifying and then prioritizing values, as required in Values-Oriented Critical Thinking (PS Pattern 3), can be the work of a lifetime. Making decisions, as spelled out in Deliberative Critical Thinking (PS Pattern 4), requires perseverance in the discipline of balancing risks and opportunities, constraints, and propelling forces.

SUMMARY

This chapter began with the identification of three aims: (1) to invite readers to reflect on their own thought processes routinely engaged when they attempt to solve problems, (2) to clarify at least one account of critical thinking, and (3) to identify three distinct types of critical thinking and their structure.

Regarding the invitation, the chapter briefly considered how critical thinking relates to some earlier developments in educational psychology and why critical thinking has become a topic of interest in educational discourse. As long as environments exist where problems remain unsolved and where issues of fact and value need to be resolved, and decisions need to be made then critical thinking will be both relevant and required for any real progress.

Regarding the clarification of critical thinking this chapter offers an account that is guided by Peter Facione's definition of critical thinking, which focuses primarily on judgment not merely as a proposition, but as a cognitive act, and the surrounding considerations which well-founded judgments will involve. The chapter expanded the consideration of judgment to include the act of decision, which has a similar structure.[35]

Regarding the identification of different types of critical thinking, the chapter describes three basic types or patterns of critical thinking: Factual (Pattern 2), Value-Oriented (Pattern 3), and Deliberative (Pattern 4). The chapter indicates the similarity of structure in the three patterns and examined their differences. The acts and operations identified in each pattern of critical thinking do not follow each other mechanically. Progress from one to other requires that the problem solver intend, or at least be willing, to follow the trajectory of each pattern. One can move one's attention back and forth until things are so clear that the reflective insight can emerge. Once that happens one is on sufficient ground to make a judgment or decision.

Critical thinking, as described in this chapter does not operate in a vacuum, but proceeds in larger personal and environmental contexts. This will be explored in greater detail in chapter 5.

There are no substitutes for the three types critical thinking specified here. While there are forms of uncritical thinking that are fast, they generally cannot replace the more extended and detailed processes of critical thinking.[36] All of the patterns of problem solving, including the patterns of critical thinking, are examples of what has been termed "system II thinking." More specifically, Factual Critical Thinking is only useful to the extent that situations require that the facts be established. For example, while accident investigators may consider many possibilities, only those that are true or likely are of lasting interest. Values-Oriented Critical Thinking is only useful only to the extent that all things are not considered equally desirable or worthwhile. A Manufacturing representative may consider many new technologies, but he is mainly interested in those that would be worthwhile for his company. Deliberative Critical Thinking is only useful in situations where responsible action is required or a decision is pending. Embedded within every decision is a trajectory of growth, remaining stationary or decline. A new college graduate will need to choose from among available job offers presented to him or her.

Moreover, the three types of critical thinking are unique, since each is guided by a different reflective question. In addition, within each type of critical thinking, each act or operation has a unique function. In particular, questions have the unique role of operator, since they guide the process by providing clues of what is sought. The insight has the unique role of integrator, since it places all the collected elements required to answer the question into a unifying perspective. The desire to know has the unique role of propelling the process forward and of insuring quality control. Later in the book, a special role for social trust will be identified and examined.

Whatever we learn about critical thinking may be transferred to and shared with others in our practice, teaching, counseling, consulting, or many other social activities. Such sharing serves to model critical thinking for others, and it allows us to test our grasp of it in concrete situations.[37] Anyone operating in light of the conditions of critical thinking specified in this chapter will increase their comprehensive learning in any field they choose. The learning thus achieved will be tested and verified, valuable, and transformative of situations and self.

Based on the discussion in this chapter, each reader might wish to address the following questions: Is critical thinking important? And, why? A first option would involve ignoring these questions altogether. The reader, in effect, will be turning attention to other matters and will not be in a position to derive any benefit in this area at this time. A second option is to answer these questions in the negative by asserting that critical thinking is unimportant, based on reasons that seem convincing. In that case, the reader is free to embark on the ultimate experiment of generally not resolving questions of fact or value and of not engaging in reasoned decision and action. However, a third option is to answer these questions in the affirmative by asserting that critical thinking is important, and for a variety of convincing reasons. In that case, the reader may wish to pursue those insights in a different, more growth-oriented ways.

NOTES

1. Portions of this chapter are based on previously published articles in *Lonergan Review* and *Method: Journal of Lonergan Studies*: "Thinking Carefully about Critical Thinking." *Lonergan Review*, IV, No. 1 (2013), 154–180; "Approaching Critical Thinking through Generalized Empirical Method." *Method*, 4, No. 2 (2103).

2. Richard Grallo, "The Absence of Question and Insight in Accounts of Knowledge." *Symposium*, XIV No. 1 (2007), 33–43; D. Moseley, Vivienne

Baumfield, Julian Elliott, Maggie Gregson, Steven Higgins, J. Miller, and D. Newton, *Frameworks for Thinking* (Cambridge, UK: Cambridge University Press, 2005); more recent work has started to examine the functional role of questions and questioning in learning: National Research Council, *How People Learn* (Washington, DC: National Academy Press, 2000).

3. Bernard Lonergan, *Insight: A Study of Human Understanding* (Toronto: University of Toronto Press, 1992).

4. Richard Meyer, *Thinking, Problem Solving, Cognition (2nded.).*(New York: W.H. Freeman & Co., 1983); Edward Smith, and Daniel Osherson, *Thinking* (Cambridge, MA: MIT Press, 1995); Robert Sternberg, *Thinking and Problem Solving* (New York: Academic Press, 1994).

5. Peter Lamont. "The Construction of 'Critical Thinking': Between How We Think and What We Believe." *History of Psychology,* 23 (2020), No. 3, 232–251.

6. Louis Leon Thurstone, *Primary Mental Abilities* (Chicago: University of Chicago Press, 1938); Louis. Leon and Thelma Thurstone, *Factorial Studies of Intelligence* (Chicago: University of Chicago Press, 1941).

7. Howard Gardner, *Frames of Mind: The Theory of Multiple Intelligences* (New York: Basic Books, 1993).

8. J. P. Guilford, "Intelligence Has Three Facets," *Science*, 160 (1968), 351–364.

9. Benjamin Bloom, M, Engelhart, E. Frost, W. Hill, and David Krathwohl, *Taxonomy of Educational Objectives. Handbook I: Cognitive Domain* (New York: David McKay, 1956).

10. Lorin Anderson, and David Krathwohl, eds. *A Taxonomy for Learning, Teaching and Assessing: A Revision of Bloom's Taxonomy of Educational Objectives* (New York: Longman, 2001).

11. Richard Arum and Josipa Roksa, *Academically Adrift: Limited Learning on College Campuses* (Chicago, IL: University of Chicago Press, 2011).

12. Middle States Commission on Higher Education, *Characteristics of Excellence in Higher Education* (Philadelphia, PA: Middle States Commission on Higher Education, 2006).

13. Lucy S. Cromwell, *Teaching Critical Thinking in the Arts and Humanities* (Milwaukee, WI: Alverno Productions, 1986); Jane Halonen, *Critical Thinking in Psychology* (Milwaukee, WI: Alverno Productions, 1995).

14. Robert Ennis, *Critical Thinking* (Upper Saddle River, NJ: Prentice-Hall, 1996).

15. Peter Facione, *Critical thinking: What It Is and Why It Counts* (Millbrae, CA: Insight Publishing, 2006).

16. David Levy, *Tools of Critical Thinking: Metathoughts for Psychology* (Boston: Allyn and Bacon, 1997).

17. Gerald Nosich, *Learning to Think Things Through: A Guide to Critical Thinking across the Curriculum (4thed.).* (Boston: Pearson, 2012).

18. Facione, *Critical Thinking.*

19. Samuel Kotz, and Norman Johnson, eds. *Encyclopedia of Statistical Sciences, v.5* (New York: Wiley, 1985).

20. Lonergan, *Insight*; Robert Sternberg and Janet Davidson, eds. *The Nature of Insight* (Cambridge, MA: MIT Press, 1998).

21. Lonergan, *Insight*, Ch. X.

22. American Psychological Association, *Dictionary of Psychology* (Washington, DC: American Psychological Association, 2015, 232).

23. On multiple criteria for judgments of value and decisions see: Joseph A. Petrick and John F. Quinn. *Management Ethics: Integrity at Work* (Thousand Oaks, CA: Sage, 1997); also Patrick Byrne. *The Ethics of Discernment: Lonergan's Foundations for Ethics* (Toronto: University of Toronto Press, 2017).

24. Albert Ellis and Robert Harper. *A New Guide to Rational Living* (Woodland Hills, CA: Wilshire Book Co., 1975).

25. On the variety of values, see Milton Rokeach. *The Nature of Human Values* (New York: Free Press, 1973); Henry Murray. *Explorations in Personality* (New York: Oxford University Press.

26. On the ranking of values, see Manfred Frings. *The Mind of Max Scheler: The First Comprehensive Guide Based on the Complete Works (Milwaukee, Wisconsin: Marquette University Press, 1997)*; Abraham Maslow. *Motivation and Personality* (New York: Harper & Row, 1954).

27. Contrast this definition with that of Stephen Covey and Fritz Perls.

28. One way of doing this is to develop a decision tree that includes all the options. See Detlof von Winterfeldt and Ward Edwards, *Decision Analysis and Behavioral Research* (New York: Cambridge University Press, 1986). For a medical example, see Theresa J. Jordan, Richard Grallo, and Richard Montgomery, "Combining Decision Analysis and Experimental Data to Study Bias in Educational Settings: Impact of Age on Medical Students' Treatment Decisions," *Journal of Research in Education*, 4, No. 1, (1994), 58–67.

29. James Prochaska, John Norcross, and Carlo DiClemente, *Changing for Good* (New York: Avon Books, 1994).

30. Prochaska *Changing for Good.*

31. Maryanne Garry and Harlene Hayne, *Do Justice and Let the Sky Fall: Elizabeth Loftus and Her Contributions to Science, Law and Academic Freedom* (Mahwah, NJ: Lawrence Erlbaum Associates, 2007); Joachim Krueger, *Rationality and Social Responsibility: Essays in Honor of Robyn Mason Dawes* (New York: Psychology Press, 2008).

32. Ennis, *Critical Thinking*; Jennifer Moon (2007). *Critical Thinking: An Exploration of Theory and Practice* (New York: Routledge, 2007); Nosich, *Learning to Think Things Through.*

33. David Rosner. (ed.) *Catastrophe and Philosophy* (New York: Lexington Books, 2019).

34. Philosopher Immanuel Kant was not optimistic about the widespread distribution of critical thinking, or what he called "reasoning." See "What is Enlightenment" *Internet Modern History Sourcebook.*

35. Jonathan Baron, *Thinking and Deciding (2nded.)* (Cambridge, UK: Cambridge University Press, 1998); T. Connolly, H. Arkes, and K. Hammond, eds. *Judgment*

and Decision Making: An Interdisciplinary Reader (Cambridge, UK: Cambridge University Press, 2000).

36. Malcolm Gladwell, *Blink: The power of Thinking without Thinking* (New York: Little Brown & Co., 2005); Daniel Kahneman, *Thinking, Fast and Slow* (New York: Farrar, Straus & Giroux, 2011).

37. D. Alan Bensley, "A brief guide for teaching and assessing critical thinking in psychology." *Psychological science*, 23, No. 10 (2010), 49–53; Brookhart, Susan. *How to Assess Higher Order Thinking Skills in Your Classroom* (Alexandria, VA: ASCD, 2010); Heide Hlawaty and Richard Grallo, "Reframing STEM Standards, Outcomes and Strategies for the 21st Century Workplace," Conference of the National Science Teachers Association, San Francisco, 2011; Kenneth Melchin, and Cheryl Picard, *Transforming Conflict through Insight* (Toronto: University of Toronto Press, 2009); Louis Tietje, Philip Nufrio, and R. Kramer, "Theory and Practice of Action Learning in the MPA/MBA Curriculum at Metropolitan College of New York." *Public Administration Quarterly*, 32, No. 2 (2008), 214–242.

Chapter 4

Experiencing and Its Functions in Learning and Problem Solving

FUNCTIONS OF EXPERIENCE IN OVERVIEW

So[1] far, this book has been an invitation to readers to be witnesses to their own experience in all its variety. Some types of experience are the patterns of problem solving already explored; others are non-problem-solving activities that call a halt to the work of problem solving. This chapter explores both experience in general and the types of experience that move away from problem solving. For our purpose, "getting the most out of our experience" specifically involves attending to it, questioning it for purposes of greater understanding, arriving at knowledge about how it works, valuing its existence as a resource in learning, and deciding to make careful use of it in the future.

In various helping professions over the last fifty years, it has become increasingly important to work with people "where they are." For example, in the twentieth century, psychologist Carl Rogers signaled a shift in counseling practice away from classification and use of a medical model to a focus on clients' lived experience.[2] More recently, the movement in education known as "differentiated instruction" takes aim at students' interests and abilities in the ongoing attempt to assist them in learning different kinds of course content.[3] In these fields and others, each person's experience will be crucial in accurately describing his or her perspective both present and past. This raises a general question: What is the role of experience in complex human learning and problem solving?

It should be noted that the word "experience" is an abstract noun and is therefore likely to have multiple uses. Common meanings include expressions such as "survived events," "conscious events," and "expert knowledge." Common dictionary definitions list these related, but distinct, referents for the term: (1) "an event or a series of events participated in or lived through," (2) the apprehension of an object, thought, or emotion through the senses or mind," (3) "active participation in events or activities, leading to the accumulation of knowledge or skill."[4]

To be more specific, one can distinguish three types of experience as defined in the general language and as reflected in philosophic and psychological literature. First, experience has been identified as the sum total of anything that is lived through. This may be regarded as the "survival definition," and it is the most comprehensive of all three. It includes anything that one lives through in the course of a time period, including dreamless sleep. This is consistent with definition (1) above. Second, a more restrictive definition of experience is given as the sum total of consciously apprehended events. This may be regarded as the "stream of consciousness definition." William James described consciousness as being constantly in flux, and being associated with a person's ability to focus on external objects as well as internal states.[5] For James,

> consciousness, then, does not appear to itself chopped up in bits. Such words as "chain" or "train" are not really appropriate descriptions of consciousness as it presents itself in the first instance. It is nothing jointed; it flows. A "river" or a "stream" are the metaphors by which it is most naturally described. In talking of it hereafter let us call it the stream of thought, of consciousness, or of subjective life.

All of this is consistent with definition (2). Some approaches to definition (2) regard the origins of conscious experience as being either in the senses or mind. Some approaches are very broad in their conception of origins, but others restrict origins to sensation alone. This latter restriction prioritizes sense experience as the origin of all other conscious events. Sense data are given a chronological, if not a causal priority, over other conscious states (or ideas). A common example of this is the persistent philosophic doctrine that nothing is in the intellect which is not first in the senses. This view had precedents in ancient and medieval philosophy and was carried into the philosophy of the British empiricists such as John Locke[6] and David Hume.[7] It is consistent with the most restrictive reading of definition (2). Finally, dictionary definition (3) covers the patterns of problem solving examined already in chapters 2 and 3.

Given that experience may be widely or narrowly defined, what functions does experience play in complex human learning and problem solving? Three functions or roles for experience in learning will be posited here. (1) Experience is a "source" and "resource" of learning. As such, it provides the material (or data) that is the content of all thinking. This aligns with the dictionary account given above of "the apprehension of an object, thought, or emotion through the senses or mind." Experience is also a resource for learning, since it includes the personal and contextual conditions that either facilitate or hinder learning efforts. This relates to the dictionary entry of "an event or a series of events participated in or lived through" already noted. (2) Experience can function as a "testing ground" for learning, by providing data that can confirm or falsify insights and can assist in engaging or refusing potential courses of action. This is consistent with the dictionary rendering of "participation in events or activities, leading to the accumulation of knowledge or skill." It is also very much the kind of thing examined in the chapters on patterns of problem solving. (3) Experience can also function as a "pause" from learning if it is the kind of "basic experience" that is mostly devoid of the problem solving activities, such as question and insight and any mental event identified in the patterns of problem solving. This type of experience also counts as a series of events lived through, but these events are not of an active problem solving nature.

This chapter offers a structure for understanding "experience," in its multiple conceptions, in relation to human learning and problem solving. More specifically, it has three related aims: (1) to explore the basic roles of experience in complex human learning: source and resource, testing ground and pause, (2) to explore how non-problem solving experience gets organized, and (3) to identify implications of making the most out of experience.

Why bother with these aims? If experience plays any role in human learning, then a deeper understanding of how it works increases not only the probability of learning in a specific area but also the probability of greater self-knowledge, especially knowledge about how one learns. Increased self-knowledge about learning increases the probability of achieving increased facility and freedom in the management of one's own learning and in becoming an independent thinker. In contrast, lack of this self-knowledge leaves learning as largely a hit-or-miss enterprise, with the likelihood of a vastly reduced cumulative beneficial effect.

Experience, broadly considered, is a source of all the materials for later understanding, judging, and deciding. More narrowly considered, experiencing becomes "basic experiencing" when there is a pause from problem solving activities. This can take a few different forms: automatic habitual activities, aesthetic absorption, and the thought cessation known as tranquil abiding. The pauses of aesthetic absorption and tranquil abiding can provide a haven from the work of problem solving and they can provide a re-creation of energy and of focus. While learning how to shift into these states of consciousness may require consistent practice, the benefits of renewed energy and clarity of focus are clear.

EXPERIENCE AS SOURCE AND RESOURCE FOR LEARNING

Experience, however defined, functions as a "source" for human learning by providing material (or data) that is the content of all thinking. This "data" is what is given in consciousness. (It includes much more than the more narrow meaning of scientific "data," which is the product of systematic observation and measurement.) Philosopher Edmund Husserl developed a method of reflective attentiveness to this data that discloses the individual's "lived experience."[8] The philosopher Franz Brentano and the psychologist J. P. Guilford argued that thinking of any sort must be about something, and that "something" is the content of thinking.[9] Brentano states it this way:

> Every mental phenomenon includes something as object within itself, although they do not all do so in the same way. In presentation something is presented, in judgement something is affirmed or denied, in love loved, in hate hated, in desire desired and so on. This intentional in-existence is characteristic exclusively of mental phenomena. No physical phenomenon exhibits anything like it. We could, therefore, define mental phenomena by saying that they are those phenomena which contain an object intentionally within themselves.

Without this content, there is no thinking. Consequently any problem solving or learning efforts that depend on thinking will collapse if it is devoid of content.

Whatever is admitted as content (or "data") then will largely depend on one's definition of "experience." Broader definitions of experience tend to admit more types of data. The narrower definitions either admit less data or give priority to one type of data over all others.

Buddhism presents one of the widest understandings of experience. This includes not only the data of the senses but the data of other conscious states as well. The Dalai Lama states the Buddhist perspective clearly when he writes, "When Buddhism speaks of empirical experience, it has a broader understanding of empiricism, which includes meditative states as well as the evidence of the senses."[10] In Buddhism, sensations are one type of conscious state among many, and they are not assigned any particular priority. William James also takes a view of experience wide enough to include all conscious states. These states flow in a "stream of consciousness." This stream is not just a succession of conscious states, but it also has a direction or tendency.[11] Bernard Lonergan also takes the wide view when he identifies what we call "data of sense" and "data of consciousness" (i.e., of conscious states other than sensations). Lonergan also accepts the directionality of the stream of consciousness and identifies a limited number of modes of lived experience that can result.[12] These are habitual modes of living in which we engage.

Experience is also a "resource" for learning. Not only does it provide the data to be understood, judged, and engaged, but it provides a conscious environment in which learning takes place. All environments surround, include, and permeate something. They are aggregates of conditions in which a person lives or in which something exists. An environment for learning will include inner and outer conditions that either promote learning or hinder it. Kant attempted to uncover conditions for the possibility of knowledge.[13] Among psychologists, Robert Gagné explicitly worked to identify factors that promote learning.[14] Allen Newell and Herbert Simon attempted to identify conditions for successful problem solving.[15] In 1990, summarizing the literature to that point, Edwin Locke and Gary Latham identified internal and external conditions for high performance in any area.[16] In 2007, Dale Schunck and Barry Zimmerman summarized this literature specifically as it concerns complex human learning.[17]

These accounts integrate well with the idea of experience as learned expertise and expert knowledge. Students who choose to go through a long professional development (as in law, medicine, nursing, or psychology) are exposed to a series of learning situations and environments. To facilitate their own learning, they must also master and manage their own inner environment of thought and emotion. Expert knowledge builds over time with specific honest feedback from teachers, mentors, and colleagues.

As useful as these accounts of complex human learning are, they generally take little notice of the important mental events of question and insight. As seen so far, questions and insights are pivotal conscious events that occur as part of our intellectual life. As events, both question and insight are quite fleeting. Yet, despite their swiftness, they are crucial in human learning and problem solving. Who would claim much learning without any insight? How can any problem said to be solved if questions were not answered?

As noted in previous chapters, a question (as mental event) is the recognition of a gap somewhere in our experience, understanding, knowledge, or practice. If this recognition is taken seriously, it functions as an operator by reigniting the effort to learn. However, since questions (as mental events) are fleeting, to derive the most benefit from them, they must be captured in some formulation (in words, symbols, formulae, etc.). The interrogative proposition is a question (mental event) expressed in words. Without questions, no gaps are recognized. Without their formulation, no persistent pursuit of them is likely to occur.

Also as noted, the insight goes hand-in-glove with questions. It provides a possible answer to a guiding question by integrating relevant information to answer the question. It functions as an integrator. Without insight there is no understanding, because insight is an act of understanding. Without insight, learning and problem solving cannot proceed because without insight they do not exist.

Together, both questions and insights provide the ongoing and developing context for understanding, comprehensive learning, and problem solving. If learning and problem solving are stripped of questions and insight, they collapse.

Oddly enough, some philosophers and psychologists have attempted to describe human learning and problem solving without any mention of either question or insight. Any account of knowledge, knowing, and human learning that fails to incorporate question and insight as mental events is incomplete to the point of misunderstanding.[18] This general neglect of question and insight as integral parts of the environment of learning continues to this day.[19]

EXPERIENCE AS TESTING GROUND FOR LEARNING

Experience may also be viewed as a "testing ground" for perceptions, memories, understanding, knowledge claims, values, and decisions. Among the ancient Greeks, Aristotle clearly profited from experience through systematic observation. Epictetus stressed the continual interrogation and testing of one's sense impressions, judgments and decisions. Francis Bacon, in his *Novum Organum*, emphasized recourse to experience through experimentation as a means for settling scientific disputes. William James indicated that testing predictions would be the best means for determining truth in any situation.

Testing in this sense often involves some version of a reflective question of fact. As indicated in chapter 3, "reflective questions of fact" are questions that admit "yes" or "no" as answers and may usually be of the form "Is P true?" or "Is X probable?" In these cases P may be any proposition, and X may be any event. If the eventual "yes" or "no" is to be well supported, it must be based on sufficient evidence and compelling reasons. Hence, in the case of reflective questions of fact, the entire enterprise is an instance of Factual Critical Thinking designed to resolve some issue of fact. Consequently some version of truth (however defined) is at play.

There are three criteria for truth that can act as aids in addressing three distinct questions about what we learn.[20] In the "correspondence account of truth" there is a search for a match between evidence and the proposed judgment. Its advantage is that, if successful, it relates our judgments to states of affairs in the world. Its limitation is that relevant evidence may be scattered across time and space, even to such an extent that it is irretrievable. This poses a real problem for any theory that is advertised as "evolutionary," whether it is in biology, psychology, or any other field.

In the "cohesion account of truth" there is a check for consistency among known propositions. Its advantage is that, if our developing knowledge is inconsistent, then we may be in the neighborhood of an error, and it is useful to identify errors. Its disadvantage is that it is difficult, or nearly impossible, to give a complete inventory of what we know.

In the "pragmatic account of truth" the search is for the impact and usefulness of a specific claim, embodied as a prediction. Its advantage lies in its focus on a specific time and place for a test (formulated as a prediction). Its limitation is that it must wait for the data to be collected, and such tests may be difficult to arrange.

Using experience as a testing ground leads to a number of effects. There is a gradual accumulation of knowledge. This knowledge may then find some practical applications that will transform the situations in which they are applied. Transformation often involves the introduction of some relatively enduring change. Finally, situations are not the only thing that is changed by such knowledge; as has been indicated, there is a transformation in the knower as well. With an accumulation of transformations of this sort, over time the novice is gradually changed into an expert.

EXPERIENCE AS PAUSE FROM LEARNING

If some wider definitions of experience include all conscious states, then in many of those states the mind is active: pursuing questions, formulating answers, calculating, testing, etc. To the extent that questions and insights are involved, complex human learning is proceeding. However, learning is work. It involves expenditures of energy and, therefore, cannot be pursued all day every day. While learning requires the extended work of perseverance, it also requires appropriate pause from this work.

This raises the possibility of conscious states devoid of virtually any kind of problem solving activity, including question and insight. What would a conscious state be like in which the mind is basically "shut off" or simply idling. Is there a "neutral gear" for consciousness? Is there a state in which one is conscious but not engaged in any problem solving activity? Can we be aware without pursuing questions, having insights or solving problems?

Such conscious experience with no questions, insights, or problem solving efforts of any kind may be termed "basic experience." Even without questions and insights, experience can organize itself into distinct modes of non-problem-solving experience. Three will be mentioned here: (1) automatic habitual routines, (2) aesthetic absorption, and (3) tranquil abiding.

ORGANIZATION OF EXPERIENCE
AS MODES OF PAUSE

For most of us, our experience tends to get structured as it flows along. There is not just a "flow of consciousness" with one thing appearing and then receding, followed by another new appearance. There is also a direction and a clustering of activities around aims and purposes.

How does our lived experience get organized into clusters of activities? Some have described how this clustering might occur. For example, philosopher Bernard Lonergan describes four "patterns of experience": biological, aesthetic, intellectual, and dramatic. More specifically, he has identified four streams or "patterns of experience": the biological pattern involves simply surviving (staying alive). It is exemplified by the soldier operating in combat situations or by others living in extremely dangerous environments. The dramatic pattern is concerned with individual and social action. It seeks to accomplish its agenda with some dignity or flair. It is clearly exemplified in the attempt to develop a career in one's chosen field and in making a reasonable living. The aesthetic pattern is a playful release from biological and social routines. It is exemplified by the artist who seeks to rise above merely biological and social routines and to envision and, perhaps, communicate other possibilities. Finally, the intellectual pattern of experience is a form of consciousness directed by the desire to know. It is exemplified by the scientist who seeks to find out how things work or by the troubleshooter who attempts to develop workable solutions to a concrete problem.[21]

Another description of how experience gets organized is provided by philosopher Mark Morelli. He describes how experience can get organized through five salient themes or "motifs of conscious performance": practical, intellectual, aesthetic, dramatic, and mystical.[22] In daily living these themes or motifs blend and merge in myriad ways, with perhaps one or two being dominant.

In contrast to these descriptions, the focus in this book has been on complex learning and problem solving in any situation. We have seen how this organizing works through questions and insights in the four patterns of problem solving. However, there is also a non-problem-solving experience. It is free of questions and insights. How does this type of experience get organized? Here too there are streams of consciousness that include their own direction and attention. When one pauses from the work of problem solving, one may return first to the more or less organized "habitual routines" of daily living. Because these routines are habitual, they are somewhat automatic and can be engaged without much effort at problem solving or complex learning.

A second form of pause occurs for many through "aesthetic absorption." This form of experience offers a diversion from the work of problem solving.[23] This absorption is a kind of contemplation on various art forms such as dance, music, painting, and sculpture. It is also the kind of absorption when someone contemplates the awesome beauty and power of nature. No novel or chronic problems intrude in this type of appreciation. It is a kind of haven from not only the push-pull routines of daily living but also from the work of problem solving.

A third form of pause from learning and problem solving may be named "tranquil abiding."[24] It also is a kind of haven, perhaps like lying on a beach just watching a cloud on a sunny day – having no particular thoughts or cares. It is defined here as an enjoyable, serene experience of free-floating attention that is devoid of problem solving activity. Achieving this state may require a great deal of practice, as many experienced meditators can attest. Achieving it may also produce a number of beneficial effects, to be determined by each person on their own. Effects of this state may include: (1) the experience of remarkable tranquility, (2) the "re-creation" of energy, (3) the inducement of sleep as a by-product, or (4) the gentle emergence of insights and more comprehensive understanding. The free-floating attention of this state may be focused on breathing alone, leading to effects (1), (2), and, sometimes, (3). Or the free-floating nature of this state may be focused on some object or event leading to effects (1), (2), and, then, (4). Based on this, one can distinguish the whole process of achieving tranquility as calming exercises from the process of focusing and following an object or event.[25] A "calming exercise" is any mindful activity designed to achieve subjective tranquility. A "focusing and following exercise" is any mindful activity wherein an object or theme is examined and conscious states are allowed to flow from that. Because of the emergence of insight, focusing, and following lead quite naturally into problem solving Pattern 1 (Seeking Understanding), as described in chapter 2.

Not all pauses from problem solving can be regarded as a rest from problem solving. Real rest would involve not only a pause but a concomitant recreation of energy and renewal of focus. Re-entry into some habitual routines may not provide rest if the routines are energy depleting or emotionally disturbing, whereas aesthetic absorption and tranquil abiding usually do provide the benefits of rest.

Both the patterns of problem solving and the modes of pause are experiences that are in stark contrast to the diminished experience of the schizophrenic[26] or the episodically disconnected experience of the severely developmentally delayed adult.[27] Therefore, the patterning of problem solving and the organization of pauses allows for the ongoing development of ever greater coherence in everyday living than is common with these special populations.

For anyone to derive the most from experience, they will need to learn to effectively manage the three functions of experience. Managing personal experience requires both attentiveness and planning. To some extent, individuals can plan the experiences they seek out and the environments in which they choose to learn. In this case, they are focusing their attention. However, uncertainty and unpredictability accompany this effort. Individuals can also choose those experiences and ideas that they will put to the test and subject them to critical thinking. Finally, they can also plan the pauses they take from learning and problem solving activities, to insure that rest is likely to be achieved. Implementing these choices will also require both a change in and maintenance of learning habits. If habits currently exist that promote learning, the maintenance will be relatively easy. If such habits do not currently exist, then the work leading to their acquisition is required.

Basic experiencing is under readers' control to the extent that they can successfully shift attention to what they choose. This can be done, for example, when one learns to postpone problem solving efforts and to switch to non-problem-solving habitual routines, aesthetic absorption, or tranquil abiding. It is not under our control to the extent that our attention is drawn away by unexpected events. It is also not under our control to the extent that questions and insights related to our problem solving efforts may come unbidden into our problem-free space. Mathematician Henri Poincaré describes how his working on problem solving was proceeded by active problem solving efforts, interspersed with pause states of consciousness.[28] Ultimate success was achieved by shifting consciousness back and forth. While the shifting was under his control, the emergence of insights was less so.

ADDITIONAL CONSIDERATIONS: IMPLICATIONS

Implications here address this question: "In light of what this chapter presents, how can we derive the most from our experience?"

1) A first implication concerns attentiveness and inattentiveness to the functions of our own experience. Three functions have been described here: source-resource, testing ground, and pause from learning. If these three functions of experience exist, then attentiveness to them and practice of them will facilitate learning, whereas inattentiveness will minimize learning.
2) If our experience is a basis for our uniqueness, then attentiveness to it increases the probability of developing greater self-knowledge, whereas inattentiveness to it reduces that possibility.
3) If there are qualities in our experience that we share with others (forming a basis for community), then attentiveness to those qualities will increase

the probability of understanding others, whereas inattentiveness to them will shrink the possibility of such understanding.
4) Other implications regard modes of pause specifically. If anything like these modes of pause exist then some people will function more naturally than other people in some modes but not in other modes.
5) Those who are proficient in some modes of pause are likely to lead very different sorts of lives than those who are not, since each mode differs from the others in its goals and methods for achieving those goals.
6) Also, if modes of pause exist and if people vary in their ability to manage each mode, then difficulties in communication are likely to follow. For example, the person of the everyday habitual routines may have some difficulty in understanding what the experienced practitioner of meditation is really doing. In addition, for such a person, artistic activities are often regarded as disconnected from "everyday life."
7) Basic experiencing (a pause from problem solving) can be made into habitual practice if one can learn to turn off problem solving efforts by switching to habitual routines of daily living, absorption in aesthetic experience, or the enjoyment of tranquil abiding achieved through calming exercises. Like the development of any new habit, this project may require a long time to achieve.[29]
8) Another implication focuses on any biasing factor that would unnecessarily choke off the stream of experience in any of its functions. By limiting a person's experiences, the "source" of learning is blocked, and what learning does take place may be vastly reduced and unduly influenced by vicarious experiences provided by the media and by secondhand reports of others.
9) If lived experience is reduced, then a succession of environments for learning is not traversed and the person does not get to practice learning and interaction with multiple environments and the people in them.
10) As discussed in chapter 3, if efforts of "testing" insights through one's own experience are blocked, there remain limited options for evaluating them, and they finally may be just accepted as true. Such options are frequently subject to the management agendas of others.
11) If there is no rest from the labors of learning, burnout is a likely result.
12) Since basic experiencing can be extended over time, it can be disrupted. Since possible disruptions can be identified in advance, measures can be taken to exercise some quality control over them. Generally, "problem solving quality control" is the extent to which activities of patterns of problem solving are guided by the desire to know. As regards basic experiencing, "quality control" means the ability to switch in and out of the desired state at will and being mindfully aware of the choices to do so. For example, experienced transportation investigators who arrive at

the scene of a train accident can switch into problem solving Pattern 1 (Seeking Understanding) when they arrive, but they switch out of it when they leave for the day.
13) Initially, efforts to assert quality control in basic experience will likely be imperfect. More specifically, beginning attempts to gain control may result in falling asleep or in being distracted.
14) However, as one becomes more proficient, the ability to summon and maintain the desired state of consciousness becomes more manageable. Distractions decrease, attentiveness is more focused, and perseverance is developed. As greater facility is developed, the practitioner can switch into any problem solving pattern or into a pause from problem solving in a matter of seconds. In addition, we come to more easily learn through our limitations, identified by gaps in our experiencing, understanding, judging, and deciding.
15) Sometimes the pause of basic experiencing will lead to problem solving Pattern 1 (Seeking Understanding). This can happen if new questions or insights or images related to our problem solving efforts emerge into consciousness while in a relaxed state. In this instance, one may choose to shift back into the work of problem solving.

SUMMARY

In summary, we began by noting that the very word "experience" is ambiguous and has been associated with a spectrum of definitions ranging from the all-inclusive "whatever is lived through" to the rather narrow "whatever is sensed." Three aims were specified: (1) to explore the basic roles of experience in complex human learning: source and resource, testing ground, and pause, (2) to explore how non-problem-solving experience gets organized, and (3) to identify implications and recommendations for making the most out of experience.

To address these objectives, three functions of experience were identified and described: experience as source and resource for learning, testing ground for learning, and pause from the work of learning. These descriptions were related to the various definitions of experience surveyed at the beginning of the chapter. Next, some attention was given to how non-problem-solving experience can organize itself by reversion to habitual routines, aesthetic absorption, or tranquil abiding. In each instance of pause from problem solving, it remains to be seen whether or not that pause is an instance of rest. Finally, implications were considered. Without an understanding of the implications, not much of the discussion in this chapter will have any force to it. Management of the functions of experience, or the lack of it, involves a positive choice or a refusal. Without any attempt at constructive management of experience and the development of an ongoing practice for growth, any insights presented here will have little long-term effect on learning.

The problem solving patterns are part of conscious experience, broadly considered. Because the problem solving patterns are guided by the desire to know, they are part of an intellectual way of lived experience. In contrast, basic experiencing is not a problem solving pattern at all, but it is a pause from the work of problem solving. It detaches the problem solver from the effort of wrestling with questions, and it provides the opportunity for re-creation of energy and the playfulness of purpose-free activity enjoyed for its own sake. Basic experiencing can send us back to automatic and often thoughtless routines of daily living, or we can enter havens from problem solving in either aesthetic absorption or tranquil abiding.

The most obvious thing about "basic experiencing" is its end products: memories and sometimes renewed energy for problem solving and learning. To work properly it assumes that one is conscious and involved in activities of daily life. It leads to an accumulation of experiences and memories that build up a unique developmental perspective. What is less obvious about basic experiencing is what is not happening: the work of problem solving is not taking place. In particular not much is happening with question and insight in this state. Morelli has described it as a "question-free mode of operation."[30]

"Basic experiencing" is nothing more than the series of mental events that constitute it. As seen, basic experiencing as a pause from problem solving may take at least three forms: (1) automatic habitual activities of daily living, (2) aesthetic absorption, and (3) tranquil abiding. Since the processes of problem solving are not taking place, more automatic habitual activities may take their place. These habitual activities may be habits not only of behavior but habits of thought and emotion as well. Moreover, these habits may or may not be in conflict with one another; they may lead to growth and flourishing of the person, or to a cramped and problematic style of living.[31] For example, consider our railroad investigators. After a day of examining and problem solving at a crash scene, one investigator may go back to the routines of managing a household, but a colleague may attend a tavern and return to a routine of social drinking.

For some individuals and small groups, a pause from problem solving is sometimes achieved by aesthetic absorption. By contemplating works of art, it is possible to soar above the push-pull of habitual routines and to move away from the focused work of complex learning and problem solving.[32] The railroad investigators may move away from their accident problem solving by aesthetic absorption in music or theatrical performances. In these instances, the problems of the train wreck are left behind as one soars to artistic possibilities above it.

For other individuals and small groups a form of pause from problem solving can be achieved by the disciplined management of consciousness achieved in some forms of meditation. In many cases, this disciplined practice can achieve a state of tranquil abiding.[33] Experienced meditators can clear their consciousness of the thoughts of the day through focused forms of mindful practice such as meditation and contemplation. These activities allow practitioners to achieve a focused state of tranquility that excludes problems, routines, and disturbing emotions.

Basic experiencing can go wrong if recreated energy is not achieved or if one is thrown back into chaotic and unmanageable states and habits. Both of these may be signals that one has not achieved much in the way of self-regulation of one's own consciousness.

The pause mode of basic experiencing is as widespread as the number of individuals who can switch at will from active problem solving to more habitual routines, aesthetic absorption, or tranquil abiding. Making this switch is itself a remarkable achievement of managing consciousness.[34] In contrast, for many, consciousness is simply not under consistent management, and in the case of psychotic states, there is not much management at all. Conscious states are particularly unruly in conditions such as borderline personality disorder, bipolar disorder, clinical depression, posttraumatic stress syndrome, and all psychotic states. Persons with these conditions suffer the unbidden onslaught of dysfunctional and unregulated mental states that result in numerous other problems with work, school, and human relations.

These extreme conditions do not imply a dichotomy. They are presented merely for clarification by contrast. There is a vast continuum of the extent to which individuals manage conscious states. Most do not suffer from the mental health conditions just mentioned, yet they do have less developed habits for managing consciousness. For them, problem solving and complex learning can be stopped by reversion to automatic habitual routines. These routines are habits that may or may not provide a rest from problem solving, and they may or may not result in a re-creation of energy. Some of these routines may be oppressive and result in greater depletions of energy, resulting in an overall feeling of being trapped. In contrast, the practices of aesthetic absorption and tranquil abiding provide a temporary release from the rock of managing problems and the hard place of oppressive routines.

NOTES

1. This chapter is partially based on an article previously published in *Symposium*: "Four Functions of Experience in Human Learning." *Symposium*, XXII(1), 2015, pp. 25–36.

2. Carl Rogers, *Client-Centered Therapy* (Cambridge, MA: The Riverside Press, 1951).

3. Association for Supervision and Curriculum Development, *Educational Leadership*, 67(5), 2010.

4. R. Costello & D. Jost (Eds.), *American Collegiate Dictionary, (3rd ed.)* (Boston: Houghton Mifflin, 1993).

5. William James, *Principles of Psychology* (New York: Dover, 1950, 239).

6. John Locke, An *Essay Concerning Human Understanding* (Claremont, CA: Pomona Press, 2008).

7. David Hume, *An Enquiry on Human Understanding* (New York: Oxford University Press, 2008).

8. Husserl, Edmund, *The Crisis of the European Sciences and Transcendental Phenomenology* (Evanston: Northwestern University Press, 1970, 240.)

9. Franz Brentano, *Psychology from an Empirical Standpoint* (ed. Linda L. McAlister) (London: Routledge, 1995, 88–89); J. P. Guilford. *The Nature of Human Intelligence* (New York: McGraw-Hill, 1967).

10. Dalai Lama, *The Universe in a Single Atom: The Convergence of Science and Spirituality* (New York: Morgan Road Books, 2005, 31).

11. William James, *Principles of Psychology* (New York: Dover, 1950).

12. Bernard Lonergan, *Insight: A Study of Human Understanding* (Toronto: University of Toronto Press, 1992, 204–214). Lonergan uses the phrase *patterns of experience* for these modes of living.

13. Immanuel Kant, *Critique of Pure Reason* (New York: Cambridge University Press, 1999).

14. Robert Gagné, *Conditions of Learning and Theory of Instruction* (Belmont, CA: Wadsworth Publishing, 1985).

15. Allen Newall and Herbert Simon, *Human Problem Solving* (New York: Prentice-Hall, 1972).

16. Edwin Locke and Gary Latham, "Work Motivation and Satisfaction," *Psychological Science*, 1(4), 1990, pp. 240–246.

17. Dale Schucnk and Barry Zimmerman, *Self-Regulation of Learning and Performance: Issues and Educational Applications* (Lawrence Erlbaum, Mahwah, NJ, 1994).

18. Richard Grallo, "Absence of Question and Insight in Accounts of Knowledge," in *Symposium*, XIV(1), 2007, pp. 33–43.

19. Some examples of this would include: Stephen Pinker, *How the Mind Works* (New York: Norton, 1997); National Research Council. *How People Learn* (Washington: National Academy Press, 2001).

20. Richard Grallo, "Truth in Perspective: Application of Interrogative Problem Representation." *Symposium*, XX(1), 2012, pp. 19–28.

21. Lonergan, *Insight*, 204–214.

22. Mark Morelli, *Self-Possession: Being at Home in Conscious Performance* (Boston, MA: Lonergan Institute, 2015, chs. 6–12).

23. An early description of it is provided by Arthur Schopenhauer, *The World as Will and Idea.* (London: Everyman Paperbacks,1995); Lonergan also describes it under the heading of "aesthetic pattern of experience." *Insight*, 207–209.

24. Rob Preece, *The Wisdom on Imperfection* (Ithaca, NY: Snow Lion Publications, 2010)

25. Richard Grallo, "Questioning as Meditation and Contemplation." *Symposium*, IX(1), 2002, 15–22.

26. John S. Brekke, Shelley Levin, George H. Wolkon, Eugene Sobel, and Elizabeth Slade, "Psychosocial Functioning and Subjective Experience in Schizophrenia." *Schizophrenia Bulletin*, 19(3), 1993, 599–608; John Cutting and Francis J. Dunne, "Subjective Experience of Schizophrenia." *Schizophrenia Bulletin*, 15(2), 1989, 217–231; P. H. Lysaker, and J. T. Lysaker, "Schizophrenia and Alterations in Self-Experience, in *Schizophrenia Bulletin*, 36(2), 2010, 331–340.

27. Reuven Feuerstein, S. Feuerstein, L. Falik and Y. Rand, *Dynamic Assessments of Cognitive Modifiability* (Jerusalem: ICELP Press, 1979/ 2002); Reuven Feuerstein, Y. Rand, M. B. Hoffman and R. Miller, *Instrumental Enrichment: An Intervention Program for Cognitive Modifiability.* (Baltimore, MD: University Park Press, 1980/ 2004).

28. Henri Poincaré, *The Foundations of Science.* Translated by G. B. Halstead (Garrison, NY: Science Press, 1924/2012.)

29. James Prochaska, John Norcross and Carlo DiClemente, *Changing for Good* (New York: Avon Books, 1994.)

30. Morelli, *Self-Possession*, 338.

31. Karen Horney, *Neurosis and Human Growth: The Struggle Towards Self-Realization* (New York: Norton, 1950).

32. Both Arthur Schopenhauer and Bernard Lonergan are among philosophers who describe how aesthetic absorption provides a type of freedom from both habitual routines and the work of active problem solving.

33. Rob Preece, *The Wisdom of Imperfection* (Ithaca, NY: Snow Lion Publications, 2006, 325).

34. Mihalyi Csikzentmihalyi, *Flow: The Psychology of Optimal Experience* (New York: Harper, 2008).

Chapter 5

Problem Solving in Larger Contexts

OVERVIEW OF LARGER CONTEXTS

Whatever problem solving and learning are, they do not operate in a vacuum. They function in wider contexts which set the background.[1] All contexts affect and can be affected by what we come to learn. This chapter examines larger contexts in which problem solving and rest from problem solving take place. Specifically, the larger contexts of personality, social trust, culture, and history will be considered.

So far, we have seen that question, insight, and the motivating desire to know are central to the four patterns of problem solving (understanding, judging facts, judging values, and deciding), and we have also seen how they are absent from the pauses of basic experiencing. Much of what has been said indicates that the activities of problem solving occur in individual minds. Therefore, the nature of those individual minds and their associated personalities is certainly important. Some personality structures facilitate learning and problem solving, while others block it. However, this is not all. Many problem solving activities operate within an accompanying social dimension, and this social dimension exerts a moderating influence on those activities by providing a social environment. This social dimension is here named "social trust," but it may equally well be named "reliance on the words of others" or "belief" or "believing." We cannot learn everything on our own, nor can we solve all problems. We are faced with the choice of relying on the efforts of others, or not. In addition, individual efforts in problem solving and their reliance on the work of others occur within even larger contexts of culture and history. For individual members, a "culture" provides a blueprint for living that is a resource in facing daily challenges. However, any culture may be growing or in decline. Hence, the resource presented is not perfect.

Finally, "history" as lived was the succession of cultures using their unique blueprints. However, history itself may be heading toward growth and development or toward decline.

A systematic study of one's own personality provides opportunity for a more mindful integration of that personality. It provides the details of greater self-knowledge and this can serve as a basis for any decisions involved in self-appropriation and more efficient self-regulation. A systematic study of one's significant social relations provides an opportunity to determine the extent to which social trust is or is not operating. It also provides an opportunity to identify those social relations that are growth-oriented and those that are growth-defeating. A systematic study of culture provides an opportunity to determine whether or not one is in harmony with one's own culture and whether one's culture is growth oriented or not. It can also suggest ways of integrating with the culture or moving to change it. Finally, a systematic study of recorded history can provide an opportunity to connect with other attempts at dealing with the problems of life exhibited by people of the past. A systematic study of one's own personal history has many benefits of achieving greater self-knowledge and more efficient self-regulation.

So far this book has addressed problem solving by inviting readers to inspect and identify specific facts of consciousness in their own experience. Within problem solving, attention was drawn to various patterns of problem solving that lead to solutions that are experience-based, deeply insightful, reasonable, guided by tested values, and transformative of problems and self. Attention was also drawn to various ways in which we pause from the work of problem solving. In some instances, such pauses may be a form of rest with its associated benefits of renewed energy and focus; however, it is not guaranteed that all pauses from problem solving will be restful. Finally, the facts of consciousness described so far coalesce into a general cycle of learning that spirals[2] through the distinct patterns of experiencing, understanding, judging, and deciding. Also included are the specific mental acts and operations by which each pattern proceeds.

The following objectives are formulated for this chapter. (1) There will be an examination of how the larger contexts of personality, social trust, culture, and history can influence learning and problem solving. (2) There will be an examination of how learning and problem solving influence the larger contexts. Both objectives are designed to facilitate personal growth.[3] This growth will include greater self-acceptance, self-knowledge, and more skillful self-regulation. It should assist readers to be witnesses of their own experience. This includes their experiences of understanding, judging, deciding, and the consequences of these as they exist in multiple contexts.

To assist with these objectives, the work of Kurt Lewin regarding force field analysis will be employed. "Force field analysis" is a method for describing, predicting, and explaining change or lack of change in persons, groups, and institutions.[4] Each of the larger contexts will be regarded as a force field. In each of these force fields (or larger contexts) there will be "units-of-analysis," which are the objects of study. These may be individual persons, groups, or institutions. In addition, there will be "driving forces" that move change in the direction of the growth through learning, as well as "restraining forces" that interfere with learning. As discussed in chapters 2 and 3, the acts and operations that make up each pattern of problem solving are personal driving forces that facilitate learning. They are supplemented by other forces in the environment that also propel learning. In contrast, both within the person and in the surrounding environment there are restraining forces that hold learning back, distort it, or prevent it altogether.

In a typical force field analysis an object of study, or unit of analysis, is identified. This could be one or more persons, groups, organizations, or institutions. Driving and restraining forces are identified that may account for whether or not a unit will change. In this chapter, the "unit of analysis" depends on the context considered. It could be the individual learner, small problem solving groups, organizations, or institutions. Also in this chapter, "driving forces" will be taken to mean forces that promote growth and learning, and "restraining forces" will be taken to mean anything that prevents growth through learning.

PERSONALITY AS CONTEXT

The first larger context for learning and problem solving is personality. "Personality" is defined here as a relatively stable constellation of cognitive, emotive, behavioral, and habitual traits associated with a unique human person. Chaplin[5] indicates that despite disagreement regarding specific definitions of personality, "there is a core agreement in considering personality as an integration of traits that can be investigated and described in order to render an account of the unique quality of the individual." For psychologists, "traits" are aspects of the person that are somewhat unchanging over time. Personality traits include those that are cognitive, emotive, and behavioral. Cognitive traits pertain not only to thought patterns but to the cognitive processes that produce them. Emotive traits refer to characteristic or predictable affective responses. Behavioral traits refer to recurrent patterns of observable behavior.

Personality is important to study in relation to problem solving and learning because it sets the conditions of inner functioning. These conditions will facilitate and propel growth through problem solving and any associated learning, or they will interfere with problem solving and learning, and block any related growth. The forces of personality tend to shape us as we develop and they affect not only what we learn but how we learn. As individual learners and as members of small problem solving groups, individuals are in a unique position to affect their own personality to some extent. Concretely, personality arrives at every problematic situation. It cannot be escaped. To the extent that an individual's personality is made up of habits that facilitate learning and problem solving it is an asset; to the extent that it is composed of habits that block or restrain learning and problem solving it is a liability.[6] For these reasons, some individuals need to learn how to learn and to study.

To the extent that personality traits are automatic, they are often rooted in habits not only of behavior, but habits of thought and emotion as well. Like all habits, they can be engaged without thinking, practiced easily and efficiently, and enjoyed in the process. Yet not all habits lead to greater success and integration of the person. For those habits that do, the person possessing them can easily, effectively, pleasantly, and almost without thinking increase the probability of achievement and become more skilled in the process. Yet for those persons with unskillful or destructive habits, they easily, effectively, pleasantly, and almost without thinking increase the probability of failure or mediocrity and become more damaged in the process. In effect, they become really efficient at mediocrity or self-destruction. This more or less stable constellation of cognitive, emotive, and behavioral habits constitutes the system referred to here as "personality."

Since personality is a system, a change in any one aspect of it is likely to reverberate with other changes throughout the system. Hence, distinctive changes in thought will likely result in changes in affect and behavior. Marked changes in emotion will likely result in changes in thought and behavior. Persistent changes in behavior will likely result in changes in emotion and thought.

Since personality is a dynamic system, it may be understood as a force field. Therefore, it may be profitably understood through the method of force field analysis. Here, the individual personality is the unit of analysis. Driving forces may be understood as forces both inside and outside the person that propel growth through learning and problem solving. Primary among inner driving forces is the desire to know. This desire is augmented by all the mental acts and operations described in chapters 2 and 3. This desire is also augmented by habits of study and learning that have been developed in the learner over time. Restraining forces would be any desire or emotion or outside force that moves one away from problem solving and associated learning.

Since personality is a background for complex human learning, some of its traits may influence attempts at such learning and may even interfere with those attempts. For example, a student who adamantly retains the thought that they "are no good at math" is less likely to be successful in that domain regardless of the truth or falsity of the claim. Or, a counseling client with unacknowledged anxiety may be less successful in achieving goals related to personal development as long as the anxiety operates unabated and unrecognized. While Lonergan indicated that bias is a major interference with an unfettered comprehensive learning, the examination of the larger context of personality (including its emotive and behavioral aspects) gives rise to a broader understanding of what might reinforce and drive the operation of bias.[7]

Comprehensive human learning, then, if we are to take it seriously, will engage us in a dance between mental acts, events, and operations, both active and passive, which make up the entire process. In some instances, we will need to exercise patience and preparation in waiting for the relevant insights and, when the insights emerge, we will need to co-operate with them by active pursuit in formulation, or testing, or deliberating, or acting. Bias, as previously discussed, blocks relevant images, questions, and evidence that would give rise to growth-producing learning.

Relatively unbiased learning is an active-passive oscillation that occurs in all modes of living or problem solving: whether it is a focusing of attention in basic experiencing, or the emergence of an intention (encapsulated in a question) in the four patterns of problem solving. For example, an important instance of the active-passive movement occurs in Problem Solving Patterns 1, 2, 3, and 4, where a learning sequence is often initiated by some sort of question (understood as a mental event). The question itself may have simply occurred to us passively or it may be a part of an active program of questioning. If we choose to pursue the question, it functions as an operator by initiating a series of events likely to result in some sort of answer borne by an insight. The insight serves to bring previous gains together, and is thereby an integrator.

The alternating emergence of question and insight in different circumstances (functioning as complementary problem solving patterns) regarding different experiences and concerns, if unhindered, will likely lead to a very thorough form of learning. That type of learning may be labeled as "comprehensive" because of its rootedness in experience, insightfulness, critical handling of fact and value, and its transformative nature. Moreover, as has been argued, each advance from question to insight, from question to knowledge, from question to reasoned action represents a transcendence of a new more comprehensive self over a less-developed, prior version.[8] Lonergan refers to this in his discussion of intellectual and moral self-transcendence.[9] The developing self here described faces the challenge of an ever-expanding horizon, suggested to consciousness by the ongoing question-insight dance. (See table 5.1.)

Table 5.1 Passive and Active Mental Events in Distinct Patterns of Problem Solving and Basic Experiencing (Read from bottom to top)

Pattern of Problem Solving	Passive (lower case) → ACTIVE (UPPER CASE) Sequence	Integrator
Pattern 4 – Deliberative Critical Thinking	QUESTION-FOR-DELIBERATION ↔ FORMULATION ↔ LISTING PROS-CONS ↔ WEIGHING PROS-CONS ↔ Deliberative Insight ↔ DECISION	Deliberative insight DECISION ACTION
Patterns 2 and 3—Factual and Values-Oriented Critical Thinking	QUESTIONS-FOR-REFLECTION (Fact, Value) ↔ FORMULATION ↔ COLLECTING ↔ WEIGHING ↔ Reflective Insight ↔ JUDGMENT	Reflective insight JUDGMENT
Pattern 1—Seeking Understanding	QUESTIONS-FOR-INTELLIGENCE ↔ FORMULATIONS ↔ Insights ↔FORMULATIONS	Insight as ENCODED FORMULATION
BASIC EXPERIENCING	Dreaming → Alertness → ATTENTIVENESS	Perceived events Images Memories

Source: author

Yet since comprehensive learning involves so many acts, events, and operations in sequence, the real possibility emerges for interference with it and for breakdowns of it.[10] Systematic exclusion of relevant further questions and insights, as "process bias," prevents the emergence of more comprehensive learning and thereby insures non-growth for the persons involved. The emergence of a more developed version of self is also blocked. The stalled and non-developing self here described faces the challenge of a static horizon, which happens to be the boundary of knowledge and concern up until the time the person stopped growing. At this boundary, the ongoing question-insight interaction has stopped.

Such systematic exclusion of relevant information, as occurs in process bias, is not simply an isolated cognitive event. Rather it is a cognitive event that occurs within a larger context of personality with its emotive and behavioral aspects. Those emotions and behaviors, especially if they are habitual and unnoticed, can work to reinforce the extended operation of bias and make it seem natural. Working with self and others to move beyond the limitations associated with process bias may be facilitated by exploration to the larger contexts of personality and personalities.

Hence we have in the human being a natural tendency to grow and to acquire knowledge, propelled by the desire to know. This can be observed in young children: at three years old, without training, they start asking questions. On the other hand, there are also functional interferences with this development. Children and adults often learn to avoid situations that may provoke anxiety or some other unpleasant emotion, and they thereby avoid problem solving situations that require increasing levels of commitment on the part of the learner. For example, students who have had difficulties reading before a class may move away from any project that involves public speaking. Or others, who have not had success in math courses, may later avoid any career that requires competence in mathematics of any kind.

If both the impetus to growth and interferences with it are operative in individuals, what kinds of personalities result? There is likely to be a wide range.[11] At the extremes of poor functioning, we regularly encounter distorted and lopsided personalities. They have been assigned various labels throughout history and they come in many varieties.[12] For most of these, their favored styles of responding to problems have become so rigid and so defended that it does not serve them well in the wide variety of situations they are likely to encounter in contemporary life. However, most persons do not fall at these extremes, yet there are differences in the presence of growth-oriented and interference-oriented aspects in most personalities. Because these response styles are habitual they are likely to encounter the same type of difficulty each time their environment does not match their response style.[13] Yet despite these difficulties they can be more or less successful in the activities of everyday living and problem solving.

If there are individual differences in personality, then one might expect individual differences in problem solving, learning, and intellectual activities of all sorts. Previous chapters indicated that these intellectual activities include facts of consciousness such as question, insight, formulating, expressing, collection evidence and reasons, weighing evidence and reasons, judging, deciding, and purposeful action. We have also seen how these facts of consciousness function in four patterns of problems solving and how they are largely absent from basic experience.

While the patterns of problem solving are functionally related to one another, it does not follow that each person will practice them with equal skill. Some may have overlearned one pattern, to the neglect of the others. In this connection a hypothesis can be formulated about individual differences in learning performance and in habitual response styles. The hypothesis can be stated as follows: "Considered singly, individuals exhibit differential performance in the four patterns of problem solving and in the modes of basic experience." Evidence to support this hypothesis would indicate that individuals show superior performance in the activities of one pattern of problem solving or mode of basic experiencing to the detriment of other patterns or modes. Evidence to falsify this hypothesis would show that no such differences exist; that is, it would show that one can perform reasonably well in most patterns of problem solving and modes of basic experiencing.

When superior performance has been achieved in any pattern or mode it is often a matter of spending time in relevant skill development. For example, diagnostic physicians will have spent years becoming quite expert in the activities and events of Pattern 1 (Seeking Understanding) and Pattern 2 (Factual Critical Thinking). Presented with the signs and symptoms, for any case they can quickly present credible hypotheses about what might be happening with a patient (Pattern 1). They can then sift through the further evidence of lab reports and test results to narrow the possibilities down to one (Pattern 2).

As a person practices the patterns of problem solving and modes of basic experiencing habitual "response styles" develop. If that person favors some activities to the exclusion of others, a biased response style will likely emerge. In this connection, a number of habitual "problem solving response styles" can be identified. Each problem solving response style indicates the extent to which an individual does or does not routinely engage effectively in each of the patterns of problem solving. For example, as explored in chapter 2, problem solving Pattern 1 (Seeking Understanding) consists of insights that grasp possible connections between data. The emphasis here is on possibility. A popular exercise for generating possibilities is brainstorming.[14] This low-anxiety exercise requires participants to generate ideas that are possibly useful to solving a problem under consideration. There is not much in the way of rules or evaluation. A person operates effectively in this pattern when they can discover and formulate multiple possibilities relevant to the problem. However, an effective thinker knows that this pattern is limited to possibilities only. In contrast, someone who has overlearned[15] this pattern, to the exclusion of others might be considered a "possibility thinker" or an "idea person." They are very effective at finding a possibility for this or that, but they rarely put these to the test.

Others may have mastered Problem Solving Pattern 2 (Factual Critical Thinking). They are most effective at collecting and weighing evidence, as well as determining which of a myriad of possibilities might be correct. They are more like scientists or detectives. They are not content with any possible understanding of a situation, but they require that understanding be tested and they require that only understanding that is tested be affirmed or denied. A group such as the National Transportation Safety Board (NTSB) functions in this role when it investigates a transportation accident. In contrast, someone who has overlearned this pattern and excels in it to the exclusion of other patterns tend to miss alternative explanations worthy of investigation. They have a problem solving response style that is almost prosecutorial in nature and forgetful of the needed work of Pattern 1 (Seeking Understanding).

A third response style emphasizes neither possibilities nor verified facts, but focuses on adherence to a specified set of values. "Consensus builders" may fall into this category. In working toward the solution of complex human problems, it is well to be reminded of approved values and to build a common agreement to work toward them. However, if this strength is practiced to the exclusion of other problem solving patterns, then the goal of consensus may also mitigate attempts to understand (Pattern 1) or to appropriately test possibilities (Pattern 2).

A fourth response style emphasizes getting things done. This is the approach of the so-called "activist" or "bottom-line thinker." Many problems require definitive solutions by specific dates and the consequences of meeting these deadlines are important. However, if this strength is practiced to the exclusion of other problem solving patterns, then the goal of getting results may interfere with attempts to understand (Pattern 1), to get our facts right (Pattern 2), or to consistently follow approved values (Pattern 3). In that case, less attention is paid to possibilities, verified facts, and values, while the overriding focus is bringing about some result.

Whether any of these response styles is biased depends upon the balance of a person's performance in all of the patterns of problem solving. If the patterns function in harmony with one another, comprehensive and unbiased learning can eventually result. As indicated, such comprehensive learning will be stimulated by experience, deeply insightful, evidence-based, guided by tested values, and transformative of problem situations and of self. In contrast, if any pattern is practiced to the systematic exclusion of others, then the functions of the excluded pattern are not set in operation and a defective result is inevitable.

SOCIAL TRUST AS CONTEXT

The[16] second larger context for learning and problem solving is the social context. The American Psychological Association defines "social context" as "the specific circumstance or general environment that serves as a social framework for individual or interpersonal behavior."[17] The definition goes on to note that this context frequently influences, to some degree, individual actions and feelings that occur in it.

When problems present themselves, they are embedded in social contexts. Attempts to solve problems may give rise to a social response through the emergence of small problem solving groups. Through participation in these groups, individuals can be influenced by and can influence the social context itself. Problem solving groups assemble in any field where groups attempt to address commonly held problems. For example, they are found in education, business, counseling, government, and the military, as well as in neighborhoods, churches, schools, and organizations of all sorts. Russian psychologist Lev Vygotsky identified the family as one of the first problem solving groups that children encounter. For him, this group constituted a "zone of proximal development," which ordinarily facilitates the child's growth into adolescence by allowing them to solve problems that they could not ordinarily solve on their own.[18] This initial idea blossomed into additional work on how small problem solving groups work.[19]

Within psychology, problem solving groups develop naturally in academic departments, stretching back to Wilhelm Wundt and the first psychological laboratory and William James' attempt to institute a laboratory at Harvard, to the psychology departments of the twenty-first century. However, small problem solving groups in psychology have also flourished in private institutes and societies[20] and in informal intellectual networks.[21]

A key element that will make problem solving groups work well is "social trust." Within specific problem solving groups, social trust may or may not occur. In psychology, "trust" is defined as a "reliance on or confidence in the dependability of someone or something."[22] However, there also exists, accompanying many individual actions, an aspect of social trust that involves reliance on the words and actions of others. Psychoanalyst Erik Ericson assigned a primary developmental role to whether or not children developed trust in their environment and the adults who populate it.[23] He predicted that success in this area would increase the probability of success in later expected tasks in life, such as developing initiative and industry. He also predicted that failure to develop a basic trust would likely result in the development of a less efficient and effective personality. Canadian psychologist Mary Ainsworth followed up this work by examining how attachment develops in infants. This research demonstrated that not all infants became attached to their caregivers and that some displayed a remarkable indifference toward them. Over time, different types of infants developed, all differentiated by levels of basic trust as indicated by attachment to caregivers. Some were secure in their attachment, while others were avoidant and others resistant to caregivers.[24] Later work differentiated these groups further.

Social trust has the advantage that, if it occurs, our problem solving and growth can be augmented by the efforts of trusted others. If such trusted others are not present, then problem solving and its associated learning is slowed to what one can learn in isolation. Social trust then is important to study in relation to problem solving and associated learning because it sets outer conditions for inner functioning. In particular, the social context provides other individuals who may be a resource or a hindrance. To the extent that others are trusted and are trustworthy they can facilitate and propel growth through learning and problem solving, or they can interfere with learning and problem solving, and block any related growth. Generally, we expect parents and teachers to work to propel learning in their charges. However, this is not always the case.

The forces of social trust tend to shape us as we develop and they affect not only what we learn but how we learn. As individual learners and as members of small problem solving groups we are in a unique position to affect these larger contexts to some extent. Regarding social relations specifically, we cannot get far in our learning and problem solving if we do not enlist the support of helpful others. Social trust, which is basically a decision, allows us to reap the benefits of thinking things through with interested other parties.

Small problem solving groups can bolster social trust by practicing the patterns of problem solving together. Through shared experiences, understanding, and work on critical thinking in relation to any content they can develop reliance upon the contributions of each other toward a shared work product. In these groups, if they are really effective at problem solving, the desire to know will be paramount in all members. For example, research teams in scientific work are examples of small problem solving groups. The members rely on each other in the development and implementation of various phases of a research program. Not all the team members can design a study or collect data or analyze it. They are required to specialize and trust the contributions of each other.

From the point of view of force field analysis, the social context is a force field. The individual and small groups may be regarded as units-of-analysis. Social trust is added as either a driving or restraining force for learning, problem solving, and growth. Whether it is a driving or restraining force depends upon who is the object of trust. If persons who pursue growth through learning and problem solving are trusted, then trust in them held by the individual will be a driving force for growth; but if persons who block growth through learning and problem solving are trusted, then trust in them held by the individual will be a force that restrains growth.

From a cognitive point of view, the way an individual taps into the social context and social trust is through the act of believing. "Belief" has been defined as "the acceptance of the truth, reality or validity of something, particularly in the absence of substantiation."[25] If we are relying on another person or persons, that trust becomes social trust. In sociology, belief is considered under the heading of the "sociology of knowledge." In these senses belief is to be understood as a conscious act or mental event. Here the focus is not so much with the contents of this or that belief but the activity of believing.

"Believing," understood as an act, is then a form of collaboration with others. For believing to work the following conditions must be in place: (1) the believer has made a prior judgment of fact that she cannot verify everything for herself, (2) the believer must have made a prior judgment of value that the collaboration is worth it in general, and (3) the believer must have made a prior judgment of value that the collaboration is worth it in this particular case because the source of the information is credible.[26] If we choose to collaborate with others then our thought can extend through space to other places and to the work done by others in those places. Our thought can also extend through time to the past and to the work done by others in bygone days.[27] In all cases of collaboration we rely heavily on the reports of others.[28] The others, on whom we rely, become part of a problem solving group. Typically, our problem solving efforts are done either individually or as part of a problem solving group. These points apply to research teams or any other problem solving group.

Consider some everyday examples that intimately involve believing. Jack wakes each morning to the sound of a radio alarm clock that announces the time. Since Jack has not taken steps to determine the time for himself, his acceptance of the word of the radio announcer is largely a matter of believing. More often than not, if he acts on this information, he will not be running late. Jill goes to the computer at work and sends an email. How is believing involved in this event? She accepts that this computer is working and that pressing the "send" button will result in a distant person actually receiving the message that she sent. Most of the time, this activity is successful. Tom drives to work each morning in a large city. How is believing involved in this activity? If he drives on highways with two-way traffic, Tom relies on other drivers to keep to their own lanes. Most of the time he actually gets to work in one piece. In all of these instances believing is a great time saver. None of these three needs to go out to verify everything on their own. In each of these instances, the lack of belief would slow basic social interactions to a halt.

Given these examples, it is useful to indicate what belief is not. First, believing is not simply experiencing. As indicated in chapter 4, experiencing is often a matter of living through something. Believing, if it is an experience at all, is a special kind of experience whereby one not only processes something meaningful but one also acts on that extracted information. Just hearing the alarm clock would be simple experience. However, regarding its sound as a signal and acting on that signal is part of believing.

Second, believing is not seeking understanding. As indicated in chapter 2, if it is done well, seeking understanding is a lengthy discursive process that involves generating and exploring multiple possibilities. To be sure Jill generated an intelligible message on her own. But in order to successfully send the message she does not also need a complete understanding of how computers actually work. She merely needs to press the "send" button and believe.

Third, believing is not immanently generated knowledge. Immanently generated knowledge is primarily a matter of finding things out for oneself. As indicated in chapter 3, it involves seeking out information and evidence and making appropriate judgments of fact. Elsewhere this has been termed Factual Critical Thinking. Tom, before driving to work, does not verify for himself that all the other drivers on the road are sober and have been properly trained to drive. He simply gets in his car and believes. Bernard

Lonergan indicates that while belief is not immanently generated knowledge it nevertheless

> resembles judgment in its mode, for it is a rational utterance of a "Yes" or a "No" that may be pronounced with certitude or with probability. But while judgment is motivated by one's own grasp of the unconditioned, the assent or dissent of belief is motivated by a decision to profit by a human collaboration in the pursuit of truth. And while judgment results with rational necessity from reflective grasp of the unconditioned, the assent or dissent of belief results from natural necessity from a free and responsible decision to believe.[29]

Fourth, believing is not pure speculation or fantasy. It is not just making things up, or affirming anything that one wants; it is a collaboration of relying on reports of others. It is based on a crowd of witnesses who affirm that this activity works out in practice, and it is also based on memories of our own successful performances in the past. Jack may want to sleep later, but both experience and the testimony of others indicate that doing that usually does not work out well. Jill may be afraid to send the email, but experience and the testimony of others weigh in on the effectiveness of sending the message. Tom may want to drive on the wrong side of the road just for fun, but experience and others warn that that is not an effective way to get to work.

Although, believing is not immanently generated knowledge, it does have a structure that is similar to a well-grounded judgment of fact. All well-founded judgments of fact share three common elements: (1) They answer reflective questions of fact such as "Is this True?" or "Is this probable?" These questions take "Yes" or "No" as possible answers. (2) Well-founded judgments of fact rest on sufficient evidence. (3) Well-founded judgments of fact require a clear criterion for assessing the evidence. However, in the case of belief, sufficient evidence is replaced by the word of another or the perceived reliability of something. If we are relying on the word of others, belief is sometimes referred to as "social trust."

Believing also has the structure of a decision. A decision is part of a process of choosing.[30] Decisions come as an answer to first-person-reflective deliberative questions. Examples of such questions would include "Should I do this?" or "Should we do that?". If taken seriously, these questions require a process to consider whether or not some putative good ought to be imported into one's life. Reasons and evidence (pro and con) can be considered, and a criterion of what is worthwhile can be applied. The entire process has been described elsewhere[31] and may be considered as Deliberative Critical Thinking. In believing, the word of another is substituted for reasons and evidence, and a criterion of the believability of witnesses is applied. The decision itself is a choice to rely on the word of another or not.

If believing enters as an important component into problem solving efforts, then like problem solving, believing can be subjected to interferences of various sorts. These would include disruptions arising within the individual person as well as interruptions emanating from the environment. As indicated, personal disruptions include fatigue, pain, emotional states, or the operation of dramatic or individual bias. Environmental interruptions include others demanding or requiring our attention, noise, various external events, and the operation of group bias. Particularly important in these lists are the various biases and the error and mislearning that result.

CULTURE AS CONTEXT

The[32] third larger context for learning and problem solving is culture. Broadly defined, "culture" consists of "the distinctive, customs, values, beliefs, knowledge, art and language of a society or a community."[33] Culture provides maps of living for its members. To the extent that individuals use these maps, they are affected by their culture. To the extent that individuals develop these maps, they are shaping the culture.

More specifically, the maps of culture address basic questions to orient members to their life in the world: Who are we? Where did we come from? Where are we going?[34] It also addresses more practical questions such as these: How am I to understand this situation? What am I to do about it?

Culture is important to study in relation to learning and problem solving because it also sets outer conditions of inner functioning. The outer conditions consist of what is available and what is taken for granted by the members of the culture. These outer conditions will facilitate and propel growth through learning and problem solving or they will interfere with learning and problem solving and block any related growth. Consequently, an entire culture could be on a trajectory of growth or decline, depending on how it handles complex human learning and problem solving.

The forces of culture tend to shape us from a distance as we develop by influencing not only what we learn but how we learn. They do this largely by providing options and materials for learning. As individual learners and as members of small problem solving groups we are in a unique position to affect these larger contexts to some extent as we move forward in time. Specifically, culture provides a blueprint for living by supplying generally accepted answers to questions about our origins, identity, and destiny. In addition, culture provides mores and traditions that are ready-made, pretested ways of doing things. Accepting these mores and traditions is a form of social trust, and it saves time by not requiring us to reinvent the wheel.

From the point of view of force field analysis, the culture is a force field of force fields. Again, individuals and small groups may be regarded as units-of-analysis, but organizations and institutions are also units-of-analysis. If individuals invest social trust in an organization and if that organization is committed to learning and problem solving, then the organizations may serve as a driving force for learning, problem solving, and growth within the culture. In contrast, if social trust is not invested in an organization or if that organization is not committed to learning and problem solving, then it may serve as a restraining force for problem solving, learning, and growth. Whether an organization or institution is a driving or restraining force depends upon the presence or absence of a commitment to problem solving and its associated learning. If organizations and institutions that pursue growth through learning and problem solving are trusted, then their accomplishments are likely to win widespread approval throughout the culture, but if organizations and institutions that block growth through learning and problem solving are trusted, then their accomplishments will not be as successful and will generate greater distrust within the culture.

From a problem solving point of view, insights are the vehicle by which intelligence enters a culture. Reasonable judgments and policies are the means by which a way of life becomes respectful of evidence and facts. Responsible decisions and acts are the way in which growth through knowledge comes to enter a culture. In contrast, poorly formulated insights, rash judgments, and impulsive decisions may also enter and affect the culture. The result is often a mixed bag of what is insightful and absurd, reasonable and unreasonable, responsible and irresponsible.

More specifically, culture has cognitive, behavioral, and emotive components as well as a habitual aspect. Culture has a "cognitive" (or information processing) component insofar as ideas and attitudes are involved in it. Such ideas and attitudes, as shared by many people around us, greatly influence our views of the world, of others, and of ourselves. In exercising this powerful influence, these ideas and attitudes tend to exclude competing and alternate worldviews. Culture has a "behavioral" component insofar as it also consists of behaviors and traditions. It shows how things are and are not to be done. Since ideas and attitudes, behaviors, and traditions are rarely associated with the complete absence of affect, culture also inevitably involves a massive "emotional" component involving shared feelings and pride. Finally, culture involves a habitual aspect: as ideas and attitudes, behaviors, and traditions become repetitive they also become habitual. As habits, these aspects of culture can be practiced with ease and efficiency and without much thinking. The ease and efficiency of cultural habits tend to produce order in society. The fact that they can be practiced without thinking tends to promote a general lack of reflection on one's own culture—taking it for granted.[35]

Culture, understood broadly, implies that "a large group of people" are involved. Five people living on a hilltop would not constitute what is normally considered a general culture. Even though one may speak of the "culture of an organization," usually cultures involve many thousands or millions of people, often associated with a geographical area and a specific language or dialect. Moreover, this mass of people is actively involved in passing shared ideas, attitudes, behaviors, and traditions to the next generation, who originally arrived in the world knowing none of it.

However they come into being, cultures transmit to their participants widespread expectations regarding the meaning of life and the behavior of individuals. To the extent that these expectations are taken seriously there results a measure of order in the activities of the general population. Expectations become customs and eventually traditions. In addition, cultures present to their adherents general answers to the basic questions regarding the group's origin, present situation, and destiny.

The differences observed between cultures will therefore be largely differences in the expectations and practices of people. With such differences in meanings, behaviors, and values the possibilities for cross-cultural misunderstandings are numerous, often complex, and always present when differing cultures come into contact.

HISTORY AS CONTEXT

The last larger context to be considered for learning and problem solving is history. "History" is defined here as "what has happened." More specifically, we can refer to two definitions for "history" and their associated "pasts." In the widest and most inclusive sense, the past and history refer to the same thing: all events that have occurred. We can refer to this as "complete history." To know the past in this sense would be to know every event that has ever occurred—an achievement that is clearly beyond human knowledge. Following from this, "human history" would be the sum total of all events that have occurred involving human beings. This type of knowledge too seems beyond human achievement. In a more limited sense, "the past" may refer to a more limited subset of events of interest, and "history" may refer to accounts of such events. This is "recorded history." For example, in the United States there is a past associated with railroads: this is a subset of all events that have occurred in the United States. There are also written accounts of those events. Such accounts are "histories" in the more limited sense. So while the past and history in the broad sense are beyond us, we can develop and actively recover elements of that vast ocean of events known as "the complete past." Such recovery is the process of doing history in the more limited sense—a kind of detective work designed to answer correctly specific questions of interest about the past.

Complete history provides layers of physical and social environments that one can use in the present. Recorded history provides ready-made interpretations of those environments. Through these environments and interpretations, history affects the individual. To the extent that individuals develop these environments and these interpretations, they are shaping history.

History is important to study because a deep interest in the past is not just a matter of reminiscence and nostalgia, but also a springboard to complex human problem solving. If we are serious about the past and about using the past in a constructive manner, then we are more likely to attend to it, to inquire into it, and to use its insights to address a complex present and an unknown future. The forces of history tend to shape us from a distance by influencing not only what we learn but how we learn. They do this largely by providing options and materials for learning. Individual learners and small problem solving groups are in a unique position to affect these larger contexts to some extent through the contributions of their work.

Regarding history specifically, this chapter has distinguished four purposes that may be addressed in attending to the past: (1) reminiscing, (2) seeking a deeper understanding, (3) resolving issues of fact and value, and (4) importing knowledge and value into one's life to transform situations and self. Of those who achieve knowledge of some aspects of the past, an even smaller group will ask how that knowledge of fact and value can be imported into the present to transform both present and future. The primary focus here is on what might reasonably be done at this point, informed by what we understand, know, and value about the past.

From the point of view of force field analysis, history is the succession of force fields over time. Again, individuals, small groups, organizations, and institutions may be regarded as units-of-analysis, but distinctive cultures may also be units-of-analysis. Recorded history can present the rise and fall of individuals, groups, organizations, institutions, and cultures. The functioning of question, insight, desire to know, and social trust can be regarded as driving forces in complete history if the goal was the attainment of authentic learning and problem solving. Restraining forces would be all those events and activities that prevented authentic learning and problem solving.

From a problem solving point of view, insights are the vehicle by which intelligence enters history. Reasonable judgments and policies are the means by which a way of life becomes respectful of evidence and facts. Responsible decisions and acts are the way in which growth through knowledge comes to enter any historical period. In contrast, poorly formulated insights, rash judgments, and impulsive decisions also have entered and play a role in both complete and recorded history.

Engaging in the activities of complex human learning about the past may not change the past, but it can change the learner. Being more attentive to the past makes us more attentive in general. Continuously seeking understanding makes us more understanding. Greater understanding of our past leads to greater "self-acceptance," which is a relatively objective sense or recognition of one's abilities and achievements, together with acknowledgment and acceptance of one's limitations.[36] Pursuing knowledge of fact and value makes us a better judge of what is real and valuable. Pursuing knowledge of fact and value about the past makes us a better judge of what was both real and valuable in previous times. Transforming situations makes us habitually proactive and engaged. Transforming ourselves through greater knowledge of our past promotes greater compassion. If we engage repeatedly in these activities, then we slowly acquire a kind of practical wisdom. "Wisdom" can be defined here as the developing application of the knowledge of how to live life well.

If we view the past as we would an inheritance from a distant relative, questions of what we are going to do about the inheritance naturally arise. What is our specific purpose in attending to the past, in giving this "inheritance" at least some of our attention? Will we regard it as a burden or as a potential windfall? Will we neglect it or mine it?

An easy way out is to quote Henry Ford and assert, "History is more or less bunk."[37] In this way, none of the problem solving activities involved in understanding, knowing, valuing, or using the past need to be engaged. A great deal of effort is saved. A more challenging way is to take seriously George Santayana's caution, "Those who cannot remember the past are condemned to repeat it."[38] This approach involves attending to our historical inheritance and engaging the processes of understanding, knowing, valuing, and choosing in relation to the past and to a present and future informed by and emerging out of that past.

Many will choose to merely reminisce about the past and to experience the secondary highs and lows of delight and regret. A much smaller number will choose to mine that inheritance. If we choose to mine our inheritance, as best we can, with the resources of time and talent available, we can approach this psychologically, philosophically, and/or contemplatively.

From a psychological viewpoint, our memories will remind us of fragments of the past. Some of these we may wish to honor and carry forward and others we may wish to change. Such musing can inform the resolution and decision to bring forward into our future the valuable elements and to leave behind the worthless. For example, we may be reminded of a departed relative and are saddened. We inquire into what was best about this person and then resolve to import that quality into the future in honor of them. In contrast, if we can think only of bad qualities in that person, then we might select the worst and ask about its opposite. We then resolve to import that opposite quality into the future in honor of what might have been. These activities will tend to improve both mood and self-regulation.[39]

From a philosophical point of view our memories will raise all the great philosophic issues of life and death, education, relationships, society, and religion. What was the role of each of these in my life? Were they helpful or not? How have I come to interpret them after a lifetime?

Finally, from a contemplative viewpoint, those who make a point to mine their inheritance can practice gratitude for the past they have encountered and for what they have learned from it.[40] They can use their memories as an occasion to advocate for and bring forward what they have found to be best about the past.

To further this kind of interest in history, whether personal or collective, this section has two aims: (1) to attend to some clues regarding the past and how we "carry it" with us and (2) to elucidate some limits of our knowledge of the past.

Clues about the Past and How We Carry It with Us

First, we are all emerging from the past. A walk through any city, while surely an activity of the present, is also an encounter with the residual judgments, decisions, and actions of the past. The buildings we pass may exemplify the architecture of bygone eras. Even the people we pass wear clothes that exemplify a particular fashion coupled with a very recent decision to wear these items today. The newspapers we buy refer to events that have just happened. Even the coffee we buy is often not brewing as we speak but has been sitting around for a while, however short. Our view then of the past is much clearer than our view of the future. As Coleridge would have it, we back into the future, seeing more clearly the past: "Human experience, like the stern lights of a ship at sea, illumines only the path which we have passed over."[41]

Second, most of us carry at least some portion of the past with us through memories primarily, and through archives and artifacts secondarily. Since for each of us our life journeys are different, so is our store of memories of the journey. That store of memories contributes a great deal to what may be termed our unique "developmental perspective."

Third, memory and its products are useful—allowing us to extend our reach from the confines of the here-and-now. The infant confined to a crib, with not many memories and not many ideas, is imprisoned in the limits of the present. She/he lives on a tiny island surrounded by the unknown: an unknown past, future, and an unknown world of abstract ideas. For an adult, such confinement is debilitating. The film *50 First Dates* illustrates this within the context of a romantic comedy[42]; and the film *Memento* illustrates this within the context of a murder mystery.[43]

Fourth, memory is part of a larger process of comprehensive learning. Whatever cognitive processes are involved in human efforts at comprehensive learning, they work with presentations of current states (e.g., sensations) or re-presentations of the past (e.g., memories) or as imaginary transformations. Therefore, however achieved, our knowledge is firmly rooted in the past.[44] Regarding history specifically, let us distinguish four purposes that may be addressed in attending to the past: (1) reminiscing, (2) seeking a deeper understanding, (3) resolving issues of fact and value, and (4) importing knowledge and value into one's life to transform situations and self.

In "reminiscing" we recollect events of the past and sometimes experience either delight or regret over what has happened. The act of reminiscing may be done individually or in a group; it may involve telling stories or reviewing artifacts such as letters or photographs. It may or may not involve writing. Reminiscing itself may be enjoyable and lead to a recommitment to values and goals. It may also be difficult and lead to a desire for a new beginning. The act itself often raises further questions that, if taken up, may lead to a deeper understanding of recollected events and to a clearer knowledge of what was really going forward at that time. It may even lead to a decision to address both present and unknown future in a new way.

Of those who reminisce, many will not be satisfied with mere memory but will seek a deeper understanding of the past. Such a deeper understanding of the past is achieved when we come to see events within larger contexts of uneven human development, social relations, and changing environmental conditions. Whereas previously some events may not have made sense, they now become part of a more meaningful trajectory in which intelligible life paths can be discerned. Such paths may exemplify growth or growth-avoidance. This deeper understanding of our past leads to a finite number of narratives about what was possibly going forward at a given time.

Of those who achieve a deeper understanding, a still smaller group will not be satisfied with a collection of merely possible narratives. Based on information available, they also seek to resolve issues of fact and value. In resolving an issue of fact, one seeks to know what really happened, as opposed to merely what might have happened. In resolving an issue of value, one seeks to know whether something done was worthwhile, as opposed to just seeming so at the time. The resolution of issues of fact and value constitutes knowledge (factual and moral) about aspects of the past. An additional benefit of this is the extraction of criteria to reasonably judge what is real and what is valuable in any past sequence of events.

Of those who achieve knowledge of some aspects of the past, an even smaller group will ask how that knowledge of fact and value can be imported into the present to transform both present and future. The primary focus here is on what might reasonably be done at this point, informed by what we understand, know, and value about the past.

Fifth, memory is fallible. Knowledge of the past is incomplete, fragmented, probabilistic, selective, and largely passive. Benaji & Crowder have summarized the literature on memory to show how permeated with forgetting and confabulation memory is.[45] Freud classically was concerned with important memories being repressed; in contrast, Elizabeth Loftus and her associates have been more recently concerned with the presence of false memories in our memory banks.[46] Yet for all these difficulties, memory remains an important basis of knowledge and knowledge acquisition,[47] even if it is not to be identified with knowledge.[48] As we emerge from the past our knowledge of it is like Swiss cheese—mainly empty space with here and there a bit of verified knowledge. It is augmented by active learning about the past and it is diminished by forgetting and failure to learn.

Sixth, as has been argued elsewhere human memory and the complex human learning of which it is a part together help to constitute our store of knowledge as well as our personality.[49] The various dementias provide what has been described as a "natural experiment"[50] that clarifies the role of memory in human personality.[51]

Seventh, recovering the past may require active learning and problem solving. Active learning requires sustained effort on the part of the learner to formulate and pursue correct answers to challenging questions.[52] This type of activity as applied to the data of the past characterizes the historian—assembling memories, artifacts, and archives, coupled with raising and answering questions.[53]

Eighth, such active learning and problem solving require special attitudes: a sustained desire to know, an ability to distinguish treasure from yesterday's trash, and an attitude toward historical inheritance as either burden or challenge. The lack of a habitual desire to know regarding the past will leave it as it was, diminishing daily through neglect. An attitude of inheritance-as-burden might result in its being neglected, undervalued, undiscovered, and unused.

Ninth, learning about the past can become derailed. Active learning and problem solving about the past not only require work but they suggest adjustments to situations and to self that may be uncomfortable and difficult. It is much easier to coast, in which case the process of learning is dramatically slowed, sometimes even to a stop. In this trajectory emotions can serve as clues to whether or not learning is proceeding. Often, depression can signal that learning has stopped, anxiety can signal that learning might bring new demands, and anger and resentment can signal that learning poses a threat. While on the other hand, enjoyment may signal that learning is proceeding apace.

Some Limits of Our Knowledge of the Past

Given that our knowledge of the past is limited, what are some of its aspects? Knowledge can be understood as a matter of asking and correctly answering questions.[54] Our knowledge of the past, then, should address specific questions about past events.

As seen in chapter 3, knowledge involves evidence. Therefore we can expect that knowledge of the past will also involve evidence. However, what evidence is relevant to knowledge of the past? Would it include memories, artifacts, and archives? Personal or collective memories, artifacts, and archives can all serve as evidence of some aspect of the past. In fact, anything can be evidence for something. The task in acquiring knowledge is to match available evidence with an appropriate judgment about what happened. Error results from a data-judgment mismatch.

Knowledge acquisition regarding the past can also be interfered with and distorted by desires, fears, and other disturbances that eclipse or run counter to the desire to know. As indicated previously, this interference and distortion become process biases when relevant further questions, insights, images, or evidence are systematically excluded from consciousness. Because the process of learning can be interfered with, and because at best it develops through a process from question to insight, our efforts at knowledge acquisition may be understood as successive approximations to the truth.

Sometimes clarification is achieved by contrast. Therefore, let us compare an instance of concrete knowledge of the present with an instance of concrete knowledge of the past. Moreover, let us make this contrast in terms specified above: the field of content, asking and answering questions, the place of evidence, the role of purpose, and the threat of process bias.

Consider two examples: (1) a subway operator goes to work today and as she drives the train she is concerned with the condition of the track and the traffic ahead, (2) a retired subway operator no longer works at that job and remembers what things were like while he was doing it. Operator #1 has knowledge of the present, whereas operator #2 has knowledge of the past. How do these compare?

First, consider the field of content. Operator # 1 is concerned with the here and now. This field of content may be labeled "the present." In the broad sense, "the present" is the class of all events that are happening now. Operator #1 is concerned with a small subset of those events, namely those that affect the operation of the train (e.g., track conditions and traffic). Operator #2 is concerned with the past. But he is concerned not with all of the past, but only with that subset of events related to the way things used to be on the job.

Second, consider the activities of asking and answering questions. Knowledge of both present and past is a matter of asking and answering questions. Operator #1 will likely have different questions than Operator #2. For Operator #2, however, knowledge of the past is more a matter of reconstructing past events. While the questions they both can ask about the past may be of many varieties, not just any answer can count as knowledge. Only answers supported by evidence can be regarded as approaching at least a probable knowledge of events.

Third, consider the role of evidence. If knowledge is regarded as something approaching justified true belief, then the answers supplied to questions about either the present or past must be supported by available evidence. Not just any possible answer will do, but only those that best conform to the facts. For Operator #1, the facts will be found in present conditions but for Operator #2 it will be found in memories and a narrative that is most consistent with available evidence regarding past events.

But what constitutes evidence of past events? And to whom should this evidence be available? In general, evidence of past events includes not only individual and collective memories, but also monuments, artifacts, and archives. Moreover, this evidence should be widely available to various persons to examine. For example, a personal memory is available only to the person who has it; moreover, it may be quite fleeting. Hence it is not public (i.e., available to other persons) and it is not stable (i.e., available across occasions). In comparison, archives are more public and stable. The best evidence for the purposes of constructing an historical record is whatever is relatively public and stable.

Fourth, consider the purposes of investigation. Our knowledge, whether of present or past, may be used to serve varied purposes, including theoretical purposes of increasing our understanding and knowledge and practical purposes of changing the present and emerging future. For Operator #1, the purposes are likely to be highly practical and related to safe conduct of the current train run. For Operator #2, these purposes may be more theoretical and related to settling issues of past fact and value. The purposes may well determine the kinds of questions asked, and by extension, the kinds of evidence to be associated with any answers.

Fifth, consider the threat of process bias. As argued previously, "process bias" is a systematic exclusion of relevant further questions, images, insights, and evidence from our approach to the study of anything, including present and past. As such, process bias is a threat to the very process of the acquisition of knowledge. Once a series of questions is asked, if what is relevant to those questions is systematically excluded from consideration, then what emerges, if it is the truth, will not be the whole truth or nothing but the truth. Significant portions of the story will be left out, thus rendering a skewed account. One way in which Operator #1 could exhibit this bias would be by routinely being distracted away from attention to current track conditions.

Operator #2 could exhibit process bias by ignoring significant portions of his past that, if known, would provide a significantly different account of what happened.

Yet process bias is difficult to detect. Since it is a systematic exclusion of what is relevant to a series of questions, it can only be detected in a collection of investigations spread out over time. Evidence of process bias would include over time: (1) the emergence of a series of questions, and (2) a collection of studies that excluded important further questions, images, insights, or evidence that would facilitate answering the original series of questions. Process bias can be mitigated by re-examining what is both relevant and systematically excluded and then including this material in future work.

ADDITIONAL CONSIDERATIONS: KEY POINTS AND SOME IMPLICATIONS

1) A first set of key points regards personality. Understood as a force field, the personality contains driving forces that promote growth through learning and problem solving.
2) The personality will also contain restraining forces that inhibit this growth.
3) Included among these driving and restraining forces are all intellectual habits and the learning response styles each person may have developed.
4) The individual person can affect and be affected by the forces in personality.
5) One person may be compared with another in terms of a profile of their "learning response style." This kind of profile would indicate the extent to which the learner employs each pattern of problem solving. Any differences noted would not be just a matter of learning style, which is a preference for specific types of data.
6) An implication here is that if any two persons have markedly different learning response styles, then the probability for miscommunication is dramatically increased.
7) A second set of key points regards social trust. Understood as a force field, social contexts contain driving forces that promote growth through learning and problem solving. Social trust can be one of those driving forces if the persons trusted are themselves committed to authentic learning.
8) Social contexts will also contain restraining forces that inhibit this growth, especially to the extent that suspicion and mistrust are prevalent.

9) The individual person can affect and be affected by the pro-growth and no-growth forces in social contexts to the extent they participate in them and believe them.
10) An important implication here is that small problem solving groups can provide a way to both practice patterns of problem solving and to rely on the work of others as they also practice.
11) A third set of key points regards culture. Understood as a field of force fields, culture contains widely distributed pro-growth and no-growth forces operative throughout its sphere of influence. Hence, they can affect the individual learner.
12) A culture in development will contain more pro-learning forces than no-learning forces.
13) A culture in decline will contain more forces that inhibit learning and problem solving.
14) An implication here is that individuals and small groups can also affect the cultures in which they live by making problem solving contributions to cultural mores, traditions, and interpretations of events.
15) A fourth set of key points regards the study of history. Understood as a succession of fields of force fields, the past will also contain both pro-learning and anti-learning forces.
16) Individuals are affected by the pro-growth and no-growth forces of the past through the world presented to them that was the result of those forces.
17) An implication here is that individuals can affect the pro-growth and no-growth forces in history going forward through their specific contributions or lack of them.
18) Another set of implications involves making the study of all four contexts into habitual practice.
19) This practice can exhibit quality control. As indicated in previous chapters, quality control in any of the patterns of problem solving involves the guiding influence of the desire to know. This desire facilitates the natural unfolding of all of the relevant facts of consciousness.
20) Quality control is this area can also be abandoned. In contrast, the study of these larger contexts can go wrong by relinquishing guidance of the desire to know. Quality control can also go wrong by failing to distinguish what facts of consciousness are and what are not in our control. For example, insights are not in our control; whereas questions sometimes may be in our control. Quality control can also go wrong by eliminating or ignoring relevant questions and insights, or by eliminating or ignoring entire patterns of problem solving. Finally, poorly formulated insights, rash judgments, impulsive decisions and dominance by anything other than the desire to know insure defective results.

SUMMARY

This chapter examined larger contexts in which the patterns of problem solving and the modes of basic experiencing take place. Specifically, the larger contexts of personality, social trust, culture, and history were considered. Related to this general aim, the following objectives were set out: (1) an examination of how the larger contexts of personality, social trust, culture, and history can influence learning and problem solving and (2) an examination of how learning and problem solving influence the larger contexts. Force field analysis was used to assist in interpreting each of these objectives. Then, implications were considered.

The most obvious thing about these larger contexts is their pervasiveness. All four exert a continual influence on individuals, and it is nearly impossible to avoid them. What is less obvious about the four contexts is how they operate and how we might influence them. Some individuals and problem solving groups, guided by the desire to know, will seek to understand and come to know the larger contexts better and to make unique contributions to them. Many others will passively drift through them.

Anyone who studies the larger contexts can bolster social trust by practicing the patterns of problem solving together with interested others. In these groups, if they are to be really effective at problem solving, the desire to know will be guiding all members. Through shared experiences, understanding, and work on critical thinking in relation to any context they can develop reliance upon the contributions of each other toward a shared knowledge of personality, social relations, culture, or history.

Can examination of the larger contexts of personality, social trust, culture, and history be made into habitual practice? Here some may simply give up, invoking the claim that these topics are too vast to be examined comprehensively and that the individual is too weak to really influence any of them. Regarding personality, many will simply claim that "people do not change" and leave it at that. Regarding social relations and culture they may refer to them as all too overwhelming. Regarding history, they may cite the all-too-reasonable motto "What is done is done."

The project of mining all of these four contexts may or may not be pursued by any given individual or problem solving group. They may or may not be valued by any given culture or social milieu. Moreover, some are far easier to pursue than others are. For example, reminiscing is a largely passive affair and one can continue with it until one sleeps, becomes bored, distracted, or uncomfortable. The other projects related to mining one's inheritance in the four contexts require both effort and perseverance to proceed beyond any but the most shallow of levels. This mining includes not just reminiscing, but more especially seeking a deeper understanding of the context, resolving issues of fact and value that present themselves, and importing knowledge and value into one's life to transform situations and self in the present.

NOTES

1. Urie Bronfenbrenner. *The Ecology of Human Development: Experiments by Nature and Design* (Cambridge, MA: Harvard University Press, 1979).

2. Jerome Bruner, *The Process of Education* (Cambridge, MA: Harvard University Press, 1976); Bernard Lonergan. "Theories of Inquiry" in *A Second Collection* (Toronto: University of Toronto Press, 33–42); Bernard Lonergan. "The Subject" in *A Second Collection* (Toronto: University of Toronto Press, 69–86).

3. Karen Horney. *Neurosis and Human Growth: The Struggle towards Self-Realization* (New York: Norton & Co., 1950).

4. Kurt Lewin. "Defining the 'Field at a Given Time.'" In *Resolving Social Conflicts and Field Theory in Social Science* (Washington, DC: American Psychological Association, 1997).

5. J. P. Chaplin, *Dictionary of psychology (2nd Ed.)* (New York: Laurel Books, 1985, 334).

6. Anna Freud. *The Ego and the Mechanisms of Defense* (New York: International Universities Press, 1966/1936); M. Scott Peck. *The Road Less Traveled* (New York: Simon & Schuster, 1978).

7. Karen Horney. *Our Inner Conflicts* (New York: Norton Co., 1993/1945); John B. Watson. "On personality." In Robert W. Marks (Ed.) *Great Ideas in Psychology: The Most Significant Writings of the Founders of Modern Psychology* (New York: Bantam Books, 1966, 400–431). These authors present accounts from very different traditions. Horney emphasizes conscious and unconscious motives in the psychodynamic tradition. Watson emphasizes the construction of behavioral habits, without any reference to conscious or unconscious motives.

8. Richard Grallo "Reframing applied psychology in terms of self-transcendence: Selected challenges, problems and prospects." Paper presented at 37th Lonergan Workshop, Boston College, 2010.

9. Bernard Lonergan, *Method in Theology* (New York: Herder & Herder, 1972, 35.)

10. Bernard Lonergan, *Insight: A Study of Human Understanding* (Toronto: University of Toronto Press, 1992, Ch. 6.) Hereafter, *Insight*.

11. James L. Adams. *The Care and Feeding of Ideas: A Guide to Encouraging Creativity* (Reading, MA: Addison-Wesley, 1986).

12. American Psychiatric Association. *Diagnostic and Statistic Manual of Mental Disorders (5th ed.)* (Washington DC: American Psychiatric Association, 2013).

13. Karen Horney. *Neurosis and Human Growth* (New York: W.W. Norton, 1950, ch. 7); DiGiuseppe, Ray. Workshop on "Treatment of Personality Disorders" (New York: Albert Ellis Institute, 2006).

14. Alex Osborne. *Applied Imagination: Principles and Procedures of Creative Problem Solving* (New York: Scribner, 1953.)

15. American Psychological Association. *APA Dictionary of Psychology* (Washington, DC: American psychological Association, 751). Overlearning is "a practice that is continued beyond the point at which the individual knows or performs the task as well as can be expected."

16. Parts of this section are based on an article previously published in *Symposium*: Richard Grallo. "The Role of Belief in Problem Solving." *Symposium*, XXIII, No. 2 (2015): 23–32.

17. American Psychological Association, *APA Dictionary of Psychology (2nd ed.)*, American Psychological Association: Washington, DC, 2015, p. 993.

18. Chaiklin, S. "The Zone of Proximal Development in Vygotsky's Analysis of Learning and Instruction." In Kozulin, A., Gindis, B., Ageyev, V. & Miller, S. (Eds.) *Vygotsky's Educational Theory and Practice in Cultural Context* (Cambridge: Cambridge University, 2003, 39–64).

19. Bruner. *The Process of Education.*

20. A few examples include: various psychoanalytic institutes and the Institute for Rational Emotive Behavior Therapy in New York.

21. Krista Rodkey and Elisa Rodkey. "Family, Friends and Faith Communities: Intellectual Community and the Benefits of Unofficial Networks for Marginalized Scientists." *History of Psychology*, 23 No. 4, 2020, 289–311.

22. American Psychological Association. *APA Dictionary of Psychology (2nd ed.)*, 1110.

23. Erik Erikson. (1963). *Youth: Change and Challenge* (New York: Basic Books, 1963).

24. Mary Ainsworth and Associates. *Patterns of Attachment: A Psychological Study of the Strange Situation* (Hillsdale, NJ: Erlbaum, 1978).

25. American Psychological Association. *APA Dictionary of Psychology (2nd ed.)*, 119.

26. Bernard Lonergan. *Insight.* 728–735.

27. Alfred Shutz, *The Phenomenology of the Social World* (Evanston, IL: Northwestern University Press, 1967).

28. S. I. Hayakawa. *Language in Thought and Action.* Enlarged ed. (San Diego: Harcourt Brace Jovanovich, 1978); Alfred Korzybski. *Science and Sanity: An Introduction to non-Aristotelean systems and general semantics (5th ed.)* (Fort Worth, TX: Institute for General Semantics, 2010).

29. Bernard Lonergan, *Insight*, ch. XX.

30. A. S. Reber and E. S. Reber, *Dictionary of psychology.* New York: Penguin Classics, 2001.

31. Bernard Lonergan. *Insight: A study of human understanding.* University of Toronto Press, Toronto, ON, 1992; Richard Grallo. "Thinking carefully about Critical Thinking"; Mark Morelli, *Self-possession: Being at Home in Conscious Performance* (Lonergan Center at Boston College, 2015).

32. A previously published article in *Symposium* served as a basis for this section: Richard Grallo. "How to Think about Culture." *Symposium*, X, No. 1 (2003): 19–26.

33. American Psychological Association. *Dictionary.* 274.

34. Joseph Flanagan. *Quest for Self-Knowledge* (Toronto: University of Toronto Press, 1997, 205–206.)

35. Edward T. Hall. *The Silent Language* (Garden City, NY: Doubleday, 1959); Geert *Hofstede. Culture's Consequences: Comparing Values, Behaviors, Institutions, and Organizations across Nations (2nd ed.)* (Thousand Oaks, CA: Sage, 2001).

36. American Psychological Association, *Dictionary of Psychology*, 951.

37. Henry Ford. Interview, *Chicago Tribune, May 25, 1916.*

38. George Santayana. *The Life of Reason, v.1* (Cambridge, MA: MIT Press, 1905/2011).

39. Roy Baumeister and Kathlenn Vohs. *Handbook of self-regulation* (New York: Guilford Press, 2004).

40. Richard Grallo. "Questioning as a Cognitive Process: Implications for Learning and Culture" *Symposium, XVI(1)*, 2009, 13–23.

41. Samuel Taylor Coleridge. The Friend. *The Complete Works, v. 2* (New York: Harper & Bros. 1854).

42. Peter Segal. *50 First Dates* (Hollywood, CA: Film, Columbia Pictures, 2004).

43. Christopher Nolan. *Memento* (Santa Monica, CA: Film, Summit Entertainment, 2000).

44. J. P. Guilford (1968)

45. Mahzarin Benaji and Robert Crowder. The Bankruptcy of Everyday Memory. *American Psychologist, 44*, 1989, 1185–1193.

46. Maryanne Garry and Harlene Hayne (Eds.) *Do Justice and Let the Sky Fall: Elizabeth Loftus and Her Contributions to Science, Law and Academic Freedom* (Mahwah, NJ: Lawrence Erlbaum Associates, 2006).

47. J. P. Guilford. "Intelligence Has Three Facets." *Science, 160*, 1968, 615–620.

48. Plato. *Meno* (Indianapolis, IN: Hackett Publishing, 1980).

49. Lonergan. *Insight*, 30–31.

50. William Shadish, Thomas Cook, and Donald Campbell. *Experimental and Quasi-Experimental Designs for Generalized Causal Inference* (Boston: Houghton-Mifflin Co., 2002).

51. Walter Conn. *The Desiring Self* (New York: Paulist Press, 1998); Jenni Ogden. *Fractured Minds: A Case Study Approach to Clinical Neuro-psychology* (New York: Oxford University Press, 2005); Oliver Sachs. *The Man Who Mistook His Wife for a Hat and Other Clinical Tales* (New York: Pocket Books, 1998).

52. Michael Marquardt. *Optimizing the Power of Active Learning: Solving Problems and Building Leaders in Real Time* (Mountain View, CA: Davies Black, 2004); Louis Tietje, Philip Nufrio, and R. Kramer. Theory and practice of action learning in the MPA/MBA curriculum at Metropolitan College of New York. *Public Administration Quarterly*, 32(2), 2008, 214–242.

53. R. G. Collingwood. *The Idea of History* (New York: Oxford University Press, 1994).

54. Ibid.

Chapter 6

Examples of Facts of Consciousness in Other Perspectives

This chapter explores how some other thinkers have dealt with the general self-correcting cycle of complex human learning and associated mental acts and operations. Specifically, the ancient philosopher Epictetus and contemporary organizational psychologists Edwin Locke and Gary Latham will be considered.

TWO ILLUSTRATIVE EXAMPLES: OVERVIEW

As used in this book, the phrase "facts of consciousness"[1] refers to a number of distinct but related phenomena. (1) There are distinct mental events that make up problem solving and complex human learning. Some of these events are instantaneous and others are processes extended over time. Some are in our control while some are not. Premier among these events are question, insight, the desire to know, and social trust. (2) These mental events coalesce into four natural, functional groupings of events labeled here as "patterns of problem solving." As explored in chapters 1, 2, and 3, this grouping takes place through the agency of the desire to know. (3) Chapter 4 makes clear how the patterns of problem solving emerge from experience as a source and return to it as a testing ground. (4) The experience-based patterns of problem solving form a self-correcting general cycle of learning that spirals[2] through experiencing, understanding, judging, and deciding. (5) The facts of consciousness also reveal how we can pause from the problem solving treadmill through basic experiencing and its modes of living through habitual routines, aesthetic absorption, or tranquil abiding. (6) The facts of consciousness also reveal specific ways in which problem solving and complex human learning can be disrupted or distorted.

If the facts of consciousness, whether subtle or not, are available to most individuals, then it is reasonable to ask about the independent discovery of them. To what extent have other relatively independent thinkers discovered and described the facts of consciousness considered here? To what extent have other relatively independent thinkers placed these facts in an explanatory context resembling (or departing) from the account presented in this book?

There are other accounts of learning which to a greater or lesser extent presuppose, mention, or describe the facts of consciousness and place them in an explanatory context. Examination of these theories can provide a clarification of the patterns of problem solving and their associated facts of consciousness by similarity and contrast. Two bodies of work have been selected as illustrative examples from two diverse fields: the work of Epictetus from ancient philosophy, and that of Edwin Locke and Gary Latham from contemporary organizational psychology.

Each of these authors developed a general theory of problem solving or complex human learning. In each, there is some version of a self-correcting cycle of learning that incorporates facts associated with experiencing, understanding, judging, and deciding. The work of each has sufficient detail to allow for the identification of this cycle along with feedback mechanisms and checks and balances in service to self-correction and quality control. Finally, each body of work places an emphasis on self-management of learning.

Epictetus is explored here because he is very clear about the importance of impressions, managing impressions, judging, and choosing. In particular, Epictetus' "impressions" correspond to experience as source of knowledge, "managing impressions" corresponds well with Problem Solving Pattern 1, "judging" with Problem Solving Patterns 2 and 3, and "choosing" with Problem Solving Pattern 4. Locke and Latham are examined because their "High Performance Cycle" is quite explicitly a general learning cycle that includes many of the facts of consciousness. Of particular importance are the setting of specific high goals which can correspond to the guiding questions of each pattern of problem solving. The entire cycle is a feedback loop that allows for testing insights and judgments in experience.

Both theories provide corroborating evidence, presented by independent investigators, for the identification and verification of the existence and operation of the functional groups of problem solving acts and operations, and of the facts of consciousness. These investigators are "independent" in the sense that they show no evidence in their writing that they were familiar with one another's work. Moving into the twenty-first century, theories such as these that enjoy wide use will likely continue with slight modification but will also be applied in new learning environments such as online environments.

The following objectives are set out for this chapter. (1) There will be a presentation of the basic doctrines of Epictetus regarding impressions, managing impressions, judging, and choosing. (2) There will be an examination of the High Performance Cycle of Edwin Locke and Gary Latham. These objectives are designed to illustrate how other thinkers come across the same basic facts of consciousness and use them to facilitate personal growth in themselves and others.[3] This growth includes greater self-acceptance, self-knowledge, and more skillful self-regulation. It should assist readers to be witnesses of their own experience. This includes their experiences of understanding, judging, deciding, and the consequences of these as they exist in concrete contexts.

EPICTETUS

Introduction

Imagine[4] the last time you encountered any of these annoyances of contemporary city life: (a) you are delayed on a train, (b) someone cuts you off while you are driving, (c) you hold a door for a stranger, who passes through saying nothing, or (d) a friend is forty minutes late for lunch.

The work of Epictetus has a number of aims that enhance not only our self-knowledge but also the regulation of our consciousness. (1) His teachings identify how annoyances and other emotions work. (2) These teachings provide direction of how to apply this kind of self-knowledge in a variety of contexts.

Epictetus (55–135 C.E.) became an influential Stoic philosopher in ancient Rome, until he was exiled from the capital in 71 C.E. by the Emperor Vespasian. He lived and taught the remainder of his life in the small Greek town of Nicopolis. He wrote no books, but his teachings were captured by his student Arrian in two books: The *Handbook* (or, *Enchiridion*) and the *Discourses*.

The *Handbook* is a brief compendium of maxims, collected in fifty-three sections. The *Handbook* gives the impression of Epictetus as a no-nonsense personal trainer whose goal is the development of personal excellence and virtuous character in his students. The *Discourses* are more extensive classroom notes and dialogues with students, collected into four "books." The Discourses reveal a more nuanced thinker who drew freely upon his predecessors but who remained practical in his ends and in his methods. In both books, distractions from the goals of personal development are clearly identified and ruthlessly dismissed, and sound mindful practice substituted in their place.

His entire teaching centered on philosophy as a way of life and not so much as an academic discipline. Practitioners of this way of life were compared with seasoned athletes, not academics.[5] The achievement of self-knowledge was central and was to be used as a means to achieve self-appropriation.[6] Self-appropriation serves as a basis for effective self-management and the freedom that goes with it. This way of life involves learning what is "in our control" and what is "not in our control," attending mainly to what is in our control and less to what is not in our control. On this basis one incorporates growth-oriented habits into one's character and development.

Since for Epictetus philosophy is a way of life, not so much an academic discipline,[7] it became important to distinguish it from various distractions, including some that may seem "philosophic."[8] Consequently the practice of philosophy is a kind of "mindfulness" or disciplined focusing of attention.[9]

Paramount among his teachings is the exhortation that we learn to distinguish events that are in our control from those that are not in our control.[10] As shocking and disheartening as it may be to the beginner, it is a fact that most events in the universe are simply not in our control. This includes the weather and astrophysical events, the meanderings of microbes, the economy, changes in geography, and most of human politics and social interactions. The injunction includes the thoughts, feelings, and behaviors of others including the noisy neighbors and barking dogs. It includes all past events and most future events. It even includes many of our own automatic thoughts, feelings, and behaviors. The very fact that they are automatic makes them not under our control.

More generally, instead of worrying about any X which is not in our control, he advises that we focus on what is in our control. This change of focus allows one to eliminate distractions and not waste time, while simultaneously marshalling forces in our control to better engage individual and group problem solving. The specific exercises that he prescribes are methods to do this.

The question then arises, what is in our control? For Epictetus, our own thoughts, feelings, and behaviors are in our control, but only if we work to bring them under our control. This is no easy task. It may take months or years of practice to develop a discipline of mindful attention to those aspects of ourselves that are candidates for self-control. To assist in this large task of gaining self-control a really useful philosophy concentrates study in four areas: (1) our impressions, (2) our interpretations of them, (3) our judgments, and (4) our choices.[11] Following Epictetus, the discussion of this chapter will leave out the gray area of social influence[12] as opposed to outright control.

Managing Impressions

The first crucial area for philosophic studies is the management of impressions. This refers to "experience as a source and resource" for all learning.

For Epictetus "impressions" are anything that comes to consciousness (or is given and might be called "data"). These include sense impressions (or sense data) of all sorts, as well as feelings, desires, and aversions.[13] The frequency, intensity, and duration of impressions are highly varied and their constant presence may seem as on ongoing storm.[14] This state of affairs is identified by William James as the "buzzing, booming confusion" of consciousness.[15]

Impressions are important for a variety of reasons. First, they orient individuals toward judgments and choices by filling out a landscape of meaning and concerns in which we are to operate. Impressions provide the raw material whereby persons can identify gaps between their current situation and a more desirable future state. The recognition of such gaps transforms into questions. Hence impressions play a formative role in the construction of goals (in this case, the answering of questions). Second, impressions can be a strong motive force. Included among impressions are desires and aversions which are easily recognized as sources of internal motivation. As such, they can serve as either driving or restraining forces for learning and growth. Finally, impressions can be misleading. Frequently things are not as they initially seem; that is, the interpretations that individuals ascribe to their impressions are often uselessly vague or false.[16]

Since impressions can influence the construction of goals, are a strong motive force, and can be misleading, it is important to manage them carefully. The management of impressions begins with managing personal attention through noticing, focusing, wondering, and following.

In his account of impressions, Epictetus exhibits a grasp of the facts of consciousness by associating impressions with experiencing as a source and resource for learning.

Managing the Interpretation of Impressions

Impressions come to consciousness largely unbidden and often in the context of routines or habits. Managing them is really a matter of "managing interpretation" of them. For this activity Epictetus assigns a major role to questions and questioning. By interrogating personal impressions individuals come to understand how the impressions arise and where they lead if left unchecked and unchallenged.[17] Such interrogation involves resisting automatic thoughts,[18] as well as renouncing a know-it-all attitude,[19] and the general bias.[20] Automatic thoughts are "thoughts that are instantaneous, habitual, and non-conscious." They are "thoughts that have been so well learned and habitually repeated that they occur with little cognitive effort."[21] The "general bias" is an often unstated belief, used as an operating principle, that one is sufficiently knowledgeable in an area so as to need no further learning. In its extreme form it can crystallize as a "know-it-all attitude"[22] and become operative as a hidden agenda which tends to shut down conversation, exploration, and learning.

In his account of managing the interpretation of impressions, Epictetus exhibits a grasp of many facts of consciousness. For example, he has a clear role for guiding questions and the desire to know. Because the entire process is a search for understanding and its insights, it is in fact a consideration of Problem Solving Pattern 1 (Seeking Understanding). However, in his discussion, Epictetus does not use the language associated with this book's description of Pattern 1; moreover, in his consideration of facts of consciousness, he does not place too much emphasis on the formulation of interpretations and their re-framing.

Managing Judgments

The third major area for philosophic study is judgment. "Judgments" are answers to yes-no questions (also known as "reflective questions"): "Is this true?" "Is that good?"

The proper function of judgment is not to be confused with a blaming attitude or with rash judgment. A blaming attitude is often an attempt to condemn persons for this or that trait or action. A rash judgment is a rush to affirm or deny the truth of something, or it is a rush to approve or disapprove the value of something without much in the way of considering evidence and reasons.

As previously indicated, there are two basic types of judgment: judgments of fact and judgments of value.[23] "Judgments of fact" affirm or deny the truth of some proposition.[24] "Judgments of value" approve or disapprove of something as worthwhile.[25] Regarding judgments of fact Epictetus indicates that truth resides in a judgment and in the appropriate application of a criterion of truth.[26] Regarding judgments of value Epictetus argues that "good" and "evil" reside in a judgment and in the appropriate application of a criterion of what is valuable.[27] Both these types of judgment are important because they settle for us the facts and values needed to guide further actions. They provide a way for learning to inform and guide our choices and actions. Without them nothing is ever settled as being factual or worthwhile. The one who refuses to make any judgment remains adrift in a sea of possibilities with no facts or values to consult or to use as a frame of reference.

Managing judgments is also an art and a discipline that can be improved. It requires sustained practice to improve the quality of personal judgments.[28] This often involves (1) making fewer judgments, (2) making judgments evidence-based, and (3) regarding any other thought as mere hypothesis until it is filtered through appropriate forms of critical thinking that lead to well-founded judgments of fact and value. Because judgments can be defective they need a critical review.[29]

Judgments play a key role in human living. They contribute to attitudes and set the stage and justification for decisions and choices.[30] However, judgments also often lead to high emotions, or if they are made properly, they can lead to tranquility.[31] In addition, judgments will support or deny interpretations of impressions and decisions made, and could therefore lead to cognitive dissonance.[32] "Cognitive dissonance" is "an unpleasant psychological state resulting from inconsistency between two or more elements in a cognitive system."[33]

In his account of judgment, Epictetus exhibits a grasp of many facts of consciousness associated with problem solving Patterns 2 and 3 (Factual Critical Thinking and Values-Oriented Critical Thinking). For example, in making judgments he gives primacy to the available evidence and confirmed reasons. He encourages the desire to know to follow evidence and reasons where they may lead. However, he does not spend much time on the nature of reflective questions or on alternate formulation of judgments.

Managing Choices

The fourth key area for philosophic study is choice. "Choice and refusal" are the premier acts of individual freedom.[34] Exercising choice always involves the existence of goals.[35] Exercising choice and moving toward goals is not always easy and often involves some opposition.[36] Choices are so important that anyone's life can be accurately mapped out as a series of choices extended over time.[37]

Managing one's freedom of choice is an art and a discipline.[38] It is often not easy.[39] It involves setting and managing goals[40] and remaining true to one's moral purpose.[41] It involves an accurate judgment about what is in our power and what is not. It involves identifying and weighing options. It involves a decision or commitment to act for our good. To be effective these decisions must be preceded by relevant questions and insights, evidence and criteria for evidence.[42] In contrast, poorly made decisions fail to accurately identify what is in our control. The result is often a desperate attempt to "move against people" because they interfere with one's uncontrolled desires.[43]

In his account of choice, Epictetus exhibits a grasp of many facts of consciousness associated with problem solving Pattern 4 (Deliberative Critical Thinking). For example, he encourages examination of available options associated with any choice and a review of the evidence and reasons that could be offered in support of each. Again, the desire to know should allow this process to lead where it will. However, he does not give an account of deliberative reflective questions or on how to handle multiple options in decision-making.

Whatever decisions and choices are made there will be consequences both in the world and in developing habits within oneself. To the extent that decisions and choice are in our power we can have some influence over these consequences. By way of prediction, if any reader ignores the lessons Epictetus has to teach once they have been presented, then any memory trace of them is likely to slowly evaporate over time. In addition, any system of self-management that was present at the time of forgetting is likely to continue in force as a matter of habit. If those habits are inimical to learning, then the practitioner of those habits will not only block future learning, but will continue bringing about effects based on sustained ignorance. In contrast, if the lessons of Epictetus are applied consistently then a new system of self-management will develop. This new system will be superior to its predecessor since its will result in greater freedom[44] and effectiveness,[45] and less emotional disturbance[46] and improved social relations.[47]

Return then to some of the annoyances presented above: (a) you are delayed on a train, (b) someone cuts you off while you are driving, (c) you hold a door for someone, and they say nothing, or (d) a friend is forty minutes late for lunch. In each instance some event occurs, maybe by surprise, and it is accompanied by a strong emotional response. Such a response could be anger, anxiety, or depression. Epictetus encourages us to examine our responses to see if patterns emerge. Do we get angry often? Do we get anxious often? Do we get depressed often? If so, and if we allow it to go forth, we are then practicing being angry, or anxious or depressed. We are developing emotional habits of anger, or anxiety or depression. Week by week, month by month we are becoming a habitually angry, or anxious, or depressed person.

Are we content with this state of affairs? If we are, then we will be stuck with this situation well into the future.[48] If not, is there anything that we can do about it? Epictetus would ask: Is there anything about these annoyances that is in our control? For him the answer is affirmative: we can manage our interpretations of impressions, we can manage our judgments and our choices. If one is delayed on a train, one can interrogate one's impressions and one interpretation of them. Why is the train delayed? What is useful about this? How might I constructively use my time? What judgment am I making to feel this emotion? Is that judgment sound? What other judgments can I reasonably make? How do I choose to be in this situation? Is there anything interesting or amusing about this situation? What is great about it? The delay then instantaneously changes from being a mindless, unpleasant, out-of-control emotional experience into a playful contemplation about current circumstances and how I am choosing to interact with and in those circumstances. For the neophyte, this contemplation may seem difficult and anything but playful, but for the seasoned practitioner it is an exercise in freedom—the freedom of not being emotionally controlled by chance events.[49] It is the freedom of bringing a measure of tranquility to any situation,[50] including delayed trains, erratic drivers, rude passers-by, and late friends.

The teachings of Epictetus can be used by individuals seeking greater personal growth and by those seeking professionally to improve theory and practice in various human service disciplines. "Human services disciplines" here include all the branches of applied psychology and social science, medicine, nursing, education, and business-related disciplines. For those seeking greater personal growth, Epictetus clearly identifies four areas of conscious activity that are under our control: impressions and the attention given to them, interpretations of impressions and the formulation of them, judgments, and choices. By attending to the facts of consciousness studied in basic experiencing and the patterns of problem solving one is moving to take the lessons of Epictetus seriously. For those seeking to improve theory and practice in various human service disciplines, Epictetus invites the study of how exactly impressions (or data) are managed and interpreted, and of how judgments and choices are made within each discipline.[51] The conclusions of Epictetus could be studied in relation to field-specific codes of ethics and methodological precepts. Since the cognitive revolution of the 1970s, there has been an avalanche of research on these areas of human cognition and problem solving.

Readers who have followed the teachings of Epictetus so far are then faced with a number of choices. (1) They may explore these ideas further or not. To do nothing is the path of least effort. To choose further exploration would require sustained effort in examining how we actually attend to and interpret our own impressions and manage our judgments and choices. This examination will involve "positive" events such as desires fulfilled, correct judgments made, and choices completed. It will also involve "negative" events such as desires frustrated, defective judgments, and choices gone awry. To summon that sustained effort will likely be no easy task because it is often a slow process.[52] This is especially true if the advantages of seeking self-knowledge appear far off and if one is subjected to censure and ridicule by others for attempting such an enterprise.[53] (2) Beyond just exploring ideas they may do the further work of changing habits or not. This is a more difficult enterprise, but again, to do nothing here is also a path of least effort. To change habits requires not only perseverance but sustained commitment in the face of possible failure.[54] (3) Finally, beyond just changing a habit here or there, some readers may commit to becoming a learning personality, while others will not. To become a "learning personality" is a way of life that orients daily activity around learning and problem solving. This is a very steep climb. Many will choose a path of least effort and evade it. Becoming a learning personality requires settled establishment of an entire collection of new habits that foster comprehensive learning. This includes taking responsibility to nurture one's own desire to know and giving it primacy, making time and space to study in depth, associating with other learning personalities and getting in the habit of improving habits as experience and learning require. These new habits embrace Epictetus' call to take responsibility for one's desires, interpretations, judgments, and choices.

LOCKE AND LATHAM'S HIGH PERFORMANCE CYCLE

Introduction

In 1990 Edwin Locke and Gary Latham presented an important literature review in the area of work motivation and satisfaction. In the course of this review they introduced what has come to be known as the "High Performance Cycle" (HPC).[55] In it they summarized developments in both theory and empirical research in this area, and demonstrated how it could be subsumed into a more comprehensive general theory of work motivation and satisfaction. At the end of the review, however, they raised the possibility of generalizing the theory to apply to any high performance whatever in any area of human endeavor.

More specifically, these authors identified personal and environmental conditions for the presence of high performance in work settings. They also suggested that the HPC could be extended to performance in non-work settings as well. It could be regarded as a matrix of testable predictions regarding learning and individual differences in learning. As such, it could provide a map of a person-environment interface.

Part of the power of the theory they developed is that, by implication, the lack of any combination of these conditions would provide sufficient explanation for mediocre or low or no performance in any area. Consequently, HPC is a theory that is designed to describe, predict, and explain levels of performance and to pinpoint areas for possible interventions to improve performance. As such, it fits well with efforts to develop a "science of improvement."[56]

If the performance examined can also be considered as an instance of problem solving or complex human learning then the HPC can be regarded as a theory of complex human learning and problem solving. As such, it should be of particular interest to researchers and practitioners in education, counseling, and organizational and personal consulting. Moreover, if the HPC can be reframed in terms of "conditions for human learning," then it stands in a line of intellectual work stretching at least from the Enlightenment to our own postmodern era. For example, in 1781 philosopher Immanuel Kant attempted to specify conditions for human knowledge.[57] More recently the focus shifted to cognitive processes as conditions for human learning[58] and problem solving.[59]

Any potentially useful theory should be subject to ongoing and rigorous assessment. Since its introduction the theory has undergone continuous test and confirmation. In addition, it is easily adaptable to both in-person and online contexts. In the spirit of assessment, one can ask the following additional questions: What specifically is involved in this theory? To what uses could an updated version be put in the future?

The HPC

The HPC specifies conditions for excellent performance in work settings. In it both environmental and personal causes and effects of performance are identified. For example, high performance itself generally leads to rewards. These rewards may be dependent on others (extrinsic rewards) or may be dependent on the one engaged in the performance (intrinsic rewards). For example, an accomplished musician may experience the joy of playing complicated musical scores (intrinsic reward) but may also enjoy the acclaim of audiences in doing so (extrinsic reward). The capture of rewards increases the probability of work satisfaction, which in turn brings re-commitment to specific high goals.

In addition, the HPC theory specifies causes and antecedent conditions for high performance. Initial among these antecedent conditions are specific high goals. These can be task accomplishment goals or learning goals. This account of specific high goals is consistent with the guiding questions in the four patterns of problem solving since they too are goals. For the authors, goals "direct attention towards goal-related activities and away from unrelated activities."[60] In the patterns of problem solving, questions serve as guiding intentions to move the learner through the mental events or each pattern on the way to the goal of an answer. Since authentic questions are an expression of the desire to know, which is an ongoing intention to learn, work of the learner is kept on track toward the goal.

The authors also identified "mechanisms for achievement." These include choice/direction, effort, persistence, and strategies. This account of mechanisms for achievement is consistent with facts of consciousness elaborated so far. More specifically in the language of chapter 3, the pursuit of questions is itself a choice which provides "direction" to problem solving activities. If the desire to know is an established desire, and not just a fleeting emotion, then it motivates the "effort" and "persistence" needed to see problem solving through to completion. The specific mental events that make up the chain of events for each pattern of problems solving guide the specific actions to be taken as next steps. For example, if the general goal of railroad crash investigators is to definitively determine the cause of a crash, then they will be involved in testing a number of hypotheses. One such hypothesis might be that the crash occurred because of mechanical failure, another that it occurred because of human error. The reflective factual questions "Did this crash occur because of mechanical failure?" and "Did this crash occur because of human error?" will be questions that are pursued along with questions about other hypotheses. The desire to know will propel the effort and persistence to collect and weigh all available relevant evidence. The process is brought to a conclusion with a reflective factual insight that the evidence is sufficient to support one hypothesis over others, and with the judgment of fact that answers the reflective question.

Finally, the authors identify "moderating influences." These include goal importance, goal commitment, self-efficacy, feedback, and task complexity. This account of moderating influences is also consistent with facts of consciousness presented so far. More specifically, the choice of questions to pursue is itself evidence of the learner's value of the "importance" and "commitment" to the activity of answering the chosen question or solving the selected problem. In addition, there is "high self-efficacy," which is the belief that one is competent enough to achieve the established goals (i.e., answer the posed questions). An individual is unlikely to proceed through the tasks of each pattern of problem solving for very long without the belief that she/he is competent to succeed. As one proceeds through each pattern of problem solving one is in a position to collect "feedback" on how the process is going. Finally, the process has all the "task complexity" of assembling the mental events required in each pattern. For example, one can reasonably expect that railroad crash investigators value and are committed to the overall value of transportation safety. In line with this value, they select relevant questions to pursue and they eliminate questions that are irrelevant to this particular crash. Because of their experience with these types of investigation, the investigators are reasonably certain that they can competently do this job ("high self-efficacy"). The investigators will acquire "feedback" on how they are doing as they collect and weigh all available relevant evidence.

When the entire process is brought to a conclusion with a reflective factual insight and a related judgment of fact, the team members are likely to experience the "satisfaction" of a job well done. Negotiating the entire process of Factual Critical Thinking itself is, in the words of Locke and Latham, a "high achievement."

Part of the power of the HPC is that it predicts and explains complex achievements of all sorts. However, another part of the power of the theory is that, by implication, the lack of any combination of these conditions would both predict and provide sufficient explanation for mediocre or low or no performance in any area. Consequently, the HPC is a theory that is designed to describe, predict, and explain levels of performance and to pinpoint areas for possible interventions to improve performance. As such, it fits well with efforts to develop a "science of improvement."[61] While this concept was initially developed in medicine, its principles can be applied to any human service discipline.

If the performance examined can also be considered as an instance of complex human learning or problem solving then the HPC can be regarded as a theory of complex human learning and problem solving. As such, it should be of particular interest to researchers and practitioners in education, counseling, and organizational and personal consulting. By way of prediction, if any reader ignores or forgets the lessons of the HPC and its conditions for learning, then an opportunity for greater self-knowledge will have been lost. In addition, any system of self-management that was present at the time of forgetting about HPC is likely to continue in force as a matter of habit. If those existing habits are inimical to learning, then the practitioner of those habits will not only block future learning but will continue bringing about effects based on sustained ignorance. In contrast, if these lessons are applied consistently then a new and more effective system of self-management will develop.

The lessons of the HPC can also be used by individuals seeking greater personal growth and by those seeking professionally to improve theory and practice in various human service disciplines. For those seeking greater personal growth, the HPC provides at least a checklist of conditions that individuals can examine for their presence or absence in personal efforts at problem solving and complex human learning. Conditions that are present will indicate areas of strength, while conditions that are weak or absent constitute areas that need further attention and development. For those seeking to improve theory and practice in a human service discipline, an updated version of the HPC might be labeled the "All Performance Cycle." The HPC is useful for describing conditions of high performance, for making predictions about the likelihood of high performance and for explaining how high performance occurs. The All Performance Cycle would be a generalization of the HPC. It would describe conditions for any performance: high, medium, low, or no performance. It would predict whether any action is likely to be or to result in high, medium, low, or no performance. It would explain whatever level of performance is or is not achieved. Use of the All Performance Cycle should prove quite useful diagnostically in practical situations, as well as useful to more precisely target assessment and further research.

Readers are also faced with choices emanating from an application of the HPC to their own experience. (1) They may explore these ideas further or not. As indicated, to do nothing is the path of least effort. To choose further exploration would require sustained effort in examining the extent to which we actually fulfill mediating and moderating conditions for high achievement. This examination will also uncover whether or not goals are clear and realistic. This study will also uncover missing elements, many of which could have been supplied. To engage in the sustained search for that kind of self-knowledge will likely be no easy task because it is often a slow process and because it will likely reveal imperfections in our efforts. (2) In the light of this investigation, readers may do the further work of changing habits or not. Again, to do nothing is the path of least effort. In contrast, changing habits requires not only perseverance but sustained commitment in the face of possible failure. Here the HPC reveals clearly what the conditions for success happen to be. (3) A few may commit to becoming a learning personality. Many will not. To do nothing is a way out of this work. Becoming a "learning personality" requires settled establishment of new habits that foster comprehensive learning: (1) taking responsibility to nurture one's own desire to know and giving it primacy, (2) making time and space to study in depth, (3) associating with other learning personalities, and (4) getting in the habit of improving habits as experience and learning require. These new habits embrace the importance of all the conditions for high performance as identified by the HPC, and the importance of doing something about them.

ADDITIONAL CONSIDERATIONS: KEY POINTS AND IMPLICATIONS

1) Taking the teachings of Epictetus seriously can increase self-knowledge. It provides methods for self-appropriation and the freedom of greater self-regulation.
2) By way of implication, taking the teachings of Epictetus seriously can increase knowledge of what adequate complex human learning is. It raises questions that must be addressed by other accounts of learning.
3) Since the cognitive revolution of the 1970s there has been an explosion of interest in the very areas of human functioning explored by Epictetus.
4) Another implication is that in various human service professions (e.g., teaching, counseling, medicine, and nursing), the four areas of study highlighted by Epictetus can be used to diagnostically identify the presence or absence of conditions for transformative problem solving and complex human learning.
5) In human service professions, such as teaching or counseling, the four areas of study highlighted by Epictetus can be used to help compensate

and strengthen those areas where conditions for transformative problem solving and complex human learning seem to be weak or absent.
6) Taking the HPC seriously can also increase self-knowledge. It pinpoints areas where gains can be made in self-appropriation and the freedom of greater self-regulation.
7) By way of implication, taking the HPC seriously can increase knowledge of what adequate complex human learning is. It raises questions that must be addressed by other accounts of learning.
8) Since the cognitive revolution of the 1970s there has been an explosion of interest in the very areas of human functioning explored by the HPC. For example, science of improvement in medicine.
9) In various human service professions the HPC can be used to diagnostically identify the presence or absence of conditions for problem solving and complex human learning.
10) In human service professions the HPC can be used to help compensate and strengthen those areas where conditions for problem solving and complex human learning seem to be weak or absent.
11) In research, a generalized All Performance Cycle could be used to guide research on any attempts at learning whatever. It could be regarded as a matrix of testable first- and third-person predictions regarding learning and individual differences in learning. It can be used to describe, predict, and explain not only high performance, but mediocre, low, and no performance.

SUMMARY

The following objectives were set out for this chapter. (1) There was a presentation of the basic doctrines of Epictetus regarding impressions, managing impressions, judging, and choosing. (2) There was an examination of the HPC of Edwin Locke and Gary Latham. These objectives are designed to illustrate how other thinkers come across the same basic facts of consciousness and use them to facilitate personal growth in themselves and others. The teachings of Epictetus, the HPC, and the patterns of problem solving all provide a blueprint for learning that is transformative of problems and of self. This transformation includes not only change in problem situations but also personal growth in the learner. The work of these authors is also useful in the professional development of many human service disciplines.

Regarding personal development, to the extent that habits of learning are automatic, they are often rooted in habits not only of behavior but habits of thought and emotion as well. Like all habits, they can be engaged without thinking, practiced easily and efficiently, and enjoyed in the process. Yet not all habits lead to greater success and integration of the person. For those habits that do, the person possessing them can easily, effectively, pleasantly, and almost without thinking increase the probability of achievement and become more skilled in the process. Such a person, in terms of Epictetus, would be skillful in managing impressions, interpretations of them, judgments, and choices. Such a person, in terms of the HPC, would be skillful in establishing specific high goals and in fulfilling the mediating mechanisms and using the moderating conditions to achieve those goals. In other words, such a learner would be self-knowing, self-possessed, self-appropriated, and self-regulated.

Yet for those persons with undeveloped or destructive habits, they easily, effectively, pleasantly, and almost without thinking increase the probability of failure or mediocrity and become more damaged in the process—in effect, they become really efficient at non-growth and sometimes self-destruction. Such a person, in terms of Epictetus, would be generally unskillful in managing impressions, interpreting them, making sound judgments, and implementing responsible choices. Such a person, in terms of the HPC, would be unskillful in establishing specific high goals and in fulfilling the mediating conditions and using the moderating conditions to achieve those goals. In other words, such a learner would tend to be less self-knowing, not self-possessed, not self-appropriated, and rather chaotic and unregulated in the way they approach problems.

Four areas of cognitive functioning have been examined according to teachings offered by Epictetus. These areas are (1) impressions, (2) interpretations of impressions, (3) judgment, and (4) choice. If the reader verified the existence of these operations in his or her own experience then the points made here constitute knowledge, because they are verified. They also constitute self-knowledge because it is knowledge about aspects of one's own functioning. Self-management and self-regulation[62] rely heavily upon accurate self-knowledge.[63] Both self-management and self-regulation are forms of self-control. The alternatives to self-control are problematic. They include being out of control or being controlled by others. In this light then self-control emerges clearly as a form of freedom.

Other facts of consciousness have been emphasized in the HPC. The setting of specific "high goals" is reminiscent of questions serving as guiding intentions for the patterns of problem solving. Under the heading of "mechanisms for achievement," "choice/direction" relates to the pursuit of questions, "effort and persistence" relate to a well-established desire to know, and "strategies" relate to the specific mental events of each pattern of problem solving. Under the heading "moderating influences" are included goal importance, goal commitment, self-efficacy, feedback, and task complexity. "Goal importance and goal commitment" relate to a judgment of value to pursue of specific question or problem. "Self-efficacy" is a judgment of fact, regarding oneself, that one is or is not competent to pursue this question or solve this problem. Like all judgments of fact, it may or may not be true. "Feedback" refers to the fact that as problem solving proceeds new information is gained about how learning is going. "Task complexity" refers to the fact that many problems are complex, but also to the fact that the patterns of problem solving are complex functional groupings of mental events designed to answer specific questions. In particular, the authors suggest how the HPC can be used to check on our progress in problem solving.

Regarding the professional development of human service disciplines, the areas of study identified by Epictetus zero in on areas of conscious operation which are largely under our control. Examining how data, interpretations of data, judgments, and choices are handled in any discipline will provide useful information for assessment and improvement. The conditions of high achievement identified by HPC can be used for practical problems of productivity, cost improvement, performance appraisal, and selection.[64] Hence, if a condition or area is neglected in any discipline, it immediately suggests that something can be done to fill in that gap.

A final question prompted by this chapter is: How can one search for the facts of consciousness in the works of others? A preliminary step is to investigate the role thinkers assign to question, insight, social trust, and the desire to know in their work. Are these even mentioned? Are they given credit in their work? Are they described at all? Are they placed in an explanatory context? Beyond this one can investigate how other facts of consciousness are handled, such as working in problem solving groups and the formulation of questions and insights that is required in problem solving. One can examine how collecting and weighing evidence is managed, as well as how decision-making is regulated.

NOTES

1. An early use of the German equivalent of this phrase was employed by philosopher J. Fichte in his book *Die Thatsachen des Bewusstseyns* (translated as *Facts of Consciousness.*) See Johann G. Fichte, *Facts of Consciousness* (Gloucester, UK: Dodo Press, 2008/1817). The project of Fichte's book was to elucidate various mental events and the nature of the world they reveal. However, the specific mental events of *question* and *insight*, *judgment* and *decision*, the *desire to know* and *social trust*, and other related events are not highlighted as they are here.

2. Jerome Bruner, *The Process of Education* (Cambridge, MA: Harvard University Press, 1976).

3. From psychodynamic psychology, the work of Karen Horney describes the challenges associated with personal growth. Karen Horney, *Neurosis and Human Growth: The Struggle Towards Self-Realization* (New York: Norton, 1950/1990).

4. This section is based on an article previously published in *Symposium*: "Epictetus in the City." *Symposium*, XXIV(1), 2017: 15–25.

5. Epictetus, *Discourses*, II–xii, II–xvii. Cambridge, MA: Loeb Classical Library, vs. 131, 218, 1925, 1928; See also Pierre Hadot, *Philosophy as a Way of Life: Spiritual Exercises from Socrates to Foucault* (Hoboken, NJ: Wiley-Blackwell, 1995).

6. Bernard Lonergan, *Insight: A Study of Human Understanding* (Toronto: University of Toronto Press, 1992).

7. Epictetus, *Discourses*, I–xv, I–xx, IV–x

8. Ibid. II–xix, II–xx

9. Ibid. III–xxiii

10. Epictetus, *Handbook*, 2, 14 (Cambridge, MA: Loeb Classical Library, v. 218, 1985).

11. Epictetus, *Discourses*, III–ii, III–xii.

12. Steven. Covey, *Seven Habits of Highly Effective People* (New York: Free Press, 1989).

13. Epictetus, *Handbook*, 1, 8, 15 v. 218; *Discourses*, IV–viii.

14. Epictetus, *Discourses*, II–xviii.

15. William James, *Principles of Psychology* (Eastford, CT: Martino Fine books, 2010).

16. Epictetus, *Discourses*, I–xx, I–xxviii, II–xviii; *Handbook*, 1.

17. Epictetus, *Handbook*, 8, 15; *Discourses*, III–xxiv.

18. B. A. Alford & Aaron Beck, *The Integrative Power of Cognitive Therapy* (New York: Guilford Press, 1998).

19. Mathew McKay, Martha Davis & Patrick Fanning, *Messages: The Communication Skills Handbook (2nd Ed.)* (Oakland, CA: New Harbinger Publications, 1985).

20. Lonergan, *Insight*, esp. 250–268.

21. American Psychological Association, *APA Dictionary of Psychology (2nd ed.)*. (Washington, DC: American Psychological Association, 2015), 97.

22. McKay, David and Associates. *Messages*, ch. 6.

23. Epictetus, *Discourses*, III–iii, III–xxiv.

24. Ibid. II–ii.

25. Ibid. II–ii, II–iii.

26. Ibid. II–ii, II–xi.

27. Ibid. II–ii, II–iii, II–xvii, II–xxii.

28. Ibid. II–xix, III–ix, III–x.

29. Ibid. II–xix, II–xxii, III–xvii, IV–ii.

30. Ibid. III–ix, III–x.

31. Epictetus, *Handbook*, 5; *Discourses*, II–xvi, III–xix, IV–I, IV–iv.

32. Leon Festinger, *A Theory of Cognitive Dissonance* (Stanford, CA: Stanford University Press, 1957).

33. *APA Dictionary of Psychology*, 203.

34. Epictetus, *Handbook*, 3, 5; *Discourses*, III–xxiv.

35. Ibid. 4; *Discourses*, III–xv.

36. Ibid. 20, 22; *Discourses*, IV–i.
37. Epictetus, *Discourses*, I–i, I–iv, III–ii, III–xii, IV–x; *Handbook*, 14, 31, 35.
38. Ibid. II–i, IV–I.
39. Ibid. IV–i.
40. Ibid. III–xv.
41. Epictetus, *Handbook*, 4, 35.
42. Epictetus, *Discourses*, I–vii, I–xvii, I–xxviii, II–xi, III–ix.
43. Horney, *Neurosis and Human Growth*.
44. Epictetus, *Discourses*, II–i, IV–I; Victor Salva (director), *Peaceful Warrior* (Los Angeles, CA: DEJ Productions, 2006).
45. Covey, *Seven Habits of Highly Effective People*.
46. Epictetus, *Discourses*, IV–iv; Albert Ellis, *How to Stubbornly Refuse to Make Yourself Miserable About Anything. Yes, Anything!* (New York: Citadel Press, 1988).
47. Robert Wise (director), *The Day the Earth Stood Still* (Hollywood, CA: 20th Century Fox, 1951).
48. Epictetus, *Discourses*, II–xxiii; III–xxiv.
49. Epictetus, *Handbook*, 48, 51; *Discourses*, II–i, II–ii, II–xvi, II–xviii; II–xiv; III–xii, III–xiv, III–xxiv; IV–iv, IV–vii, IV–xi.
50. Ellis, *How To Stubbornly Refuse*.
51. On managing judgment: Epictetus, *Discourses*, III, IV. On managing choices: Epictetus, *Discourses*, IV.
52. Epictetus, *Discourses*, IV–viii.
53. Epictetus, *Handbook*, 20, 22; *Discourses*, II–xii.
54. Edwin Locke and Gary Latham, "Work motivation and satisfaction," in *Psychological Science*, 1(4), 1990, 240–246; James Prochaska, *Changing for Good: A Revolutionary Six-Stage Program for Overcoming Bad Habits and Moving Your Life Positively Forward* (New York City: William Morrow, 2007).
55. Edwin Locke and Gary Latham, "Work Motivation and Satisfaction." *Psychological Science*, 1(4), 1990, 240–246.
56. Martin Marshall and Associates, "Promotion of Improvement as a Science." *Lancet*, 381(Feb 2), 2013, 381–421.
57. Immanuel Kant, *Critique of Pure Reason*, trans. Norman Kemp Smith (New York: Palgrave-Macmillan, 1781/2003).
58. Robert Gagné, *Conditions of Learning* (New York: Holt, Rinehart and Winston, 1965).
59. Herbert Simon and Alan Newall. *Human Problem Solving* (Englewood Cliffs, NJ: Prentice-Hall, 1972); Lorin Anderson, David Krathwohl and Associates, *A Taxonomy for Learning, teaching and Assessing: A Revision of Bloom's taxonomy of Educational Objectives* (New York: Pearson, 2000).
60. Edwin Locke and Gary Latham. "Building a Practically Useful Theory of Goal Setting and Task Motivation." *American Psychologist*, 3(9), 2002, 705–717.
61. Martin Marshall and Associates. "Promotion of Improvement as a Science."
62. Roy Baumeister & Kathleen Vohs, eds., *Handbook of Self-Regulation: Research, Theory, and Applications* (New York: Guilford Press, 2006); D. Schucnk

and B. Zimmerman, *Self-Regulation of Learning and Performance: Issues and Educational Applications* (Mahwah, NJ: Lawrence Erlbaum, 1994).

63. *Handbook of Self-Regulation: Research, Theory and Applications.*

64. Locke and Latham, "Building a Practically Useful Theory of Goal Setting and Task Motivation." 711–712.

Epilogue
Problem Solving as Mindful Practice

SUMMARY REMARKS ON TRANSFORMATIVE PROBLEM SOLVING: INTRODUCTION

This book has been a series of reflections on what it really means to attempt to solve problems and achieve complex human learning. It concerns what many are capable of doing, although they may not typically do it. It concerns what can be achieved if one has the desire to know and a concomitant desire to grow. These reflections approached the mental events of problem solving by addressing six aims: (1) to identify and distinguish some basic facts of consciousness, (2) to describe some aspects of the experience of each fact of consciousness, (3) to place these facts of consciousness in an explanatory and functional relation with one another as these exist in distinct patterns of problem solving, (4) to identify possible interferences with cognitive functioning and describe how they work, (5) to describe a mode of pause from problem solving, and (6) to describe some larger contexts in which the patterns of problem solving and the mode of pause function.

As indicated in the Introduction, this book may assist readers in two ways. First, it should facilitate attaining a special type of self-knowledge. This would be knowledge of the acts, operations, and processes involved in one's own problem solving efforts. Second, it should offer some guidance in self-management, allowing the reader to put this knowledge to use by better coordinating the mental events which enable human problem solving. With this self-knowledge and self-management one is positioned to develop a "learning personality," which is a habitual approach to problem situations; a learning personality is focused on problem solving and the constructive change it invites. This habitual approach becomes a form of mindful practice. In contrast, without this kind of self-knowledge, future problem solving is likely to remain a hit-or-miss affair. Without a related self-management, the self-knowledge will be ineffective.

It turns out that the facts of consciousness coalesce into an iterative cycle of learning that spirals through experiencing, understanding, judging, and deciding. They also include the specific mental acts and operations by which each pattern of problem solving proceeds and which have been examined in chapters 2 and 3. It is the attention to all these details that is designed to increase self-knowledge and the effective self-regulation of learning and freedom that goes with it. Attention to and regulation of these key mental events result in transformative problem solving. "Transformative problem solving" is a form of complex and comprehensive human learning that is attentive to experience, deeply insightful, supported by evidence, guided by time-tested values, and transformative of situations and self. It is not simply stimulus-response learning, or concept attainment, or information transfer.

In addition, the mental events of transformative problem solving are either instantaneous acts or operations that are extended over time. These events are invisible and not sensible in any way. Moreover, they are best described in temporal rather than spatial terms: they have a clear beginning and end. They naturally coalesce into patterns of problem solving that may be regarded as cognitive processes: seeking understanding, judging facts, judging values and deciding. In addition, there is a mode of consciousness, basic experiencing, in which no problem solving activity of any kind is present. Experiencing can function as source and resource for learning, a testing ground for possible solutions and as a haven from the work of learning itself.

The patterns of problem solving (involving acts, operations, and processes) occur over time, and therefore they may be subject to interference. Such interference may come from disruptions within the learner or through interruptions from the environment.

We learn significantly more about ourselves by learning about the four patterns of problem solving and about how we pause from them. This very specific kind of self-knowledge may also facilitate our work with others because of our common humanity. Hence, teaching, counseling, consulting, and any human service discipline or social enterprise may become a matter of facilitating the occurrence of relevant mental events in others. No one can experience these events for another person, but, in the spirit of Socrates, we may be able to assist their emergence in others.

Whatever has been discussed in this book will have no lasting effect unless it is put to use. Moreover, it must be put to use on a consistent basis so as to form habits of problem solving and to establish what may be called the mindful practice of a learning personality.

RECAPITULATION OF MAJOR THEMES OF CHAPTERS 1–6

More specifically, chapter 1 presents an overview of four patterns of problem solving that are involved in any attempts at comprehensive learning. Going through each pattern is not an easy process. Philosopher Bernard Lonergan expressed it this way:

> To learn thoroughly is a vast undertaking that calls for relentless perseverance. To strike out on a new line and become more than a weekend celebrity calls for years in which one's living is more or less constantly absorbed in the effort to understand, in which one's understanding gradually works round and up a spiral of viewpoints with each complementing its predecessor and only the last embracing the whole field to be mastered.[1]

The central themes of chapter 1 are as follows: (1) The patterns of problem solving are integrated groupings of mental events. (2) The patterns of problem solving are related to one another functionally. (3) The patterns of problem solving are not developmental stages. (4) The desire to know is crucial to the operation of all the patterns of problem solving. (5) Engaging in the patterns of problem solving has immediate, medium-term, and long-term effects. Let us examine these claims more closely.

First, the patterns of problem solving are integrated groupings of mental events. Each pattern works to achieve a specific purpose. The events may be instantaneous or extended across time. The events may be in our control or not. It saves time to focus learning on what is in our control, and it creates more realistic attitudes for what is not in our control. The patterns are differentiated by guiding intention, end-products, and elementary acts and operations. The aim of chapter 1 is to provide an overview of problem solving in its component parts and patterns.

Second, the patterns of problem solving are related to one another functionally. The processes of experiencing, understanding, judging, and deciding are related through what is known as sublation. "Sublation" is a process whereby new goals and new operations are introduced, without negating the work of previous patterns.[2] More specifically, Problem Solving Pattern 1 (Seeking Understanding) presupposes and uses the materials presented by experiencing. This pattern does not interfere with or destroy experiencing, but adds to it by considering possibilities and making experiences understandable. Problem Solving Patterns 2 and 3 (Factual Critical Thinking and Values-oriented Critical Thinking) presuppose the multiple possibilities presented by Pattern 1. However, these patterns do not interfere with or destroy the work of Pattern 1, but they add to it by subjecting the possibilities of

Pattern 1 to further tests of truth (Pattern 2) and worth (Pattern 3). Problem Solving Pattern 4 (Deliberative Critical Thinking) presupposes and uses what has gone before: the presentations of experience, the possibilities of Pattern 1, the judgments of Patterns 2 and 3. Pattern 4 does not interfere with or destroy the work of prior processes.

Because the patterns of problem solving are related in this way by sublation, it is generally not a good idea to ignore any one of them. However, individuals, in their varied learning response styles, often do just that. Some individuals overlearn the activities Problem Solving Pattern 1 (Seeking Understanding). There may be any number of reasons for this overlearning: a fascination with the large number of possibilities involved, an experience of a kind of freedom to explore, the ease with which possibilities arise. However, individuals who overlearn Pattern 1 tend to neglect the functions and purposes of the other patterns of problem solving. So it is with each pattern, as discussed in chapter 3.

Third, the patterns of problem solving are not developmental stages. A "developmental stage" can be described as a relatively discrete period of time, in the development of an individual, in which functioning is qualitatively different from functioning during other periods. The period of time mentioned usually spans a number of months or years. Also, when a later stage emerges, previous stages are abandoned. The work of Jean Piaget and Eric Ericson are classic examples of stage theories in the area of intellectual and personality development respectively. In contrast, individuals can shift in and out of the patterns of problem solving as the need arises.

Fourth, the desire to know is crucial to the operation of all patterns of problem solving. (1) It is playful in the sense of letting things unfold. It is tolerant of uncertainty and of not knowing as learning proceeds. It is the essence of the Socratic attitude. (2) It is not compulsive, demanding, or commanding, especially about how learning is to proceed or about what the products of learning must be. Ideologies are excluded. (3) It is a desire to "get things right." As such, it excludes deception by self and others, and it highlights the eventual and inevitable importance of critical thinking.

Fifth, engaging in the patterns of problem solving has immediate, medium-term, and long-term effects. These effects not only serve to change the problem situation by illuminating it in all its complexity, but they also change the problem solver. Individuals become more experienced, insightful, knowledgeable, and skillful in the process of practicing the patterns of problem solving, and long-term effects of a habitually changed personality begin to appear.

Chapter 2 argues that achieving understanding is not a simple or easy state to achieve; in contrast, it is a multifaceted process that can easily go wrong. More specifically, chapter 2 described Problem Solving Pattern 1 (Seeking

Understanding). The guiding intention of this pattern is to grasp a preliminary understanding of what might be happening in a problem situation. For example, railroad investigators arriving at the scene of a train wreck seek to gain a preliminary understanding of what happened there. They proceed through mental events such as multiple questions for understanding and insights about the accident scene. Sometimes there are "inverse insights" that indicate that there is something wrong with the questions themselves, and so they need to pursue better formulated questions. Their work terminates in a preliminary narrative that answers most questions arising out of the accident. Quality is assured in this pattern if all further relevant questions are carefully pursued and if all likely hypotheses are investigated. Things go wrong if and when relevant questions are ignored and relevant hypotheses are not examined. There are three goals of this chapter. (1) It explores the process of Seeking Understanding in concrete detail. The specific acts and operations associated with this pattern of problem solving are identified, described, and then related functionally to one another in a sequenced pattern. (2) In consequence it promotes an understanding of our own capability to understand anything by introducing quality assurance checks to our own thinking. (3) It identifies some practical steps that can be taken to solidify this knowledge and make it part of a habitual approach to learning and problem solving. In terms of more concrete objectives, by the end of the chapter the reader should be able to (1) compare and contrast the component acts and operations of Process 1 and (2) provide examples of the component acts and operations of Process 1 from personal experience as well as the reported experience of others.

If individuals value their own ability to seek understanding then they attend to it, cultivate it and employ it. Specifically, they will make note of their recurrent questions and adopt a plan to systematically pursue them and keep track of progress. They will actively pursue questions and wait for insights to arrive. They will record both when they are present. Sometimes, they will have an inverse insight that their questions are on the wrong track—formulated with unnecessary vagueness or based on a falsehood. They will value clarity and precision in what they think. They will value and follow the desire to know. They will look for these qualities in others, and will view with caution those who do not possess them. In contrast, if individuals do not value their own ability to seek understanding, then they will not bother much about questions at all. They will neglect the desire to know and follow other pursuits. They will not be disturbed if they engage in sloppy thinking and inhabit a world of epidemic vagueness. They will concede to others the work of posing questions.

Chapter 3 argues that there are three types of critical thinking: Factual Critical Thinking (Pattern 2), Values-oriented Critical Thinking (Pattern 3), and Deliberative Critical Thinking (Pattern 4). Chapter 3 also argues that each type of critical thinking acts as a distinctive filter for the possibilities presented in Pattern 1. This chapter has three related aims: (1) to invite readers to reflect on the thought processes they routinely use when they seriously attempt to solve problems, (2) to clarify what is meant by "critical thinking," and (3) to describe in detail the three distinct types of critical thinking and the processes associated with them. Some comments can be made on each of these goals.

Chapter 3 describes Problem Solving Pattern 2 (Factual Critical Thinking). The guiding intention of this pattern is to answer a reflective question of fact and to determine whether or not a specified possibility is correct. For example, of all the possible explanations of a train crash, which one is correct? The filter here is one of truth and falsity. Pattern 2 proceeds through mental events such as the reflective question of fact, collecting and weighing evidence, and the reflective factual insight. Pattern 2 terminates in a judgment of fact as its end-product. Quality is assured in this pattern if its mental events unfold under the desire to know. Things go wrong if and when key mental events are left out, or if the process is guided by any emotion or concern other than the desire to know.

For persons who value their own ability to judge facts, they attend to it, cultivate it, and employ it. In particular, they will attend to it if they have a desire to know and if they value truth, versus some beautiful or convenient illusion. They will cultivate this ability in areas of interest and will map out a landscape of knowledge and ignorance and raise appropriate factual reflective questions. They will employ this ability by the practice of making modest judgments based on evidence, and by avoiding the errors of lack of clarity, overgeneralization, under-generalization, rash judgment, and judgment avoidance. Actual learning will be more important to them than "winning arguments" and appearing right in the estimation of others. They will look for these qualities in others and will view with caution those who do not possess them. In contrast, for persons who do not value their own ability to correctly judge facts, they do not attend to it, they neglect it, and do not make the most of it. Appearing correct to others and winning arguments will be more important to them than actual learning. They often inhabit a world of dueling conclusions and clashing egos.

Chapter 3 also describes Problem Solving Pattern 3 (Values-oriented Critical Thinking). The guiding intention of this pattern is to answer a reflective question of value and to determine whether or not a specified possibility or fact is worthwhile. The filter here is one of value or disvalue. For example, a manufacturer seeks to purchase the most efficient new technology as part of his production process. Careful reflection about any potential purchase will proceed through mental events such as the reflective question of value, collecting and weighing reasons and evidence, and the reflective values insight.

Pattern 3 terminates in a judgment of value as end-product: "Yes, product X would be useful for us" or "No, product X is not useful for us." Quality is assured in this pattern if the mental events of this pattern unfold under the desire to know. Things go wrong if and when key mental events are left out, or if the process is guided by any emotion or concern other than the desire to know.

Some persons value their own ability to judge values. They attend to this ability, cultivate it, and employ it. They attend to it by identifying what they value and making a record of that for further study. They cultivate the ability by discerning a scale of values embedded in the history of their value judgments. They employ the ability by making modest judgments of value based on reasons and evidence, and by avoiding the errors of lack of clarity, rash judgment, and judgment avoidance. They look for these qualities in others, and will view with caution those who do not possess them. In contrast, there are those who do not value their own ability to judge values. They do not attend to it; they neglect it and do not make the most of it. For them, their judgments are best, no matter how badly they are made, or they will practice a submission to the expressed value judgments of others.

Finally, chapter 3 also describes Problem Solving Pattern 4 (Deliberative Critical Thinking). The guiding intention of this pattern is to answer a reflective question of deliberation and to determine whether or not a specified course of action is worthy of being engaged or refused. The filter here pertains to whether or not a specific possibility is to be imported or exported from one's life. Embedded within every decision is a trajectory of growth, remaining stationary or decline. For example, a college student is faced with the decision to accept a job in a big city or a small town. Careful deliberation about any potential job choice will proceed through mental events such as the reflective deliberative question, collecting and weighing reasons and evidence, and the reflective deliberative insight. Pattern 4 terminates in a decision as end-product: "Yes, I choose the job in a big city." or "No, I reject the big city job." Quality is assured in this pattern if the mental events of this pattern unfold under the desire to know. Things go wrong if and when key mental events are left out, or if the process is guided by any emotion or concern other than the desire to know.

Anyone who values the ability to responsibly decide pays attention to it, cultivates it, and employs it as needed. They attend to it by recalling the major decisions of life and making a record of that for further study. They cultivate it by discerning a scale of values embedded in the history of their decisions. They employ it by making responsible decisions based on reasons and evidence, and by avoiding the errors of impulsivity and indecision. They focus on what is in their control or possible influence, and leave aside what is not. They value practical solutions over getting credit. Finally, in focusing on what is in their control, they act responsibly by adjusting their decisions and actions to their ever-increasing knowledge. Here also, they will look for these qualities in others, and will view with caution those who do not possess them. In contrast, there are many who do not value their own ability to responsibly decide. They do not attend to this ability, they neglect it, and they do not make the most of it. Their actions are more a matter of being triggered, defense mechanisms, behavior shaping, and suggestion. They value getting credit more than they value practical solutions to any problem. They do not distinguish what is in their control versus what is not. They irresponsibly adjust their judgments to conform to the actions they prefer.

Figure E.1 compares the mental events involved in each type of critical thinking. Some of these are instantaneous acts, others are discursive processes. The three types of critical thinking are compared in terms of these elementary conscious acts, operations, and events.

Each of the cognitive acts and operations discussed above has a distinct function within the sequence. To eliminate or avoid that function will be to

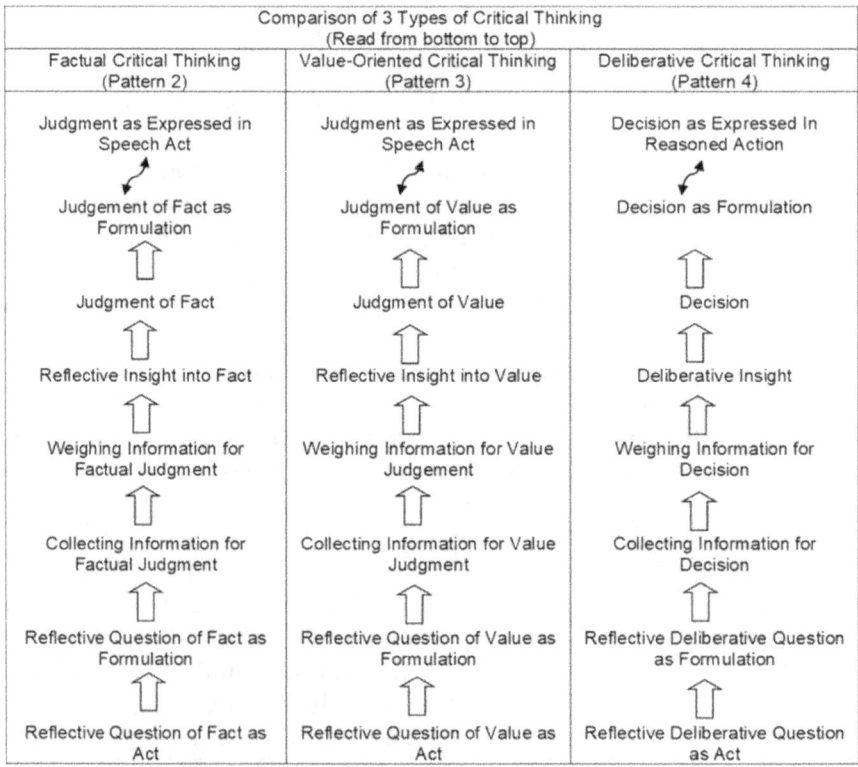

Figure E.1 Comparison of Three Types of Critical Thinking.

disrupt the process of critical thinking. Moreover, of all of these acts and operations, questions, insights, and the desire to know play central roles. The question functions as an operator for each pattern if it is pursued. That pursuit will happen only if there is a sustained desire to know. The insights function as an integrator, bringing prior elements together in a comprehensive grasp.

Moreover, while questions may be under our control, sometimes they are not and they burst into consciousness unbidden. In contrast, insights are not directly under our control, although we can set up conditions to facilitate them. When mental events are not under our control, we are more passive in relation to their occurrence. When mental events are under our control, we are more active regarding them by taking action to follow up on them.

Chapter 4 argues that there are three broad functions to "experiencing": (1) source and resource for learning, (2) testing ground for learning, and (3) pause from learning. Chapter 4 also argues that we can pause from the work of learning in at least three ways: return to habitual routines, aesthetic absorption, and the practices of tranquil abiding. This chapter offers a structure for understanding "experience," in its multiple conceptions, in relation to human learning and problem solving. More specifically, it has three related aims: (1) to explore the basic roles of experience in complex human learning: source and resource, testing ground and pause, (2) to explore how non-problem-solving experience gets organized, and (3) to identify implications with some recommendations for making the most out of experience.

If individuals value their own experience they attend to it, cultivate it, and employ it. They will notice what draws their attention and where and with whom they spend time. Insofar as they can, they will actively choose experiences wisely. They will be in a position to make the most out of it. They will pay attention to those who value their own experience and encourage others to do the same. They will view with caution those who dismiss anyone's experience, without really considering it, or who routinely attempt to draw attention away from it. In contrast, if individuals do not value their own experience, they do not attend to it, neglect it, and do not make the most of it. They are free of any burden of managing it. They will be in a position to waste it. They will be more available to be swayed by others.

Chapter 5 argues that problem solving occurs within the larger contexts of personality, social relations, culture, and history. The chapter indicates how we are affected by each of these larger contexts, and how we can each make our contribution to these larger contexts. The following two objectives are set out in chapter 5. (1) There is an examination of how the larger contexts of personality, social trust, culture, and history can influence learning and problem solving. (2) There is an examination of how an individual's or small group's learning and problem solving influence the larger contexts.

While all of these contexts are important, those of personality and social trust are closest to the problem solver. Activities in effective problem solving groups will be organized around questions, insights, the desire to know of its members, and social trust. Multiple individuals will be working on the same problem: collectively examining data, raising questions about it and having insights, recording intellectual progress on the problem, formulating and testing the insights, and coming to joint conclusions and actions. When group members make judgments and decisions they will be evidence-based and free of vagueness and overgeneralization. Investigative teams for the National Transportation Safety Board provide examples of this sort of group.

Problem solving groups go wrong when they are biased by some preestablished ideology, when the desire to know is not dominant, when groupthink prevails, and when alternative viewpoints are not taken seriously. In short, these groups fail in quality control when the patterns of problem solving do not unfold as guided by the desire to know, and when they are disrupted or disturbed or eliminated. Defective problem solving groups generally do two things: they claim to be working on a problem but they also are working on a political or financial agenda. They may reach a problem solution, but only after and to the extent that the pre-set agenda is served first. The desire to know is not first.

Chapter 6 offers two illustrative examples of how other thinkers have independently discovered and used the facts of consciousness described in this book. The first example is the ancient philosopher Epictetus; the second example is the High Performance Cycle of psychologists Edwin Locke and Gary Latham. The chapter also provides a model for those who may be interested in identifying the facts of consciousness in the work of others. The following two objectives appear in chapter 6: (1) There is a presentation of the basic doctrines of Epictetus regarding impressions, managing impressions, judging, and choosing. (2) There is an examination of the High Performance Cycle with its antecedents, mediating mechanisms, moderating conditions, and consequences.

CLARIFICATION BY CONTRAST

The view of problem solving and complex human learning presented in this book contrasts markedly other viewpoints. This book was written because recent pervasive attitudes and approaches to learning and problem solving have only focused on some facts of consciousness to the neglect of others, and few have attempted to place all in an explanatory account that relates them to each other. More specifically, it should be noted that (1) Question and insight are very important among the facts of consciousness. Questions move learning forward by identifying gaps that need to be addressed. Insights provide a unifying synthesis that illuminates the viable answers. Both question and insight are central to complex human learning and any effort at problem solving. (2) Questions and insights naturally organize themselves into four patterns of problem solving and a mode of pause from the work of problem solving. (3) Since problem solving often requires perseverance, the role of the desire to know is crucial. (4) Since problem solving often occurs as part of problem solving groups, social trust is also an important fact of consciousness. (5) Knowledge of the facts of consciousness and their related patterns can provide a blueprint for all past, present, and future problem solving and complex human learning.

Other presentations of problem solving and complex learning often ignore, confuse, or conflate the facts of consciousness. They emerge mainly from the disciplines of philosophy and psychology.

Some accounts of learning and problem solving ignore the facts of consciousness. Examples from psychology would include the radical behaviorism of B.F. Skinner and John B. Watson.[3] In this view, mental events are simply banished, either because supposedly they do not exist or they are not regarded as acceptable data for a science of psychology. In philosophy, John Locke's (1967/1690) *Essay Concerning Human Understanding* and David Hume's (1951/1751) *Enquiry Concerning Human Understanding* were both designed to examine human understanding and the kinds of processes that result in this understanding.[4] Yet in these classic works of modern Western philosophy the mental event of insight is not considered in any detail, either descriptively or in an explanatory context. Moreover, the process of questioning is simply overlooked. These authors were very intelligent people who themselves were on a quest for understanding. They were in fact asking questions. However, perhaps that fact was so close to them that they did not "get it." Another example also comes from philosophy in Gilbert Ryle's 1949 classic *The Concept of Mind*.[5] While this work did provide a rather complete list of the cognitive operations that make up the everyday activities of mind, facts of consciousness such as insight, questioning, desire to know, and social trust are neither mentioned nor described.

While all of these accounts eclipse question and insight, they also fail to emphasize distinct groupings of mental events guided by distinct intentions; here, these groupings of mental events have been named patterns of problem solving. In addition, these accounts fail to highlight learning as a self-correcting process that incorporates feedback. Finally, they provide little insight into social trust and problem solving groups.

Other accounts of learning and problem solving confuse the facts of consciousness. Confusion suggests the lack of clear and useful definitions of terms. For example, chapter 4 has identified distinct meanings for the word "experience." If they are confused with one another then any claim that knowledge is based on experience, or that a particular person is experienced has no clear meaning. As another example, from philosophy various definitions of judgment are offered, but they are often confused with the account presented in chapter 3. There is also confusion about "responsibility." In the discussion of Pattern 4 in chapter 3, responsibility is presented as an ongoing adjustment of our actions to ever expanding knowledge of fact and value. It is certainly not the adjustment of our judgments to our currently favored actions. Nor is it the simplistic account that it is the "ability to respond."[6] If the "ability to respond" definition were useful, then an oyster would have responsibility.

Some forms of applied psychology have identified a desire for confusion and a flight from understanding that is designed to maintain a status quo and to reduce anxiety.[7] Individuals engaged in this flight have a vested interest in not knowing about specific aspects of their own lives. Instead, they prefer to drift as in a fog.

Still other accounts conflate the facts of consciousness with each other. "Conflation" in this context is the substitution of one mental event for another, or the merging of two distinct mental events into one. Three examples are presented here. One common conflation is merging experiencing with understanding. The expectation here is that because someone has experienced something, they will understand it. But general experience is one thing, getting an insight into it is quite another matter. A second common conflation merges experiencing with knowledge. If knowledge is a matter of experiencing, understanding, and correct judgment, then it cannot be identified with experiencing alone. As one grows in knowledge, however, the processes involved in learning may be forgotten, and in retrospect one may simplify and mis-remember learning as experiencing alone. A third common conflation is to merge understanding with judgment. In this conflation, a person who has an insight affirms immediately that it is true, bypassing the work of critical thinking (Patterns 2 and 3). They fail to grasp that the insights of Pattern 1 are only possibilities. Another form of conflation is to fail to distinguish between judgments of fact and judgments of value. Anyone who makes this conflation will have a difficult time affirming facts without tacking on a value judgment. Their first response is to assert a value judgment, often without bothering to get the facts right.

ADDITIONAL CONSIDERATIONS: IMPLICATIONS

In light of this chapter, implications are presented as a list with three aims. First, the list recapitulates the main points developed in our discussion of transformative problem solving. Second, it encourages readers to mindfully practice the patterns and modes associated with transformative problem solving. Third, it invites readers to adopt a Socratic attitude of bearing witness to personal experience, and making a series of judgments about themselves as problem solvers. In sum, these aims work to facilitate greater self-knowledge and self-appropriation. To stress the transformative aspect of authentic problem solving and to emphasize its personal nature, the list is mainly written in first-person language.

1) I am a questioner.
2) Because of limited time and energy I can pursue questions in some areas of interest, but I cannot pursue all questions.
3) Sometimes, my questions are defective—based on unclear or false assumptions. I need to reformulate them.
4) When it comes to questioning, I rely on the credible work of others.
5) I am insightful. Although the appearance of insights is sporadic and beyond my control, I remain open and receptive to them as they appear.
6) Because of limited time and energy, I can pursue insights in some, but not all, areas of interest.
7) Although I am insightful, I do not have insights into everything. My insights are limited in their number and quality.
8) I also rely on the credible insight of others.
9) I am a judge of fact.
10) Because of limited time and energy, I can judge facts well in some areas of interest, but not all.
11) I also rely on the credible factual judgments of others.
12) Because I have a history of judging facts, there is a track record in this area that can be examined.
13) If I have a desire to know, I am willing to revisit my factual judgments.
14) On examination, some of my key factual judgments about self, others, or the world will be true.
15) I can reaffirm judgments of fact that are true.
16) On examination, some of my key factual judgments about self, others, or the world will be false.
17) I can deny judgments of fact that are false.
18) I am a judge of value.
19) Because of limited time and energy, I can judge values well in some areas of interest, but not all.
20) I also rely on the credible value judgments of others.
21) Because I have a history of judging values, there is also a track record in this area that can be examined.
22) If I have a desire to know, I am willing to revisit my value judgments.

23) Because I have a history of judging values, my value judgments contain at least an implicit scale of values.
24) On examination, some of my key value judgments about self, others, and the world will stand the test of time and not be reversed.
25) I can re-approve my judgments of value that withstand reversal over time.
26) On examination, some of my key value judgments about self, others, or the world will be reversed in time with good reason.
27) I can disapprove of my prior judgments of value that call for reversal over time.
28) I am a decider.
29) Because of limited time and energy I can make well-founded decisions in some areas.
30) In decision making, I am also fallible.
31) I also rely on facts and values as reported by others in making decisions.
32) Because I have a history of making decisions, there is also a track record in this area.
33) If I have a desire to know, I am willing to revisit my decisions.
34) On examination, some of my key decisions about self, others, or the world will stand the test of time and not be reversed.
35) I can re-endorse those decisions that stand the test of time and resolve that I would do it again.
36) On examination, some of my key decisions about self, others, and the world will lead to regret and would be reversed if I could.
37) I can refuse to endorse those decisions that did not work well over time and I can indicate that I would not do it again.
38) I can improve. Because parts of experiencing, understanding, judging, and deciding are under my control, I can regulate what is in my control and thereby improve my overall performance as an attentive, insightful, reasonable, responsible, enthusiastic problem solver. To the extent that I continue to do this, I am developing habits, which are long-term effects of my efforts. To the extent that I do this, I am engaged in mindful practice.
39) My learning through experiencing, understanding, judging, and deciding changes me as a person. In the long run, if I choose, I can develop a "learning personality." I can become someone who gives a central place to learning in all aspects of life.
40) If what I have learned about my problem solving and learning is useful for me, it may be useful for others.
41) To the extent that the problem solving and learning of others occasionally involves the desire to know, questions, insights, social trust, and the other facts of consciousness, then their learning experience may be similar to mine.

42) I occasionally participate in problem solving groups.
43) What I have learned about my problem solving and learning is useful for identifying, classifying, and studying learning and teaching interventions.
44) What I have learned about my problem solving and learning is useful for teaching problem solving, self-directed learning, and meta-cognition to others.[8]
45) What I have learned about my problem solving and learning is useful for counseling, consulting, other human service work, and many other social enterprises.
46) To the extent that various environments are associated with various knowledge claims, I can exercise my own skills in the patterns of problem solving with regard to those claims.

SUMMARY

What kind of world is revealed by the patterns of problem solving and basic experiencing described in this book? Basic experiencing reveals a world of data, impressions, and established habitual routines. It also reveals whether or not a reader has made use of the resources of rest available through aesthetic absorption and tranquil abiding. Problem Solving Pattern 1 (Seeking Understanding) reveals a world that is meaningful, understandable, and intelligible through the process of asking and answering questions. Problem Solving Pattern 2 (Factual Critical Thinking) reveals a world of facts and errors. Problem Solving Pattern 3 (Values-oriented Critical Thinking) reveals a world populated by what is valuable and what is not. Problem Solving Pattern 4 (Deliberative Critical Thinking) reveals a world in which decision and action enable personal input to the twists and turns presented in life.

Establishing or reinforcing a learning personality would be the major long-term effect for readers of this book, if they choose it. As indicated, a "learning personality" is an individual who is routinely attentive to experience, deeply insightful, reasonable in making sound judgments of fact and value, and responsible in action. This "responsibility" is not the mere "ability to respond" of some writers,[9] but it is the ever-refined adjustment of action to the expanding development of knowledge of fact and value.[10] To the extent that I am developing a learning personality I am engaging in a mindful practice and a way of life. Such individuals are skillful in recognizing their own conscious states and processes and in habitually putting that self-knowledge to use for greater personal effectiveness and freedom.[11] By engaging in this mindful practice they take steps toward partial self-appropriation. For any new problem, they would ask, "What would a learning personality do in this situation?"

Another question a learning personality would ask is, "Given my talents and abilities and limited time and energy, what is it that I can uniquely do in life with attentiveness, intelligence, reason, responsibility and enthusiasm?" If anyone values their time and unique talents, then they can practice four interventions to develop a learning personality. First, they can reconnect with the desire to know. It existed at three years of age. Second, they can make appropriate opportunities to explore and study and to pause and rest from problem solving. Third, they can associate with those who promote and practice authentic transformative learning and problem solving, and avoid those who do not. Finally, they can make an effort to improve their own personal habits, maintaining what is beneficial to growth and replacing what interferes with growth. This includes not only habits of behavior but also habits of thought and emotion. They will have achieved a change in disposition that social psychologist M. Csiksentmihalyi describes in this way: "People who learn to control inner experience will be able to determine the quality of their lives, which is as close as any of us can come to being happy."[12]

In contrast, those who do not care about either their time or unique talents will ignore all of the above and continue to waste time, drift, and pursue mediocrity.

NOTES

1. Bernard Lonergan. *Insight: A Study of Human Understanding* (Toronto: University of Toronto Press, 1992, 210).

2. For an elaboration of some history of sublation, see Patrick Byrne. Consciousness: Levels, sublations and the subject as subject. *Method*, 13(2), 1995, 131–150; Bernard Lonergan. "Cognitional structure." In *Collected Works of Bernard Lonergan V. 4: Collection* (Toronto: University of Toronto Press, 1967/1993); Mark Morelli. "Beyond the Metaphor of levels of Consciousness: Appropriation of Sublative Transformations." *Method*, 9(2), 2018, 47–74.

3. John B. Watson. *Behaviorism* (Chicago: University of Chicago Press, 1930); B.F. Skinner. *Science and Human Behavior* (New York: Simon & Schuster, 1953).

4. John Locke. *Essay Concerning Human Understanding* (London: Oxford University Press, 1967/1690); David Hume. *Enquiry Concerning Human Understanding* (London: Oxford, 1951/1751).

5. Gilbert Ryle. *The Concept of Mind* (New York: Barnes & Noble, 1949).

6. Fritz Perls. *Gestalt Therapy Verbatim* (Lafayette, CA: Real People Press, 1969); Stephen Covey. *Seven Habits of Highly Effective People* (New York: Simon & Schuster, 1989).

7. For example, see Karen Horney. *Neurosis and Human Growth: The Struggle Toward Self-Realization* (New York: W.W. Norton, 1950/1990), Ch. 7; Bernard Lonergan. *Insight*, Ch. 7.

8. Mervin Lynch. "Some Effects of Applications of Metacognitive Monitoring Skills on Frequency of Error Detection." *Journal for the Adavncement of Educational Research*, 3(1), 2007, 60–66; M. Marquardt. *Organizing the Power of Active Learning: Solving Problems and Building Leaders in Real Time* (Mountain View, CA: Davies Black, 2004).

9. Fritz Perls. *Gestalt Therapy Verbatim* (Lafayette, CA: Real People Press, 1969); Stephen Covey. *Seven Habits of Highly Effective People* (New York: Simon & Schuster, 1989).

10. Lonergan. *Insight.* 642.

11. Schwartz, Tony and McCarthy, Catherine. "Manage Your Energy, Not Your Time." *Harvard Business Review* 2007, October, 61–78.

12. Mihalyi Csikzentmihalyi. *Flow: The Psychology of Optimal Experience* (New York: Harper & Row, 1990), Ch. 1.

Bibliography

Adams, James. *The Care and Feeding of Ideas: A Guide to Encouraging Creativity.* Addison-Wesley, Boston, 1986.

Adams, Marilee. *Change Your Questions—Change Your Life.* Berrett-Koehler Publishers, San Francisco, 2009.

Ainsworth, Mary and Associates. *Patterns of Attachment.* Hillsdale, NJ: Erlbaum, 1978.

Alford, B. A. and Beck, Aaron. *The Integrative Power of Cognitive Therapy.* New York: Guilford Press, 1998.

American Psychiatric Association. *Diagnostic and Statistic Manual of Mental Disorders* (5th ed.). Washington DC: American Psychiatric Association, 2013.

American Psychological Association. *Dictionary of Psychology.* Washington, DC: American Psychological Association, 2015.

Anderson, Lorin and Krathwohl, David. eds. *A Taxonomy for Learning, Teaching and Assessing: A Revision of Bloom's Taxonomy of Educational Objectives.* New York: Longman, 2001.

Aristotle, *De Anima.* Cambridge, MA: Loeb Classical Library, 1964.

Arum, Richard. and Roksa, Josipa. *Academically Adrift: Limited Learning on College Campuses.* Chicago, IL: University of Chicago Press, 2011.

Association for Supervision and Curriculum Development, *Educational Leadership*, 67(5), 2010.

Baron, Jonathan. *Thinking and Deciding* (2nded.). Cambridge, UK: Cambridge University Press, 1998

Baumeister, Roy and Vohs, Kathleen. (eds.) *Handbook of Self-Regulation: Research, Theory, and Applications.* New York: Guilford Press, 2006.

Benaji, Mahzarin and Crowder, Robert. "The Bankruptcy of Everyday Memory." *American Psychologist*, 44 (1989), 1185–1193.

Bensley, D. Alan. "A Brief Guide for Teaching and Assessing Critical Thinking in Psychology." *Psychological Science*, 23, No. 10 (2010), 49–53.

Bloom, Benjamin M, Engelhart, E. Frost, W. Hill, and David. Krathwohl, *Taxonomy of Educational Objectives. Handbook I: Cognitive Domain.* New York: David McKay, 1956.

Brekke, John S. and Associates. "Psychosocial Functioning and Subjective Experience in Schizophrenia." *Schizophrenia Bulletin*, 19, No. *3* (1993), 599–608.

Brentano, Franz. *Psychology from an Empirical Standpoint* (ed. Linda L. McAlister). London: Routledge, 1995, 88–89.

Bromberger, Sylvan. *On What We Know We Don't Know: Explanation, Theory, Linguistics and How Questions Shape Them.* Chicago: University of Chicago Press, 1992.

Bronfenbrenner, Urie. *The Ecology of Human Development: Experiments by Nature and Design.* Cambridge, MA: Harvard University Press, 1979.

Brookhart, Susan. *How to Assess Higher Order Thinking Skills in Your Classroom.* Alexandria, VA: ASCD, 2010.

Bruner, Jerome. *The Process of Education.* Cambridge, MA: Harvard University Press, 1976.

Burger, Edward and Starbird, Michael. *The Five Elements of Effective Thinking.* Princeton, NJ: Princeton University Press, 2012.

Byrne, Patrick. "Consciousness: Levels, Sublations and the Subject as Subject." *Method*, 13, No. 2 (1995), 131–150.

Patrick Byrne. *The Ethics of Discernment: Lonergan's Foundations for Ethics.* Toronto: University of Toronto Press, 2017.

Carter, Craig and Associates. "Behavioral Supply Management: A Taxonomy of Judgment and Decision Making Biases," *International Journal of Physical Distribution and Logistics Management,* 37, No. 8 (2007), 631–669.

Chaiklin, S. "The Zone of Proximal Development in Vygotsky's Analysis of Learning and Instruction." In *Vygotsky's Educational Theory and Practice in Cultural Context*, edited by A. Kozulin, B. Gindis, V. Ageyev, & S. Miller. Cambridge: Cambridge University, 2003, 39–64.

Chaplin, J. P. *Dictionary of Psychology* (2nd ed.).New York: Laurel Books, 1985.

Coleridge, Samuel Taylor. The Friend. *The complete works, v. 2.* New York: Harper & Bros. 1854.

Collingwood, R. G. *The Idea of History.* New York: Oxford University Press, 1994.

Conn, Walter. *The Desiring Self.* New York: Paulist Press, 1998.

Connolly, T. H. Arkes, and K. Hammond, eds. *Judgment and Decision Making: An Interdisciplinary Reader.* Cambridge, UK: Cambridge University Press, 2000.

Costello, R. and Jost, D. (Eds.), *American Collegiate Dictionary* (3rd ed.). Boston: Houghton Mifflin, 1993.

Covey, Steven. *Seven Habits of Highly Effective People.* New York: Free Press, 1989.

Cromwell, Lucy S. *Teaching Critical Thinking in the Arts and Humanities.* Milwaukee, WI: Alverno Productions, 1986.

Csikszentmihalyi, Mihaly. *Flow: The Psychology of Optimal Experience.* New York: Harper Perennial, 1990.

Csikszentmihalyi, Mihalyi and Sawyer, Keith. "Creative Insight: The Social Dimension of a Solitary Moment." *The Nature of Insight.* Cambridge, MA: MIT Press. 329–364.

Cutting, John and Dunne, Francis J. "Subjective Experience of Schizophrenia." *Schizophrenia Bulletin,* 15 No. 2 (1989), 217–231.

Dalai, Lama. *The Universe in a Single Atom: The Convergence of Science and Spirituality.* New York: Morgan Road Books, 2005, 31.

Davidson, Janet. "The Suddenness of Insight." *The Nature of Insight,* 125–156.

Dawes, Robin and Associates. "Clinical vs. Actuarial Judgment." *Science,* 243 (1989), 1668–1674.

DiGiuseppe, Ray. *Workshop on "Treatment of Personality Disorders."* New York: Albert Ellis Institute, 2006.

Duhigg, Charles. *The Power of Habit: Why We Do What We Do in Life and Business.* New York: Random House, 2014.

Ellis, Albert and Harper, Robert. *A New Guide to Rational Living.* Woodland Hills, CA: Wilshire Book Co., 1975.

Ellis, Albert. *How to Stubbornly Refuse to Make Yourself Miserable about anything. Yes, Anything!* New York: Lyle Stuart, 1988.

Ennis, Robert. *Critical Thinking.* Upper Saddle River, NJ: Prentice-Hall, 1996.

Epictetus. *Discourses.* Cambridge, MA: Loeb Classical Library, 1925, 1928.

Erikson, Erik. *Childhood and Society.* New York: W.W. Norton, 1993.

Facione, Peter. *Critical Thinking: What It Is and Why It Counts.* Millbrae, CA: Insight Publishing, 2006.

Feuerstein, Reuven and Associates. *Dynamic Assessments of Cognitive Modifiability.* Jerusalem: ICELP Press, 1979/ 2002.

Feuerstein, Reuven and Associates. *Instrumental Enrichment: An Intervention Program for Cognitive Modifiability.* Baltimore, MD: University Park Press, 1980/2004.

Festinger, Leon. *A Theory of Cognitive Dissonance.* Stanford, CA: Stanford University Press, 1957.

Fichte, Johann. *Facts of Consciousness.* Gloucester, UK: Dodo Press, 2008/1817.

Flanagan, Joseph. *Quest for Self-Knowledge* (Toronto: University of Toronto Press, 1997, 205–206.)

Ford, Henry. Interview, *Chicago Tribune, May 25, 1916.*

Frege, Gottlob. *The Foundations of Arithmetic: A Logico-Mathematical Enquiry into the Concept of Number.* New York: John Wiley & Sons, 1980.

Freud, Anna. *The Ego and the Mechanisms of Defense.* New York: International Universities Press, 1966/1936.

Frings, Manfred. *The Mind of Max Scheler: The First Comprehensive Guide Based on the Complete Works.* Milwaukee, Wisconsin: Marquette University Press, 1997.

Gagné, Robert. *Conditions of Learning and Theory of Instruction.* Belmont, CA: Wadsworth Publishing, 1985.

Gardner, Howard. *Frames of Mind: The Theory of Multiple Intelligences.* New York: Basic Books, 1993.

Garry, Maryanne and Hayne, Harlene. *Do Justice and Let the Sky Fall: Elizabeth Loftus and Her Contributions to Science, Law and Academic Freedom.* Mahwah, NJ: Lawrence Erlbaum Associates, 2007.

Gick, Mary and Lockhart, Robert. "Cognitive and Affective Components of Insight." *The Nature of Insight,* edited by Robert Sternberg and Janet Davison, 197–228. Cambridge, MA: MIT Press, 1998.

Gladwell, Malcolm. *Blink: The Power of Thinking without Thinking.* New York: Little Brown & Co., 2005.

Grallo, Richard. "Questioning as Meditation and Contemplation." *Symposium,* IX, No. 1 (2002), 15–22.

———. "How to Think about Culture." *Symposium,* X, No. 1 (2003): 19–26.

———. "Learning, Functional Interferences and Personality Dynamics." *Symposium,* XIII, No. 1 (2006), 15–22.

———. "The Absence of Question and Insight in Accounts of Knowledge." *Symposium,* XIV No. 1 (2007), 33–43.

———. "Questioning as a Cognitive Process: Implications for Learning and Culture." *Symposium,* XVI. No. 1 (2009), 13–23.

———. "Reframing Applied Psychology in Terms of Self-Transcendence: Selected Challenges, Problems and Prospects." Paper presented at 37th Lonergan Workshop, Boston College, 2010.

———. "Principle of Interrogative Problem Representation (IPR) – A Preliminary Sketch." *Symposium,* XIX, No. 1 (2012), 21–31.

———. "Thinking Carefully about Critical Thinking." *Lonergan Review,* IV, No. 1 (2013), 154–180.

———. "Approaching Critical Thinking through Generalized Empirical Method." *Method,* 4, No. 2 (2013), 59–78.

———. "On Seeking Understanding." *Symposium,* XXI, No. 1 (2014): 19–28.

———. "Four Functions of Experience in Human Learning." *Symposium,* XXII, No. 1 (2015): 25–36.

———. "The Role of Belief in Problem Solving." *Symposium,* XXIII, No. 2 (2015): 23–32.

———. "Personal Differences in the Application of G.E.M." *Lonergan Review,* VII, No. 1 (2016), 49–61.

———. "Epictetus in the City." *Symposium,* XXIV, No. 1 (2017): 15–25.

Graybiel, Ann and Smith, Kyle. "Good habits, bad habits." *Scientific American,* June (2014), 38–43.

Gruber, Howard. "Insight and Affect in the History of Science." *The Nature of Insight,* 397–432. edited by Robert Sternberg and Janet Davison. Cambridge, MA: MIT Press, 1998.

Guilford, J. P. *The Nature of Human Intelligence.* New York: McGraw-Hill, 1967.

Guilford, J. P. "Intelligence Has Three Facets." *Science,* 160 (1968), 351–364.

Hadot, Pierre. *Philosophy as a Way of Life: Spiritual Exercises from Socrates to Foucault.* Hoboken, NJ: Wiley-Blackwell, 1995.

Hall, Edward T. *The Silent Language.* Garden City, NY: Doubleday, 1959.

Halonen, Jane. *Critical Thinking in Psychology.* Milwaukee, WI: Alverno Productions, 1995.

Hamblin, C. "Questions." *The Encyclopedia of Philosophy.* New York: Collier Macmillan, 1972.

Harvey, Peter. *An Introduction to Buddhism: Teachings, History and Practices.* New York: Cambridge University Press, 1990, 246–252

Hayakawa, S. I. *Language in Thought and Action.* Enlarged ed. San Diego: Harcourt Brace Jovanovich, 1978.

Hlawaty, Heide and Grallo, Richard. "Reframing STEM Standards, Outcomes and Strategies for the 21st Century Workplace," Conference of the National Science Teachers Association, San Francisco, 2011.

Hofstede, Geert. *Culture's Consequences: Comparing Values, Behaviors, Institutions, and Organizations across Nations* (2nd ed.). Thousand Oaks, CA: Sage, 2001.

Horney, Karen. *Neurosis and Human Growth: The Struggle Towards Self-Realization.* New York: Norton, 1950/1990.

Horney, Karen. *Our Inner Conflicts: A Constructive Theory of Neurosis.* New York: W.W. Norton, 1993.

Hume, David. *An Enquiry on Human Understanding.* New York: Oxford University Press, 2008.

Husserl, Edmund. *The Crisis of the European Sciences and Transcendental Phenomenology.* Evanston: Northwestern University Press, 1970, 240.

Ippolito, Maria and Tweney, Ryan. "The Inception of Insight." *The Nature of Insight,* 433–462. edited by Robert Sternberg and Janet Davison. Cambridge, MA: MIT Press, 1998.

James, William. *Principles of Psychology.* New York: Dover, 1950, 239.

Jordan, Theresa J., Grallo, Richard and Montgomery, Richard. "Combining Decision Analysis and Experimental Data to Study Bias in Educational Settings: Impact of Age on Medical Students' Treatment Decisions," *Journal of Research in Education,* 4, No. 1, 1994, 58–67.

Kahneman, Daniel. *Thinking, Fast and Slow.* New York: Farrar, Straus & Giroux, 2011.

Kant, Immanuel. *Critique of Pure Reason.* New York: Cambridge University Press, 1999.

Kipling, Rudyard. "I have Six Faithful Serving Men" Accessed March 16, 2021. http://www.kiplingsociety.co.uk/poems_servingmen.htm

Korzybski, Alfred. *Science and Sanity: An Introduction to Non-Aristotelean Systems and General Semantics* (5th ed.). Fort Worth, TX: Institute for General Semantics, 2010.

Kotz, Samuel and Johnson, Norman. *Encyclopedia of Statistical Sciences, v.5.* New York: Wiley, 1985.

Krueger, J. *Rationality and Social Responsibility: Essays in Honor of Robyn Mason Dawes.* New York: Psychology Press, 2008.

Lamont, Peter. "The Construction of 'Critical Thinking': Between How We Think and What We Believe." *History of Psychology,* 23, No. 3 (2020), 232–251.

Leeds, Dorothy. *Smart Questions: A New Strategy for Successful Managers.* Berkley Books: New York, 1987.

Levy, David. *Tools of Critical Thinking: Metathoughts for Psychology.* Boston: Allyn and Bacon, 1997.

Lewin, Kurt. "Defining the 'Field at a Given Time'." In *Resolving Social Conflicts and Field Theory in Social Science*. Washington, DC: American Psychological Association, 1997.

Locke, Edwin and Latham, Gary. "Work motivation and satisfaction," *Psychological Science,* 1 No. 4 (1990), 240–246.

Locke, John. An *Essay Concerning Human Understanding*. Claremont, CA: Pomona Press, 2008.

Lonergan, Bernard. "Cognitional Structure." *Collection*. New York: Herder and Herder, 1967.

———. *Method in Theology*. New York: Herder, 1971.

———. *Insight: A Study of Human Understanding*. Collected Works of Bernard Lonergan, edited by Frederick E. Crowe and Robert Doran Toronto: University of Toronto Press, 1992.

———. *Collected Works of Bernard Lonergan V. 4: Collection* Toronto: University of Toronto Press, 1993.

———. *Collected Works of Bernard Lonergan V. 13: A Second Collection*, edited by Robert Doran and John Dadosky. Toronto: University of Toronto Press, 2016.

Lynch, Mervin. "Some Effects of Applications of Metacognitive Monitoring Skills on Frequency of Error Detection." *Journal for the Advancement of Educational Research*, 3 No. 1 (2007), 60–66.

Lysaker, P. H. and Lysaker, J. T. "Schizophrenia and Alterations in Self-Experience, in *Schizophrenia Bulletin,* 36, No. 2 (2010), 331–340.

Marshall, Martin and Associates. "Promotion of Improvement as a Science." *Lancet,* 2013, 381(Feb 2), 381–421.

Marquardt, M. *Organizing the Power of Active Learning: Solving Problems and Building Leaders in Real Time*. Mountain View, CA: Davies Black, 2004.

Maslow, Abraham. *Motivation and Personality*. New York: Harper & Row, 1954.

McKay, Mathew and Associates. *Messages: The Communication Skills Handbook* (2nd ed.). Oakland, CA: New Harbinger Publications, 1985.

Melchin, Kenneth and Cheryl Picard. *Transforming Conflict through Insight*. Toronto: University of Toronto Press, 2009.

Meyer, Richard. *Thinking, Problem Solving, Cognition* (2nded.). New York: W.H. Freeman & Co., 1983.

Middle States Commission on Higher Education, *Characteristics of Excellence in Higher Education*. Philadelphia, PA: Middle States Commission on Higher Education, 2006.

Miller, Bennett. (director) *Moneyball*. Film. Hollywood, CA: Columbia Pictures, 2011.

Moon, Jennifer. *Critical Thinking: An Exploration of Theory and Practice*. New York: Routledge, 2007.

Morelli, Mark. *Self-Possession: Being at Home in Conscious Performance*. Boston: Lonergan Institute, 2015.

Morelli, Mark. "Beyond the Metaphor of levels of Consciousness: Appropriation of Sublative Transformations." *Method,* 9, No. 2 (2018), 47–74.

Moseley, D., Vivienne Baumfield, Julian Elliott, Maggie Gregson, Steven Higgins, J. Miller, and D. Newton. *Frameworks for Thinking*. Cambridge, UK: Cambridge University Press, 2005.

Murray, Henry. *Explorations in Personality*. New York: Oxford University Press.

National Research Council. *How People Learn*. Washington, DC: National Academy Press, 2000.

Newell, Alan and Simon, Herbert. *Human Problem Solving*. New York: Pearson, 1972.

Nolan, Christopher. *Memento*. Santa Monica, CA: Film, Summit Entertainment, 2000.

Nosich, Gerard. *Learning to Think Things Through: A Guide to Critical Thinking across the Curriculum* (4th ed.). Boston: Pearson, 2012.

Ogden, Jenni. *Fractured Minds: A Case Study Approach to Clinical Neuro-Psychology*. New York: Oxford University Press, 2005.

Osborne, Alex. *Applied Imagination*. New York: Charles Scribner & Sons, 1953.

Pashler, Harold, McDaniel, Mark, Rohrer, Doug and Bjork, R. "Learning Styles: Concepts and Evidence." *Psychological Science in the Public Interest*, 9 (2008), 105–119.

Peck, M. Scott. *The Road Less Traveled*. New York: Simon & Schuster, 1978.

Perls, Fritz. *Gestalt Therapy Verbatim*. Lafayette, CA: Real People Press, 1969.

Petrick, Joseph A. and Quinn, John F. *Management Ethics: Integrity at Work*. Thousand Oaks, CA: Sage, 1997.

Pinker, Stephen. *How the Mind Works*. New York: Norton, 1997.

Plato. *Meno*. Indianapolis, IN: Hackett Publishing, 1980.

Poincaré, Henri. *The Foundations of Science*. Translated by G. B. Halstead. Garrison, NY: Science Press, 1924/2012.

Prebish, Charles. *The A to Z of Buddhism*. London: Scarecrow Press, 2001.

Preece, Rob. *The Wisdom on Imperfection*. Ithaca, NY: Snow Lion Publications, 2010.

Prochaska, James, Norcross, John and Carlo DiClemente, *Changing for Good*. New York: Avon Books, 1994.

Reber, Arthur and Reber, Emily. *Dictionary of Psychology*. New York: Penguin Books, 2001.

Rodkey, Krista and Rodkey, Elisa. "Family, Friends and Faith Communities: Intellectual Community and the Benefits of Unofficial Networks for Marginalized Scientists." *History of Psychology*, 23, No. 4 (2020), 289–311.

Rogers, Carl. *Client-Centered Therapy*. Cambridge, MA: The Riverside Press, 1951.

Rokeach, Milton. *The Nature of Human Values*. New York: Free Press, 1973.

Rosner, David. (ed.) *Catastrophe and Philosophy*. New York: Lexington Books, 2019.

Ryle, Gilbert. *The Concept of Mind*. New York: Barnes & Noble, 1949.

Sachs, Oliver. *The Man Who Mistook His Wife for a Hat and Other Clinical Tales*. New York: Pocket Books, 1998.

Santayana, George. *The Life of Reason, v.1.* (Cambridge, MA: MIT Press, 1905/2011).

Schooler, Jonathan W. and Associates "Putting Insight into Perspective." *The Nature of Insight,* edited by Robert Sternberg and Janet Davison, 559–587. Cambridge, MA: MIT Press, 1998.

Schopenhauer, Arthur. *The World as Will and Idea*. London: Everyman Paperbacks, 1995.

Schunk, Dale and Zimmerman, Barry. *Self-Regulation of Learning and Performance: Issues and Educational Applications*. Mahwah, NJ: Erlbaum, 1994.

Schwartz, Tony and McCarthy, Catherine. "Manage Your Energy, Not Your Time." *Harvard Business Review* October (2007), 61–78.

Segal, Peter. *50 First Dates*. Hollywood, CA: Film, Columbia Pictures, 2004.

Seifert, Colleen M. and Associates "Demystification of Cognitive Insight: Opportunistic Assimilation and the Prepared-Mind Perspective." *The Nature of Insight*, 65–124, edited by Robert Sternberg and Janet Davison. Cambridge, MA: MIT Press, 1998.

Shadish, William and Associates. *Experimental and Quasi-Experimental Designs for Generalized Causal Inference*. Boston: Houghton-Mifflin Co., 2002.

Shutz, Alfred. *The Phenomenology of the Social World* (Evanston, IL: Northwestern University Press, 1967).

Simon, Herbert and Newall, Alan. *Human Problem Solving*. Englewood Cliffs, NJ: Prentice-Hall, 1972.

Skinner, B. F. *Science and Human Behavior*. New York: Free Press, 1953.

Sobol, Andrew and Panas, Jerold. *Power Questions: Build Relationships, Win New Business and Influence Others*. Hoboken, NJ: Wiley, 2012.

Smith, Edward and Osherson, Daniel. *Thinking*. Cambridge, MA: MIT Press, 1995.

Sternberg, Robert. *Thinking and Problem Solving*. New York: Academic Press, 1994.

Sternberg, Robert and Davidson, Janet, eds. *The Nature of Insight*. Cambridge, MA: MIT Press, 1998.

Thurstone, Louis Leon. *Primary Mental Abilities*. Chicago: University of Chicago Press, 1938.

Thurstone, Louis Leon and Thurstone, Thelma G. *Factorial Studies of Intelligence*. Chicago: University of Chicago Press, 1941.

Tietje, Louis, Nufrio, Philip and Kramer, R. "Theory and Practice of Action Learning in the MPA/MBA Curriculum at Metropolitan College of New York." *Public Administration Quarterly*, 32, No. 2 (2008), 214–242.

Von Winterfeldt, Detlof and Edwards, Ward. *Decision Analysis and Behavioral Research*. New York: Cambridge University Press, 1986.

Vygotsky, Lev. *Mind in Society: The Development of Higher psychological Processes*. Cambridge, MA: Harvard University Press, 1978.

Wallas, G. *The Art of Thought*. New York: Harcourt Brace Jovanovich, 1926.

Watson. John B. *Behaviorism*. Chicago: University of Chicago Press, 1930.

———. "On Personality." In *Great Ideas in Psychology: The Most Significant Writings of the Founders of Modern Psychology*, edited by Robert W. Marks. New York: Bantam Books, 1966, 400–431.

Wise, Robert. (director), *The Day the Earth Stood Still*. Hollywood, CA: 20th Century Fox, 1951.

Wittgenstein, Ludwig. *Philosophical Investigations*. Hoboken, NJ: Wiley-Blackwell, 2009.

Glossary of Terms

NB: Some definitions are associated with an external source and an identifying code and page number as follows: [APA]—American Psychological Association, *Dictionary of Psychology*; [INS]—Bernard Lonergan, *Insight*; [MOR]—Mark Morelli, *Self-Possession: Being at Home in Conscious Performance*.

"Ability" is an existing competence or skill to perform a specific physical or mental act. [APA-2]

"Achievement" is the attainment of some goal or the goal attained. [APA-9]

"Action" is a self-initiated sequence of movements, usually with respect to some goal. It is also the occurrence or performance of a process or function. [APA-12]

"Aesthetic absorption" is a type of experience that offers a diversion from the work of problem solving through contemplation on various art forms such as dance, literature, music, painting, and sculpture. No novel or chronic problems intrude in this type of appreciative experience.

"Anxiety" is a vague sense of apprehension about the future. Anxiety is considered a future-oriented, long-acting response broadly focused on a diffuse threat. [APA-66]

"Apprehension" is the act or capability of grasping something mentally. [APA-70]

"Basic experiencing" is a kind of experience that is mostly devoid of the problem solving activities, such as question and insight and any mental event identified in the patterns of problem solving. This type of experience also counts as a series of events lived through, but these events are not of an active problem solving nature.

"Belief," "believing" [See "Social trust."]

Glossary of Terms

"Bias, confirmation," is the tendency to gather evidence that confirms preexisting expectations, typically by emphasizing or pursuing supporting evidence while dismissing or failing to seek contradictory evidence. [APA-232]

"Bias, process," is any systematic disruption, distortion, or interference of problem solving efforts. This bias frequently manifests as a systematic exclusion from an investigation of further relevant questions or insights. In contrast, unbiased problem solving efforts are described in patterns of problem solving 1, 2, 3, or 4.

"Buddhism" is the non-theistic religion and philosophy founded in India by Siddhartha Gautama, known as the Buddha. [APA-148]

"Calming exercise" is any mindful activity designed to achieve subjective tranquility. [QI]

"Character" is the totality of an individual's attributes and personality traits. [APA-175]

"Choice behavior" or "choosing" is the selection of one of a group of available options or behavioral alternatives. [APA-182]

"Cognitional structure," as described by Lonergan, is the dynamic assembly of interrelations between and among experiencing, understanding, and judging. It is part of what he refers to as cognitional theory.

"Cognitive process" is a mental function assumed to be involved in the acquisition, storage, interpretation, manipulation, transformation, and use of knowledge. [APA-205–206]

"Comprehension" is the act or capability of understanding something, especially the meaning of a communication. [APA-224]

"Consciousness, facts of" [See "Facts of consciousness."]

"Consciousness, levels of," is an older name for patterns of problem solving and a mode of rest from problem solving.

"Consciousness, management of," is an individual's control of his or her conscious states and processes, in addition to behavior.

"Consciousness, (stream of)," is the notion that the contents of subjective consciousness are a continuous, dynamic flow of ideas, images, feelings, sensations, intuitions, and so forth, rather than a series of discrete, static components. [APA-1036]

"Critical thinking" is a form of thinking characterized by the use of a *criterion* to achieve a *judgment* or *decision*. (See also *Factual critical thinking*, *Values-oriented critical thinking*, and *Deliberative critical thinking*.) [QI]

"Culture" is the distinctive customs, values, beliefs, knowledge, art, and language of a society or a community. These values and concepts are passed on from generation to generation and they are the basis for everyday behaviors and practices. [APA-274]

"Deciding" (See also "Deliberative critical thinking.")

"Decision" (or "Deciding") is a limited personal resolution, commitment, or imperative to realize some value in one's life, or to eliminate some disvalue. In this book, the associated process leading up to decision is formulated as deliberative critical thinking (problem solving Pattern 4).

"Deliberative critical thinking" is one of the three forms of critical thinking; as such it a collection of mental events designed to address reflective questions of deliberation and to choose options. In this book it is also referred to as problem solving Pattern 4.

"Desire to know" is the driving force behind authentic questions. In some contexts it is known as the intention to learn or wonder.

"Development" is a progressive series of changes in structure, function, and behavior patterns that occur over the lifespan of a human being or other organism. [APA-304]

"Developmental stage" is a period of development during which specific abilities, characteristics, or behavior patterns appear. [APA-305]

"Driving force," in Force Field Analysis, is an operating force that, when increased, alters preferences in such a way that participants act to support change in a specific direction. In the context of problem solving, a *driving force* moves change in the direction of growth through learning. [QI]

"Evidence collecting" is a mental process and fact of consciousness that serves as part of factual, values-oriented, and deliberative critical thinking. It is the assembly of material that is relevant to the making of judgments or decisions in one direction or another.

"Evidence weighing" is a mental process and fact of consciousness that serves as part of factual, values-oriented, and deliberative critical thinking. It is the comparison of collected evidence and reasons with a criterion for judgment or decision making and the application of that criterion of judgment or decision in one direction or another.

"Experience, Basic," is a form of conscious experience with no questions, insights, or problem solving efforts of any kind.

"Experiencing" is (1) the collection of conscious events or (2) the subjective impression of conscious events.

"Expressing" is a mental process and fact of consciousness that serves as part of all of the patterns of problem solving by making formulations of mental events more explicit by committing them to writing or speech, sometimes in the presence of others.

"Facts of consciousness" are mental events that can be verified in one's own experience. Included among these are questions and insights, the desire to know, sensation and perception, images and evidence, formulations, judgments and decisions, and expressive actions and habits, and finally the social trust that is necessary for all effective collaborative problem solving.

"Factual critical thinking" is one of the three forms of critical thinking; as such it is a collection of mental events designed to address reflective questions of fact and to establish facts. In this book, it is also referred to as problem solving Pattern 2.

"Factual judging" (See also "Factual critical thinking.")

"Focusing and following exercise" is any mindful activity wherein an object or theme is examined and conscious states are allowed to flow from that.

"Force Field Analysis" is a method of social-psychological analysis, developed by Kurt Lewin, designed to describe, predict, and explain change or no change in individuals and groups.

"Formulating" is a mental process and fact of consciousness that serves as part of all of the patterns of problem solving by making formulations of mental events encoded in some language or symbol system.

"Functional interferences with problem solving," types of: "Environmental interferences" involve interruptions caused by the physical environment or by the activities of others. "Personal interferences" are disruptions caused by the state of one's body, emotions, or habitual thoughts. [QI]

"Habit" is a well-learned behavior or automatic sequence of behaviors that is relatively situation specific and over time has become motorically reflexive and independent of motivational and cognitive influence. [APA-479] It is a thesis of this book that habits of cognition and emotions also exist. These would be automatic sequences of thoughts and emotions that are relatively situation specific.

"History" here means both (1) the succession of events lived by a people and (2) the scholarly discipline of investigating those events.

"Hypothetical Construct" is an explanatory model based on processes inferred from data but not directly observable. [APA-239]

"Image" is a likeness or cognitive representation of an earlier sensory experience recalled without external stimulation. [APA-524]

"Impression" is a presumed effect of stimulation on the brain. [APA-528]

"Insight" is the sudden appearance of a potential solution to a problem or answer to a question. [INS-3]

"Interrogative Problem Representation" [IPR] is a procedure for formulating problems in terms of questions that an adequate solution would answer.

"Instruction, Differentiated," is a form of instruction wherein curriculum planning and execution take students' current abilities into account.

"Irresponsibility" is the active, ongoing defense of one's current decisions and actions against newly emerging factual and moral knowledge.

"Judging" aims at factual or moral knowledge by subjecting our insights to criteria of truth or worth, respectively.

"Judgment" (See also "Judging.")

Glossary of Terms

"Judgment of Fact" is a limited affirmation or denial offered to resolve an issue of fact about states of affairs in the world or regarding self or others.

"Judgment of value" is a limited approval or disapproval of something, whether it exists or not.

"Learning" is the acquisition of novel information, behavior, or abilities after practice, observation or other experiences, as evidenced by change in behavior, knowledge, or brain function. [APA-594]

"Learning cycle" is a distinct pattern, related to learning or problem solving, within a time series of data. [APA-278]

"Learning personality" is a type of personality wherein the primary motivation is the desire to know and the related desire to grow in accordance with it.

"Learning response style." (See "Problem solving response style.")

"Learning, transformative" is a form of learning that not only transforms the problem situation but also transforms the learner in important ways.

"Meditation" is a profound and extended contemplation or reflection in order to achieve focused attention or an otherwise altered state of consciousness and to gain insight into oneself and the world. [APA-634]

"Memory" is (1) the ability to retain information or a representation of past experience, based on mental processes of learning or encoding, retention across some interval of time, and retrieval or reactivation of the memory. Memory is also (2) specific information or a specific past experience that is recalled. [APA-636]

"Mental event" is an experienced occurrence or phenomenon of consciousness that has a definite beginning and end and that involves or produces change. [APA-389,638]

"Mindfulness" is awareness of one's internal states and surroundings. [APA-655]

"Neuroscience" is the scientific study of the nervous system and its applications in psychology, psychiatry, and neurology. [APA-704]

"Overlearning" is a level of practice that is continued beyond the point at which the individual knows or performs the task as well as can be expected. [APA-751]

"Pattern-anxiety hypothesis" states that as a person shifts from basic experiencing to understanding to factual critical thinking to values-oriented critical thinking to deciding the level of personal anxiety will increase.

"Pattern of problem solving" is a functionally interrelated collection of mental events, motivated by the desire to know and designed to address questions.

"Pause from problem solving." (See also "Rest from problem solving.")

"Personality" is the enduring configuration of characteristics and behavior that comprises an individual's unique adjustment to life, including major traits, interests, drives, values, self-concept, abilities, and emotional patterns. [APA-782]

"Perspective, developmental," is the accumulation of insights, judgments, and decisions over a lifetime.

"Perspective, problem solving," is a collection of recalled insights, judgments, and decisions that seem relevant to a present problem.

"Prehension" is the act of grasping, clasping, or seizing an object or supporting the body, usually with an appendage adapted for that purpose. [APA-822]

"Problem Solving" is the process by which individuals attempt to overcome difficulties, achieve plans that move them from a starting situation to a desired goal, or reach conclusions through the use of higher mental functions, such as reasoning and creative thinking. [APA-837-838] For purposes of this book, problem solving is a type of complex human learning that addresses novel or chronic situations that confront us with gaps in our experience, understanding, knowledge, values, or practice.

"Problem solving disruptions and interferences," types of "Environmental interferences" involve interruptions caused by the physical environment or by the activities of others. "Personal interferences" are disruptions caused by the state of one's body, emotions, or habitual thoughts.

"Problem solving end-products" are the results of the unfolding of each pattern of problem solving in accordance with the desire to know; these are often answers to questions.

"Problem solving profile" is a formal assessment of a person's relative strengths and weaknesses based on the patterns of problem solving.

"Problem solving quality" is the extent to which activities of patterns of problem solving are guided by the desire to know.

"Problem Solving Response Style" is a descriptive account of the extent to which an individual does or does not routinely engage effectively in each of the patterns of problem solving.

"Problem solving, transformative." (See "Transformative problem solving.")

"Process bias" is any systematic disruption, distortion, or interference of problem solving efforts. In contrast, unbiased problem solving efforts are described in patterns of problem solving 1, 2, 3, or 4.

"Question": (1) As a mental event, a question is the recognition of a gap in our experience, understanding, knowledge, values, or practice. (See also *Question, unformulated.*) (2) As an expressed formulation, a question is an interrogative utterance that, if authentic, is a call for information to fill the recognized gap. (See also *Question, formulated.*)

"Questions, authentic versus unauthentic": An "authentic question" is a question that is an expression of the desire to know. An "unauthentic question" is an utterance that has the grammatical form of a question, without a concomitant desire to know on the part of the person who utters it.

"Questions, deliberative" are questions of the form: "Should I/we do this?" This kind of question is typically the guiding question in Problem Solving Pattern 4 (Deliberative Critical Thinking).

"Questions, expressed versus unexpressed": An "expressed question" is a formulated question that is held by one person and communicated to another. An "unexpressed question" is a formulated question that is held by one person and not communicated to another.

"Questions, formulated versus unformulated": An "unformulated question" is a recognition that there is a gap in our experience, understanding, knowledge, values, or practice. A "formulated question" is an encoding of an unformulated question into a language or some other coding system.

"Question-free mode of operation" is the mode of operation constituted by acts of seeing, hearing, tasting, touching, smelling, feeling, remembering, and imagining, and by mere presence to oneself. [MOR-338]

"Questions, guiding" are questions that coordinate all activities within a pattern of problem solving. Within Pattern 1 (Seeking Understanding) it might be a question such as: What might be going on in this situation? Within Pattern 2 (Factual Critical Thinking) it would be something such as: Is this true? Within Pattern 3 (Values-Oriented Critical Thinking): Is this worthwhile? Within Pattern 4 (Deliberative Critical Thinking): Should I/we do this?

"Questions, reflective" are questions that take "yes" or "no" as an answer. Reflective questions are typically the guiding questions in Problem Solving Patterns 2, 3, and 4.

"Questions for understanding" are the key questions in Problem Solving Pattern 1 (Seeking Understanding). They do not take "yes" or "no" as answers. They include: who, what, when, where, why, how, how many, how often, how much, how long, how far.

"Reflective insight" is the grasp of the sufficiency (or insufficiency) of reasons and evidence to support a prospective judgment or decision.

"Reminiscing" is the recalling of previous experiences, especially those of a pleasant nature. [APA-904]

"Responsibility" is the active, ongoing alignment of one's decisions and actions with one's ever-expanding factual and moral knowledge.

"Rest from problem solving, mode of," is a kind of experience that is free of problem solving activities.

"Restraining force," in Force Field Analysis, is an operating force that, when increased, alters preferences in such a way that participants act to support the status quo or resist change in a specific direction. In the context of problem solving, a *restraining force* operates to block learning and the change brought about by it.

"Seeking understanding" is a pattern of problem solving that involves the search to grasp possible meaning in various situations. In this book it is also referred to as Problem Solving Pattern 1.

"Self" is the totality of the individual, consisting of all characteristic attributes, conscious, and unconscious, mental and physical. [APA-951]

"Self-acceptance" is a relatively objective sense or recognition of one's abilities and achievements, together with acknowledgment and acceptance of one's limitations. [APA-951]

"Self-appropriation" is the self-managed developmental process of achieving ever more differentiated experiencing, understanding, judging, and deciding about one's own experiencing, understanding, judging, and deciding. [INS]

"Self-appropriation, partial" is any growth-oriented contribution to the developmental process of self-appropriation.

"Self-efficacy" is an individual's subjective perception of his or her capability to perform in a given setting or to attain desired results. [APA-954]

"Self-knowledge" is the collection of true judgments of fact that a person makes about self.

"Self-management" is an individual's control of his or her behavior, particularly regarding the pursuit of a specific objective [APA-956–957]. In this book, self-management is generalized to include control of conscious states and processes, in addition to behavior.

"Self-possession as a conscious performer" is "being at home with oneself in one's conscious performance, that is self-directing conscious performance informed and guided by self-knowledge, . . . or deliberate and reflective conscious performance." [MOR-339]

"Self-regulation of learning" is an individual's control of his or her own learning and problem solving efforts.

"Social influence" includes the interpersonal processes that can cause individuals to change their thoughts, feelings, or behaviors. [APA-996]

"Social trust" is defined here as the reliance on the word and the assumed competence of others in thinking and in getting things done.

"Society" is an enduring social group living in a particular place whose members are mutually interdependent and share and share political and other institutions, laws, and mores, and a common culture. [APA-1002]

"Sublation" is a term used in this book to refer to the interrelationships between the patterns of problem solving with each other and with *basic experiencing*: in particular, the acts, operations, and processes of one pattern of problem solving complement and do not interfere with the acts, operations, and processes of any other pattern or of basic experiencing.

Glossary of Terms 173

In general, all patterns of problem solving presuppose the data of basic experiencing. Pattern 1 presupposes complements and adds possible meanings to basic experiencing. Pattern 2 presupposes complements and adds a consideration of accuracy to the work of Pattern 1. Pattern 3 presupposes complements and adds an alignment with a scale of values to the work of Patterns 1 and 2. Pattern 4 presupposes, complements and adds something new to the work of Patterns 1, 2, and 3 by importing something valuable or discarding something as worthless from one's life.

"System I Thinking" is a mode of thought comprising, rapid, implicit, and automatic cognitive operations. [APA-1061]

"System II Thinking" is a mode of thought comprising slow, explicit, and controlled processes. [APA-1061]

"Taxonomy of educational objectives," originally developed by Benjamin Bloom and associates, is an early systematic classification of the three domains—cognitive, affective, and psychomotor—that students use in attaining educational goals. [APA-135]

"Traits" (of personality) are enduring characteristics that describe or determine an individual's behavior across a range of situations. [APA-1098]

"Transformative Problem Solving" is a form of complex and comprehensive human learning that is attentive to experience, deeply insightful, supported by evidence, guided by time-tested values, and transformative of situations and self. It is not simply stimulus-response learning, or concept attainment or information transfer. It is a form of problem solving that not only transforms the problem situation but also transforms the learner in important ways.

"Tranquil abiding" is defined here as an enjoyable, serene experience of free-floating attention that is devoid of problem solving activity.

"Trust" [See "Social trust."]

"Truth, cohesion criterion of," requires consistency among known propositions.

"Truth, correspondence criterion of," requires a match between evidence and a proposed judgment.

"Truth, pragmatic criterion of," requires a search for the impact and usefulness of a specific claim, embodied as a prediction.

"Type I and II errors" are basic errors in statistics wherein one asserts that an effect exists when there is none (type I), or that there is no effect when there is one (type II). In this book, these errors are also referred to as "errors of hallucination" (type I) and "errors of blindness" (type II).

"Understanding" (See "Seeking understanding.")

"Unit of analysis," in Force Field Analysis, is the object under study, whether it is an individual, group, or organization.

"Values-oriented critical thinking" is one of the three forms of critical thinking; as such it is a collection of mental events designed to approve and prioritize values and to address reflective questions of value. In this book it is also referred to as Problem Solving Pattern 3.

"Values judging" (See also "Values-oriented critical thinking.")

"Weighing information" is a mental process and fact of consciousness that figures prominently in the three types of critical thinking. (See also "Evidence weighing.")

"Wisdom" is defined here as the ongoing and developing knowledge of how to live life well.

"Wonder" [See "Desire to know."]

Index

ability, 47, 48, 74, 83, 84, 109, 143–46
achievement, 129–35
aesthetic absorption, 75, 79, 81–86, 88, 147, 153
Ainsworth, Mary and associates, 98
All Performance Cycle, 131, 133
Alverno College, 48–49
Anderson, Lorin, 33, 48
anxiety, 20, 21, 24, 26, 93, 94, 109, 126, 150
apprehension, 34, 74, 75
aptitude, 47
Aristotle, 34, 78
attending (attention), 19, 21, 24, 68, 73, 80–82, 93, 97, 105, 106, 108, 122, 123, 127, 129, 140, 145, 147
automatic habitual routines. *See* habitual routines

Bacon, Francis, 78
basic experiencing. *See* experiencing, basic
Beck, Aaron, 9
behaviorism, radical, 9, 14, 149
belief, believing, 99–102, 111
Benajai, M and S. Crowder, 109
Bensley, D. Alan, 3–17, 24
bias, confirmation, 15, 56, 60, 63
bias, group, 15, 24, 102
bias, personal, 24
bias, process, 15, 42, 94, 110–12
Bloom, Benjamin, 48
Brentano, Franz, 76
Buddhism, 76

calming exercises, 81, 83
careful thinking, 47–48
Chaplin, J.P., 91
character, 53, 121–22
choice. *See* decision
cognitional structure, 32
cognitional theory, 8
cognitive process, 9, 15, 20, 33, 38, 39, 47, 48, 65, 91, 108, 129, 140
cognitive response style. *See* problem solving response style
Coleridge, Samuel Taylor, 107
collecting information, 14–15, 58–59, 62–63, 65, 94, 96, 135, 144, 145
commitment, personal, 18, 20–21, 25, 49, 51–53, 95, 103, 108, 125, 127, 129–30, 132, 134
competency, 48
comprehension, 16, 33–34, 48
conflation, 150
consciousness, facts of. *See* facts of consciousness
consciousness, levels of, 32

consciousness, management of, 86
consciousness, stream of, 74, 76, 80
construct, hypothetical. *See* hypothetical constructs
contemplation. *See also* focusing and following exercises
criteria for judging and deciding, 17, 32, 45, 52, 54–60, 62–64, 78, 108, 125
critical thinking, 49–53; critical thinking, deliberative, 13, 16–19, 21–22, 26, 35, 51, 61–64, 67–68, 101, 125, 142–43, 153; critical thinking, factual, 16–17, 19, 21–22, 26, 34, 38, 41, 53–57, 61, 64–65, 67–68, 94, 96, 100, 130, 141, 144, 146, 153; critical thinking, values-oriented, 16–17, 19, 21–22, 26, 57–61, 64–65, 67–68, 125, 141, 143, 153
Cromwell, Lucy, 49
Csikzentmihalyi, Mihalyi, 26, 154
culture, 7, 20, 22–23, 46, 89–90, 102–5, 113–14, 147

Dalai Lama, 76
data, 6, 32, 74–77, 79, 96, 99, 109–10, 112, 123, 127, 135, 148–49, 153
Davidson, Janet, 12
deciding. *See* deliberative critical thinking
decision, 2–3, 18–19, 21, 27, 41, 48–53, 61–68, 94, 99, 101, 103, 105–6, 108, 113, 125–26, 135, 145–46, 148, 152–53
decision trees, 71
deliberation. *See* deliberative critical thinking
desire to grow, 3, 26
desire to know, 2–3, 5, 10–15, 19, 24–26, 38–40, 46, 53–54, 56, 58–60, 62–66, 69, 80, 83, 92, 94, 105, 109–10, 113–14, 119, 124–25, 128–30, 132, 134–35, 139, 141–45, 147–49, 151–52, 154

development, 1, 7, 9, 22, 25, 40, 53, 57, 60, 64, 66, 81, 85, 93, 94, 98, 107–8, 113, 121–22, 133, 135, 153
developmental stage, 141–42
driving force, 20, 91–92, 99–100, 103, 105, 112, 123

echo exercise, 37
Ellis, Albert, 9
engagement. *See also* deciding and action
Ennis, Robert, 49
Epictetus, 78, 119–28, 132–35
Erikson, Erik, 9
error, 21, 55–56, 59, 63, 79, 102, 110, 144–45, 153
evidence collecting, 14–15, 25, 52, 58–59, 63, 65, 94, 96, 136, 144–45
evidence weighing, 14–15, 25, 54–55, 58–59, 62–63, 65, 94, 96, 136, 144, 145
experience, basic, 7, 15, 18–19, 21–23, 35, 75, 79, 82–86, 89, 93–96, 114, 119, 127, 140, 153
experience, functions of, 73–88
experiencing, 19, 21, 23, 25–26, 73–88, 90, 100, 119–20, 123, 140–41, 147, 150, 152
expressing, 14–15, 52, 55, 95

Facione, Peter, 49, 51–52, 68
facts of consciousness, 2–3, 14, 25, 32, 39, 55, 56, 59, 63–64, 90, 95, 113, 119–40, 148–50, 152
fantasy, 101
feedback, 120
Fichte, Johan, 135n1
field notes, 41
"50 First Dates," 107
focusing and following exercises, 81
Force Field Analysis, 20, 90–91, 99, 103, 105
Ford, Henry, 106
formulating, 14–15, 38–39, 41, 65, 79, 95, 148

Frege, Gottlob, 14
functional interferences, 94

Gagné, Robert, 77
Gardner, Howard, 47
Generalized Empirical Method (G.E.M), 8, 32
Gick, Mary, 12
goals, 3, 31, 83, 93, 120–21, 123, 125, 129–30, 132, 134, 141, 143
growth, personal, 1, 90, 121, 127, 131, 133, 135n3
Gruber, Howard, 12
Guilford, J.P., 47, 76

habit, 25
habit, development of, 40, 127–28, 132
habitual routines, 79–86, 119, 123, 147, 153
Halonen, Jane, 49
High Performance Cycle, 120–21, 128–35, 148
history, 7, 20, 23, 89–90, 104–14, 147, 151–52
Horney, Karen, 9
human service disciplines, 127, 131–33, 135, 140, 153
Hume, David, 74
Husserl, Edmund, 76
hypothetical constructs, 13, 33

image, 2–3, 9, 18, 25, 34–35, 84, 93–94, 110–12
impressions, 78, 120–27, 133–34, 148, 153
improvement, science of, 131, 133
individual differences, 33, 95, 128, 133
insight, 2–3, 9, 11–13, 19, 21, 25; insight, direct, 39; insight, inverse, 38, 39, 42, 143; insight as integrator, 11, 53, 69, 77, 93–94, 147
instruction, differentiated, 73
intentionality analysis, 32
Interrogative Problem Representation, 40

irresponsibility, 61

James, William, 74, 76, 78, 98, 123
judging: judging facts. *See* factual critical thinking; judging values. *See* values-oriented critical thinking
judgment, 2–3, 45–52; judgment of fact, 17, 19, 50, 52, 54–57, 99, 101, 130, 144; judgment of value, 17, 19, 51–52, 58–60, 99, 134, 145

Kant, Immanuel, 71n34, 77, 129
Kipling, Rudyard, 35
knowledge, immanently generated, 100–101

Latham, Gary, 77, 119–21, 128–31, 133, 148
learning: learning, complex human, 1, 3, 10, 14, 73–75, 77, 79, 92, 102, 106, 119–20, 128, 131–33, 139, 147–49; learning, effects of, 25, 26, 79, 81, 129, 131, 141–42, 152; learning, transformative, 3, 7, 24, 26, 32, 69, 90, 93, 97, 132–33, 139–40, 151, 154; learning, types of (simple and complex), 1, 7, 10; learning cycle, 120; learning environment, 77, 120; learning goals and objectives (for this book), 2–3, 6, 31–33, 45, 67–68, 75, 84, 90, 114, 121, 133, 139; learning personality, 3, 7, 26, 127, 132, 139–40, 152–54
Levy, David, 49
Lewin, Kurt, 20, 90
Locke, Edwin, 77, 119–21, 128–31, 133, 148
Locke, John, 74
Lockhart, Robert, 12
Loftus, Elizabeth, 109
Lonergan, Bernard, 8, 12, 22, 32, 38, 76, 80, 93, 101, 141

Markov model, 36, 50–52
"Memento," 108

memory, 10–11, 107–9, 111
mental events, 2–3, 7, 9–15, 19, 32, 34, 36, 39, 41, 51–52, 54–55, 58–59, 62–63, 65–66, 77–78, 85, 94, 119, 129, 134–35, 139–41, 143–47, 149–50
mindfulness, 122
"Moneyball," 37
Morelli, Mark, 80, 85

neuroscience, 34
Nosich, Gerald, 49

overlearning, 95–96, 116n15, 142

pattern-anxiety hypothesis, 21, 26
patterns of problem solving, 2, 7–8, 15–20, 22–23, 26, 32, 35, 41, 45, 63, 66, 68, 73–74, 81, 89, 93–97, 113, 119–20, 127, 129, 133–35, 139–42, 146, 148–49, 153
pause from problem solving, 2, 7–8, 14–15, 18, 35, 75, 79–86, 90, 139–40, 147, 149, 154
personality, 3, 7, 9, 20, 46, 89–97, 112, 114, 146–47
perspective, developmental, 60, 64, 85, 107
perspective, problem solving, 60, 64, 85
Piaget, Jean, 34, 142
Poincaré, Henri, 82
prehension, 34
problem solving: problem solving, contexts of, 89–117; problem solving, transformative. *See* transformative problem solving; problem solving disruptions and interferences, 15, 24, 38–39, 41–42, 46, 65, 94–95, 102, 139; problem solving effects. *See* learning, effects of; problem solving end-products, 32, 35–36, 54, 58, 141; problem solving profile, 21, 112; problem solving quality, 15, 23–25, 31, 36, 40, 54, 59, 63, 66, 69, 83, 113, 120, 124, 143–46, 148

process bias, 15, 24, 40, 42, 94, 110–12
proficiency, 48

quality control in problem solving. *See* problem solving quality
questions, 77, 93, 147; question as operator, 11, 53, 69, 77, 93, 147; question-free mode of operation, 85; questions, authentic *vs.* inauthentic, 11, 129, 151, 154; questions, deliberative, 61–62, 101; questions, expressed *vs.* unexpressed, 11; questions, formulated *vs.* unformulated, 37–38, 51, 143; questions, guiding, 17–18, 35, 51, 77, 120, 124, 129; questions, reflective, 16–17, 19, 46, 49–64, 69, 78, 124, 126, 130, 144–45; questions for understanding, 19, 35, 143

Rational Emotive Behavior Therapy, 116n20
reasons, 14–18, 45–47, 52–54, 56–60, 62–64, 78, 95, 101, 125, 144–45
reflective insight, 52–54, 58, 68, 94
regret, 106, 108, 152
reminiscing, 105, 108, 114
responsibility, 61, 128, 132, 150, 153–54
rest from problem solving, mode of, 81, 83, 86, 89, 154
restraining force, 20, 91–92, 99, 103, 105, 112, 123
Rogers, Carl, 73
Ryle, Gilbert, 149

Santayana, George, 106
Schopenhauer, Arthur, 87n23, 88n32
Schunck, Dale, 77
seeking understanding, 7, 13, 15, 16, 18–22, 24, 26, 31–44, 46, 56–57, 60–61, 63–65, 81, 84, 94, 96, 100, 105–6, 108, 114, 124, 140–43, 153
self, 6, 45, 93–94, 109, 115; self-acceptance, 90, 106, 121; self-

appropriation, 6, 25–26, 90, 122, 132–33, 151; self-appropriation, partial, 26, 153; self-control, 122, 134; self-destruction, 92, 134; self-efficacy, 130, 134; self-knowledge, 3, 6, 67, 75, 82, 90, 121–22, 127, 131–34, 139–40, 151, 153; self-management, 3, 6, 120, 122, 126, 131, 134, 139–40; self-possession, 7; self-regulation of learning, 7, 140
Simon, Herbert, 77
Skinner, B.F., 9, 149
social context, 34, 97–99, 112–13
social influence, 122
social trust, 2–3, 5–7, 14, 20, 22, 25–26, 54, 67, 69, 89–90, 97–99, 101, 103, 105, 112, 114, 119, 135, 147–49, 152
society, 7, 20, 22, 102, 107
Socrates, 140
speculation, 101
Sternberg, Robert, 12
structuralism, 14
sublation, 32, 141–42
System I Thinking, 10
System II Thinking, 10, 68

Taxonomy of Educational Objectives, 33, 48
Thinking, Types of. *See* System I and System II Thinking

Thurstone, L.L., 47
traits of personality, 20, 64, 91–92
tranquil abiding, 75, 79, 81–86, 119, 147, 153
transformative problem solving, 3, 24, 26, 93, 132–33, 139–40, 151, 154
trust. *See* social trust
truth, 16–17, 21, 32, 41, 56–57, 66, 78–79, 99, 101, 110–11, 124, 142, 144
Type I and II errors, 55

understanding. *See* seeking understanding
unit of analysis, 91–92

values, scale of, 17–18, 57, 145, 152
values-oriented critical thinking, 13, 16–17, 19, 21–22, 26, 34, 51, 57–61, 64–65, 67–68, 94, 125, 141, 143–44, 153
Vespasian, 121
Vygotsky, Lev, 97

Watson, John B., 9, 149
weighing information, 52, 65
wisdom, practical, 106
Wittgenstein, Ludwig, 14
wonder. *See* desire to know

Zimmerman, Barry, 77

About the Author

Richard Grallo is emeritus professor of human services at Metropolitan College of New York. Dr. Grallo began teaching at the College in 1983. He has taught undergraduate courses in applied psychology and occasionally statistics, and graduate courses in research methods. From 1993 to 2011, Dr. Grallo also taught undergraduate and graduate-level courses in counseling, measurement, and research methodology in the Department of Applied Psychology at New York University and decision analysis to third-year medical students at New Jersey Medical School. He is a fellow and lifetime member of the Albert Ellis Institute, a past president of the Association for the Advancement of Educational Research, and a member of various scientific and professional organizations. His research interests include problem solving, decision-making, self-regulation of learning, and the application of mathematical models and multivariate methods to social science problems.

CPSIA information can be obtained
at www.ICGtesting.com
Printed in the USA
BVHW032342060122
624164BV00002B/15